CONTENTS

SHOT DOWN

The true story of pilot Howard Snyder and the crew of the B-17 *Susan Ruth*

Steve Snyder

Shot Down: The true story of pilot Howard Snyder
and the crew of the B-17 *Susan Ruth* by Steve Snyder

Books may be purchased by contacting the publisher and author at:

Sea Breeze Publishing, LLC
601 Sea Breeze Drive
Seal Beach CA 90747
SteveSnyderAuthor.com
562-598-6902

Cover and Interior Design: Nick Zelinger, NZ Graphics
Publisher: Sea Breeze Publishing
Editor: John Maling (Editing By John)
Manuscript Consultant: Judith Briles (The Book Shepherd)

Library of Congress Catalog Number: 2010904344
ISBN: 978-0-9860760-0-8 (hard cover)
978-0-9860760-1-5 (soft cover)
978-0-9860760-2-2 2 (eBook)

1) Biography 2) WWII 3) European Theater 4) B-17 Bomber

First Edition Printed in the USA

This book is specially dedicated to my father, Howard Snyder, pilot of the B-17 *Susan Ruth*, and to the nine other members of his B-17 crew: co-pilot George Eike; navigator Robert Benninger; bombardier Richard Daniels; flight engineer/top turret gunner Roy Holbert; radio operator Ross Kahler; ball turret gunner Louis Colwart; left waist gunner Joseph Musial; right waist gunner John Pindroch; and tail gunner William Slenker.

It is dedicated to all the men and women of the occupied countries who risked their lives and those of their families to help the fighting men of the Allied nations alive, but missing in action, escape capture by the Axis powers during World War II—in particular, to the brave patriots in southern Belgium who aided my father and his downed crew.

Finally, *Shot Down* is dedicated to the men of the 306th Bomb Group, the Eighth Air Force, World War II veterans, and all the men and women who sacrificed in the fight for freedom. I believe without a doubt that they truly are The Greatest Generation.

PREFACE

I was born on April 24, 1947, almost two years after V-E Day (Victory in Europe) on May 8, 1945. Growing up in the 1950s, I loved watching World War II movies (*Halls of Montezuma, Run Silent Run Deep, The Flying Tigers, Battle Cry, The Enemy Below, From Here to Eternity, Sands of Iwo Jima*—with John Wayne as Marine Sergeant John Stryker, etc.) and reading landmark books about World War II (*Thirty Seconds Over Tokyo, Guadalcanal Diary, The Battle of Britain, The Story of D-Day*, etc.). A favorite pastime was playing with little rubber toy soldiers like the ones in T*oy Story*, and one Christmas my absolute top present was a Remco Navy Pom Pom gun.

My pals and I went to Army surplus stores to get ammo belts, canteens, and helmet liners. We had authentic looking (at least to us) toy rifles. Although my father was in the Air Force, I wore his shirts to look like an infantry soldier. Looking the part, we "played Army" in vacant lots, along washes, and in the yards of people with big homes. My father (Pop) owned a small restaurant, Snyder's Coffee Shop, in Pasadena, California, at the corner of Altadena Drive and Colorado Blvd. It was about a half mile from our home, and my buddies and I would march up to it, get free ice cream and sodas, and then march back. It was all very serious stuff to us.

When young, about the only things I knew about my father's war history was that he was a captain and pilot of a B-17 bomber named after my oldest sister, Susan Ruth Snyder. He used to help me build World War II model airplanes including German fighter planes (Focke-Wulf 190 and Messerschmitt 109), but of course my favorite was a B-17 Flying Fortress.

From time to time, my parents would get together socially with friends with whom he went through pilot training or with members of his crew and their wives. He belonged to the 306th Bomb Group

Association and went to a few AFEES (Air Forces Escape & Evasion Society) reunions, but I really didn't know anything about them. He would also correspond with people in Belgium who hid him and helped him escape the Germans after his plane was shot down.

My dad didn't really talk about the war until after he and my mother took trips to Belgium in 1988 and 1989. In 1988, veterinarian Dr. Paul Delahaye, who lived in Momignies in Southern Belgium and who had formed the Belgian-American Foundation, invited my parents to attend a Belgium Liberation Celebration that year. In 1989, the following year, Dr. Delahaye built a memorial in Southern Belgium to the crew of the B-17 *Susan Ruth* and invited the four surviving crew members and their wives to attend its dedication. These two trips brought back my dad's wartime experiences, and as he began to recall and discuss them, I became more and more fascinated by and interested in them. No longer was I a little kid playing Army with my pals.

In 1994, my wife Glenda, sister Nancy, and I accompanied my parents to Southern Belgium to attend the 50th Anniversary Celebrations of the Belgium Liberation. My father was the honored guest and speaker at numerous events, and we saw many of the houses where he was hidden while missing in action for seven months in 1944. It was a fascinating and emotional experience.

In February 2003, The Collings Foundation's "Wings of Freedom Tour" came to Long Beach, California, and I paid to take a 30 minute ride in the restored B-17 *Nine-O-Nine*. It was so thrilling to get just a small taste of what it must have been like during combat.

My parents were unable to travel for the 60th Anniversary of the Belgium Liberation in 2004, but Glenda and I went to represent them. Again, it was an amazing and humbling experience. In the spring of 2004, I accompanied Dad to King of Prussia, Pennsylvania, to attend the annual AFEES Reunion which included a bus trip to Washington, D.C., and to visit the World War II Memorial just prior to its formal dedication on May 29. It was the last trip my father ever took. Both my parents died in 2007—my dad in April, and my mother, Ruth, five months later.

After my parents died, I started going through their war keepsakes that included many pictures, letters, and firsthand accounts, all of which I scanned into my computer. Of particular interest to me were all the letters Dad had written to my mother while he was stationed in England.

My retirement in 2009 after 36 years of working in sales for Vision Service Plan (VSP), afforded me the opportunity to try to locate relatives of my dad's B-17 crew. Through a variety of sources (Ancestry.com, Obituaries, Facebook, etc.), I was able to find numerous relatives of all the crew except one. Although my search was time consuming, it was gratifying whenever I found a relative. I discovered that many of them did not have much knowledge of the *Susan Ruth* story so I started emailing all sorts of information to them.

Locating these relatives further ignited my enthusiasm for my research project. As a result, I became a member of The Mighty Eight Air Force Museum in Savannah, Georgia, The World War II Museum in New Orleans, Louisiana, the Air Forces Escape & Evasion Society (AFEES), The Eighth Air Force Historical Society, and the 306th Bomb Group Historical Association.

In 2011, the 306th Bomb Group held its annual reunion in San Diego, California, and I decided to attend with my oldest son Doug who had been extremely close to my parents. Later that year, Doug and I attended the AFEES reunion in San Antonio, Texas, and in 2012 we again attended the 306th Bomb Group reunion—this time in Savannah, Georgia. Talking with veterans and listening to their stories and to the stories told by relatives of Vets no longer living was an inspiration. Nonetheless, I thought what my dad and his crew had experienced was even more compelling.

Supporting this belief was the fact the story of my father's plane being shot down had already been written about in two books: Gerald Astor's *The Mighty Eighth – The Air War In Europe As Told By The Men*

Who Fought It and Russell Strong's *First Over Germany – A History of the 306th Bombardment Group*. So beginning with all the reference material my parents had accumulated, I decided to start writing a book.

As I began writing, I felt compelled to include both historical content and side notes about World War II to provide background and context. Therefore, this book is not only the story about my father and the crew of the *Susan Ruth*, but it is also a book filled with history and facts about a global cataclysmic event which resulted in more death than any other war in world history.

This book is a nonfiction, historical documentary. Every incident about the crew members has been taken from personal letters, interviews, declassified military records, and verbal and written accounts by the people who were involved 70 years ago.

Truth is stranger than fiction.
You can't make this stuff up.

Steve Snyder

1

FEBRUARY 8, 1944

I threw the extinguisher down, climbed back from between the seats where I had been standing, held the emergency switch on and began calling through the interphone for the crew to jump.

The bursting of the Focke-Wulf's 20 mm cannons around our ship was the first indication that we had been singled out. Then the celestial dome blew up in front of me. After that I could hear 20 mm striking and exploding as they hit the ship. Pieces of equipment and parts of the ship were flying about, striking my feet and legs.

When the oxygen cylinders exploded, I didn't realize what had happened. The noise of the explosion was muffled by my helmet and headset, but the concussion stunned me for a few moments. Someone lighting a match in a gas-filled room would cause much the same effect as the explosion. Only, instead of flames decreasing immediately after the explosion, they seemed to continue all around us with the same intensity.

In a half-dazed state, I became slowly conscious that the entire cockpit was filled with smoke and flames. I must have been knocked unconscious for a period of time. It was difficult to see through the smoke and flames, but I could see the terrified face of Eike, his eyes almost out of his head, looking crazily around him as he tore frantically at his flaksuit and safety belt. I think Holbert had already jumped as I couldn't see him at all.

As I looked back at Eike, after trying to see Holbert, he seemed absolutely mad and out of his head. Then, as my mind seemed to clear a little more, I too became absolutely terrified. I had been frightened before but never completely lost my wits from terror. It was horrible. I tried to yell or scream, but the sound died in my throat and my open mouth emitted no sound. I tried to jump out of my seat, but my safety belt held me there.

My only thought was to get out of that terrible fire. I couldn't think as I clawed wildly for my safety belt. The fact that I had buckled my safety belt under my flak suit on this raid, instead of over it in my usual way, was the only reason I was able to regain a semblance of sanity. For, as I endeavored to unfasten my safety belt, I could not realize in my terrorized and stupefied mind why I could not find it. It was only with great mental effort that I figured out why and thus started my thought process again. As I looked down and realized what the trouble was, a little of the terror left me. But it wasn't until I had thrown off my flak suit and unfastened my safety belt that I regained control of myself.

As I left my seat, Eike had just taken his chute pack from beneath his seat and made his way to the nose hatch to jump. I hesitated momentarily, not knowing what to do and switched on the auto pilot. Although not terrified as before, I was still greatly shaken and afraid. I acted more from instinct; I don't recall any thoughts. I grabbed a fire extinguisher, but it had no more effect on the blaze than an eyedropper. Deciding it would be impossible to save the ship, I threw the extinguisher down, climbed back from between the seats where I had been standing, held the emergency switch on and began calling through the interphone for the crew to jump. I don't know how long I continued to call, but not getting any response, I felt they had jumped.

The fire was getting so hot I could hardly stand it. My neck was burning and I pulled my scarf over the exposed skin. My nose, cheeks, eyebrows, eyelids and lower forehead must have been burned when I was using the extinguisher. I don't recall any pain from my face until I was on the ground. It was impossible to go back through the fire to see if they had jumped from the rear of the ship, and as I couldn't get any response from anyone, I left the cockpit. As I crawled down to the escape hatch, I was surprised to see Benny and Dan still in the nose. As I made my way toward them, Benny looked down and saw me. I motioned for him to come. He hit Dan on the arm and they both dived toward their chutes. We went out through the nose hatch.

When I jumped, our bomb bay doors were still open. As I crawled through the escape hatch, I recalled the discussion we had about clearing them when jumping and I wondered if I would. I did! I had been a good while without oxygen and was feeling the effects as I fell. We were at 20,000 feet. I was determined to make a delayed jump and as I extended my arms to stop somersaulting, I caught a glimpse of what I thought were eight billowing chutes.

Someone had told me that we would fall about 10,000 feet a minute so I started counting to sixty as I fell through the clouds, vapor and then clear air. But after reaching sixty, I still couldn't see the ground. I started counting again but gave it up and watched the ground. As I came out of a cloud, the earth appeared for a second and then disappeared again as I reached another cloud. I was falling into the country. There were little clusters of white farm buildings, green squares of pasture and dark brown, irregular and leafless woods. Then as the earth appeared again, I waited until I could distinguish objects very clearly and pulled the rip cord.

It seemed natural to wonder if the chute would open. I knew soon enough as the air caught, filled the chute, and the jerk nearly snapped off my head. The rushing air roaring in my ears stopped suddenly and a most wonderful and peaceful quiet settled over me. It seemed as if I had come out of that hell above into a heaven of peace and rest.

Up above, I could now hear the heavy deep sound of the "Forts" mingled with angry rasps of the fighters. But with the peaceful country coming up to meet me, baked in sunshine, the war and all that had happened only a few seconds before seemed like a bad dream long ago. A light breeze seemed to carry me toward a wood, and I reached up to grab the shrouds in order to guide myself into a pasture. I found I was so weak I could hardly lift myself up in my harness. I was too close to the ground to pilot my course. I placed my feet together and resignedly watched the trees rush up at me.

The above is an excerpt from a diary, hand written by Howard Snyder, pilot of the B-17 Flying Fortress *Susan Ruth* several weeks after he was shot down over German occupied Europe.

As he stated,

This story is being attempted primarily to occupy my time, which hangs heavily over my head, and secondly, it may prove of greater interest than a verbal account later.

I have refrained from writing this account before, for fear that it might fall into improper hands and cause serious results to those who have so kindly befriended me. However, Maurice has assured me that he has a great many hidden secret papers in connection with his work and one—more or less—would make little difference. Of course, persons, dates and places shall remain anonymous and I shall attempt to write in a somewhat vague manner in hopes of further safety.

It is impossible to know whether I shall be able to finish writing my adventure up to the point of departure or whether I will even leave this country. At least, it will give me something to do while I wait—wait—wait—in hope of returning to England through the underground.

After the war, Howard's diary was given to Lt. Jack Creek, U.S. Army 385th Anti-Aircraft Artillery by Maurice (whom Howard mentioned in his diary) and Ghislaine Bailleux in Charleroi, Belgium. Lt. Creek mailed it to Howard's wife, Ruth Snyder, on July 4, 1945, from Cuxhaven, Germany.

The envelope (containing Howard's diary)
that Lt. Creek sent to Ruth Snyder

2
HOWARD SNYDER

The result was that the lives of Howard and Ruth Snyder, as well those of millions of others around the world, were changed forever.

Growing Up ... in the Thirties

Howard John Snyder Jr. was born in Norfolk, Nebraska, on August 6, 1915; the only child of Howard John Snyder Sr. and Minna (Zuelow) Snyder. Howard's ancestry was staunchly German. His maternal grandparents, Carl and Augusta (Krueger) Zuelow were both born in Germany, and he was very close with his maternal grandfather whom he called Boo Papa. Howard's fifth great paternal grandparents were also born in Germany. He had noteworthy ancestors on his father's side of the family. Samuel Eddy sailed to America aboard the *Handmaid*, landing at Plymouth Harbor, Massachusetts, in 1630. William Eddy, David Lindsey, and Jonathan Allen all fought in the Revolutionary War. Simon Snyder was the third governor of Pennsylvania, serving three terms from 1808 to 1817.

The Snyder family lived a comfortable life at 511 Phillip Avenue in Norfolk and "Howdy," as his parents called their son, spent his free time hunting, fishing, and riding his pony. Devout Missouri Synod Lutherans, family members attended Grace Lutheran Church. Norfolk was founded in 1866 by German settlers from Ixonia, Wisconsin, and its most famous resident was television host Johnny Carson, who attended Norfolk High School, graduated from the University of Nebraska in 1949 and started his broadcasting career in Omaha, Nebraska.

The Snyder home in Norfolk, Nebraska

After Howard Sr. suffered a nervous breakdown in 1928, the family moved to Southern California and lived at 5433 Maplehurst Avenue in Eagle Rock, near Glendale. The family attended First Lutheran Church in Pasadena, California, one of the first three Missouri Synod churches founded in Southern California in 1892 and originally named First German Evangelical Lutheran St. Paul's Church. Howard attended Glendale High School where he was a star player on the basketball team. Glendale High's most famous alumnus was Marion Morrison from the Class of 1925. Morrison, nicknamed "Duke," was senior class president and later became the legendary actor John Wayne.

While he was in high school, the country and the world was suffering from the Great Depression, triggered by the U.S. stock market crash on October 29, 1929, known as Black Thursday. It was the longest, most widespread, and deepest depression of the 20th Century, and 100,000 businesses and banks failed. Eleven million people were out of work, one out of every three wage earners. In early 1933, most countries of the world slowly began to recover, and after

Howard graduated, he was able to get a job working for Desmond's Clothing Company located at 616 Broadway Street in downtown Los Angeles, where he worked for seven years and was eventually promoted to assistant warehouse manager.

At its peak, the Desmond's chain had nineteen stores throughout Southern California and was a major apparel retailer selling men's, women's and boys' clothing. During this time, Howard also continued playing basketball in the AAU (Amateur Athletic Union) leagues. The best teams in the AAU were sponsored by corporations who gave jobs to the players, usually former college players, who could earn a living while still maintaining their amateur status.

Howard met his future wife, Ruth Hempel, while attending Walther League, the Lutheran Church Missouri Synod's youth Bible and social organization. Ruth was born in Pasadena, California, on February 7, 1919, and was one of five children of Frank and Hulda (Radig) Hempel who lived at 1239 N. El Molino Avenue in Pasadena.

After graduating from high school, Ruth continued her education at Pasadena Junior College where she was a classmate of the legendary Jackie Robinson (also born in 1919). She then transferred to UCLA, as did Robinson, where she graduated with a B.A. degree in History on June 14, 1941. Ruth would also earn a teaching credential and for a short period of time was a third grade teacher at Garfield Elementary School in Long Beach, California.

Jackie Robinson was UCLA's first athlete to win varsity letters in four sports: baseball, basketball, football and track. He was one of four black players on the 1939 UCLA football team (the others were Woody Strode, Kenny Washington, and Ray Bartlett) who made up three of the team's four backfield players. Because only a handful of black players participated in mainstream college football, UCLA was college football's most integrated team at the time. Although baseball was Robinson's "worst sport" at UCLA (he hit .097 in his only season), he played major league baseball for nine years (1947 to 1956) and was inducted into the Baseball Hall of Fame in 1962. When the Brooklyn Dodgers started him at first base on April 15, 1947, he became the first African American to play Major League Baseball, breaking the baseball color line. In 1997, Major League Baseball "universally" retired his uniform number 42, across all major league teams; the first pro athlete in any sport to be so honored. Another first came on April 15, 2004, when Major League Baseball adopted the annual tradition of "Jackie Robinson Day" when every player on every team wears #42.

While Howard was working at Desmond's and Ruth was going to college, much of the world was at war. Italy invaded Ethiopia in 1935. The Spanish Civil War began in 1936 when fascist Francisco Franco attempted to overthrow the democratic government. Japan invaded China in 1937 and the Soviet Union in 1938. Germany occupied Austria in 1938, took over Czechoslovakia in May 1939, invaded Poland the following September, and then conquered Denmark, Norway, France, Belgium, and the Netherlands in 1940.

Still reeling from the Depression, the United States wanted to avoid foreign entanglements and favored a policy of noninvolvement in European affairs. Americans envisioned a repeat of World War I and desired to stay out of the never ending quarrels between European nations. Charles Lindbergh was the leader in the anti-war America First movement and a particularly outspoken critic about entering the war. Lindbergh had gained fame in 1927 for the first non-stop solo flight across the Atlantic Ocean from New York to Paris in the monoplane Spirit of Saint Louis. In addition, the kidnapping and murder of his infant son in 1932 was called the "Crime of the Century." It led to Congress passing the "Lindbergh Law" making kidnapping across state lines a federal offense.

Even though Americans wanted to stay neutral in the face of the blatant aggression by the Axis Powers (mainly Germany, Italy, and Japan) in Europe and the Pacific, President Franklin Delano Roosevelt (FDR) understood that the U.S.'s involvement in the war was inevitable and began to prepare for it. At the time, America's military was woefully weak; in 1939 it ranked only 18th in the world, behind Romania. In the fall of 1940, FDR pushed Congress to approve the first peacetime military draft in U.S. history which required the registration of all men between the ages of 21 and 35 (about 16 million men). Howard Snyder registered on October 16, 1940.

He decided to join the military, and in Los Angeles on April 1, 1941, was inducted into the United States Army. His last day working for Desmond's was April 7, and on April 12 he reported to Fort Lewis, Washington, for Basic and Advanced Training as a member of the 163rd Infantry Regiment, 82nd Infantry Brigade, 41st Infantry Division. While on leave, he and Ruth got married on July 3, 1941, at First Lutheran Church in Pasadena.

Ruth and Howard Snyder's
Wedding Photo

Ruth and Howard Snyder
on their Honeymoon

A Date That Will Live in Infamy

Later that year, on December 7, 1941, the Japanese bombed Pearl Harbor, Hawaii, and the United States officially entered World War II. The Japanese surprise attack was a devastating shock to America. From six aircraft carriers, 353 Japanese planes hit Pearl Harbor on a quiet Sunday morning in an attempt to neutralize the U.S. Pacific Fleet. All eight U.S. battleships were damaged, with four being sunk. More than 2,400 Americans were killed and almost 1,300 injured. Fortunately, the entire fleet of American aircraft carriers was not in port at the time of the attack on Pearl Harbor.

Prior to the attack, the Japanese ambassador to the United States was supposed to deliver a note officially breaking diplomatic relations with the United States; however, it was delivered late, after the bombing attack on Pearl Harbor. Americans were traumatized that the Japanese would do such an under-handed sneak attack. Upon hearing of the mistiming of the communiqué breaking diplomatic relations with the United States, Admiral Isoroku Yamamoto, commander-in-chief of the Japanese naval fleet, purportedly said, "I fear all we have done is to awaken a sleeping giant and fill him with a terrible resolve." It prophetically turned out to be absolutely true.

The following day, President Roosevelt addressed a joint session of Congress and called December 7 *a date that will live in infamy.* The Pearl Harbor attack immediately galvanized a divided nation into action. Although public opinion had been moving towards support for entering the war during 1941, there was still considerable opposition. However, after the attack, Americans immediately united against Japan. On the strategic level, the attack on Pearl Harbor ended up being a disaster for Japan.

The bombing of Pearl Harbor surprised even Germany. Although Chancellor Adolf Hitler had made an oral agreement with his Axis partner, Japan, that Germany would join a war against the U.S., he was uncertain as to how war would be declared against the United

States. Japan's attack on Pearl Harbor answered that question. Hitler didn't want the United States to beat him to the punch and declare war on Germany, and he despised Roosevelt for his repeated verbal attacks against his Nazi ideology. Mistakenly, Hitler believed that Japan was much stronger than it was and that once Japan had defeated the United States, it would help Germany defeat Russia. So on December 11, Germany and its other Axis partner Italy declared war on the U.S. Strategically, this was a huge mistake since there was almost no chance the U.S. would have declared war on Germany for quite some time. It would have devoted all its resources to the Pacific theatre in order to defeat Japan.

The result was that the lives of Howard and Ruth Snyder, as well those of millions of others around the world, were changed forever. Not only would the young couple's lives be dramatically changed by the war, but also by Ruth becoming pregnant during her visit with Howard at Fort Lewis that 1941 Christmas. Ruth had pleaded with Howard, "Let's not use anything just once" and bingo! Having the responsibility of a new bride and a baby on the way, Howard felt he needed to make more money to support them. The next year, he decided to leave the Army and become a pilot in the Air Force because the pay was much better. He volunteered to enter the Army Air Corps Aviation Cadet Training Program in June 1942.

3

PILOT TRAINING

Successful completion of pilot training was not easy. Almost 40 percent of those that entered failed to complete the Primary, Basic or Advanced stage of pilot instruction.

Becoming a Military Pilot

Howard received pre-flight training from June 18 to September 29, 1942, at Santa Ana Air Force Base in Santa Ana, California, under the 81st Flying Training Wing of the Army Air Forces Training Command. In the beginning classification stage when cadets were processed, it was decided whether they would go on to train as pilots, navigators, or bombardiers. Regardless of the outcome, pre-flight school was attended by all three. Candidates who failed the advanced physical were sent back to the regular Army.

The first six weeks of training concentrated on physical conditioning and military discipline. This was followed by three weeks of academics involving the mechanics and physics of flight and courses in mathematics, physics, aeronautics, and other disciplines. Cadets' skills were measured by 10 hours in a crude flight simulator called a "blue box." Those that passed, which Howard did, were given cadet wings and were then promoted to Pilot, Bombardier or Navigator School. During this time, Ruth and Howard's first child, Susan Ruth, was born on September 19, 1942.

Frank and Hulda Hempel, Howard and Minn Snyder, and Howard and Ruth Snyder with baby Susan Ruth

Pilot School involved four phases of training: *Primary, Basic, Advanced,* and *Transition.* In Primary training, cadets learned to fly a small aircraft of low horsepower; in Basic, they transitioned to a heavier plane with more complex controls; in Advanced, they learned to fly a still more powerful machine which approximated the characteristics of combat aircraft.

Primary Pilot Training, conducted by contract schools (civilian pilot training schools), taught basic flight using two-seater training aircraft. In Primary, cadets got around 60 to 65 flight hours in various types of bi-planes before advancing on to Basic Training. Howard received his Primary Flight Training in a Stearman PT-13 (PT for Primary Training) at Hancock College of Aeronautics in Santa Maria, California, from October 2, 1942, to December 2, 1942. He flew his first solo flight on October 22 and graduated as a part of Class 43-D on December 3, 1942.

Howard Snyder at Primary Flight Training School

It was the mission of the Basic schools to make military pilots out of

Primary graduates; hence, these schools were completely controlled and operated by the military. Basic Pilot Training taught cadets to fly in formation, fly by instruments or by aerial navigation, fly at night, and fly for long distances. Instrument training was doubtless the most important part of the Basic curriculum. The experience of combat missions underlined the necessity of flying at night and under all weather conditions. As such, missions required the operation of aircraft by instruments. For instrument flying, a black hood was put over the cadet's head so they couldn't look out the window.

Cadets completed about 70 flight hours in single wing Vultee BT-9 or BT-13 training planes (BT for Basic Trainer) before being promoted to Advanced Training. Howard flew a Vultee BT-13 Valiant which was more complex, had a more powerful engine, was faster, and heavier than the Stearman PT-13 Primary Trainer. Howard went through Basic Flight School from December 6 to February 6, 1943, with the 35th Flying Training Wing at Lemoore, California, with some flying time at Marana Army Air Field in Arizona because of the persistent fog in California.

Although Howard was able to see Ruth and Susan occasionally, he really missed being with them and went through some depressing moments. The day after Christmas, 1943, he wrote,

> *Yesterday was one of the hardest partings we have had as far as I am concerned, Baby. I wanted to stay with you so! You have been hard enough to leave and now little Susan makes it even more difficult. I am getting to the point where I don't care about anything but you. I have tried to think of the future and do what I thought would be the best for us in the days to come. Now I don't care whether I get a commission or not. I would just as soon be a buck private if I could be with you.*

Later he wrote,

You'll get a kick out of this. I was doing some navigation earlier today when a fellow walked in looking for someone. My shirt was off as it was quite warm in the barracks. He suddenly asked, "Are you married?" I was surprised but answered yes, as I thought he was looking at your and Susan's picture.

He said, 'Your wife sure put a 'hicky' on your neck." I just about fell off the chair! He said, "I raise hell with my wife when she does that." I told him I didn't think many knew what the mark was, but he seemed to think everyone knew what they were. It really is a big one—about an inch and a half long and half an inch wide."

Basic Pilot School was confined to training on single-engine aircraft and one of the responsibilities of the basic schools was the selection of students for single- or two-engine Advanced Training. Advanced Pilot Training placed the graduates in two categories: single-engine pilots flew the AT-6 (AT for Advanced Trainer), and multi-engine pilots learned to fly the AT-9, AT-10 or AT-17. Howard flew both the Curtiss-Wright AT-9 and Cessna AT-17 Bobcat which were twin-engine AT aircraft used to bridge the gap between single-engine trainers and twin-engine combat aircraft.

Cadets were supposed to total about 75 to 80 flight hours of training before graduating and earning their pilot's wings. Howard attended the 83rd Flying Training Wing Advanced Flight School at Douglas Army Airfield, Arizona, and trained on multi-engine planes from February 7 to April 11. He graduated in Class 43-D and received his pilot wings and commission as a Second Lieutenant (2nd Lt.) on April 12, 1943. On that day, Howard officially entered active duty in the armed forces of the United States. His pilot identification card listed him at Height 6' 2 1/2"—Weight 182 lb.—Color Eyes blue—Color Hair blonde/brown—Complexion Fair. In those days, Howard was considered a tall person, and he was proud of his height. Even later in life, he always proudly included that half inch whenever stating his height.

(Top) Pilot Training Class 43-D, Howard Snyder, second row, third person from left;

(Right) Howard Snyder after graduation from Advanced Pilot Training and receiving his pilot wings

Howard's future co-pilot, George W. Eike, from Rochester, New York, went through Basic Flight Training at Chico Army Air Field in California and flew Vultee BT-13s. He took Advanced Training in two-engine medium bomber aircraft at Ardmore, Oklahoma, and Douglas, Arizona. While at Douglas, George wrote,

This post is right on the edge of Mexico and all the country around here is desert. It sure is plenty hot and very dry. I went across the border to Mexico once, but there is not much to see other than poverty and dirt. It is just as you see in the picture postcards.

He received his pilot wings and commission to 2nd Lt. as part of Class 43-F on June 22, 1943. Eike's parents, Derwood and Ella, and his fiancée, Helen Prietz, flew in from Rochester, New York, for his graduation and afterwards he and Helen were married. He had a ten day leave so they went to Los Angeles and visited Hollywood for their honeymoon.

Helen and George Eike

Successful completion of pilot training was not easy. Almost 40 percent of those who entered failed to complete the Primary, Basic, or Advanced stage of pilot instruction. Most of the students eliminated from pilot training were reassigned to other types of instruction or service. The majority of men who had the qualifications were sent to bombardier or navigator schools where they joined those who were assigned to these schools during classification at pre-flight training. Those who didn't have the qualifications were assigned to other combat crew positions—positions which required courses in flexible gunnery and one of the various companion specialties, such as airplane mechanics. Aviation cadets who washed out of navigator or bombardier training were usually sent to gunnery school.

The three stages—Primary, Basic and Advanced—were integral to the training of all Air Corps pilots, and upon graduation from Advanced, students received their wings and 2nd Lieutenant bars (called gold but made out of brass). This step, however, did not signify the end of their training. The new pilots were given additional periods of specialized instruction suited to their military assignments. In Transitional Pilot Training, single-engine pilots transitioned to fighters and fighter-bombers and multi-engine pilots transitioned to transports or bombers. Transition to combat planes was a larger undertaking than previous transitions to training planes. It involved not only learning to fly a complex, high-performance aircraft, but also the mastering of complex flying techniques.

4

FOUR ENGINES

... this included 120 hours of air training in which the cadet began with practice runs and ended by performing bombing runs with live ordnance.

Combat Training

Both Howard and George were transitioned to the four-engine B-17 heavy bomber, the specific aircraft they would fly in combat. For whatever reason, Howard was selected to be a first pilot and George a co-pilot. Transition to a B-17 was the last stage of their individual training. After two months of training here, they were ready for Operational Unit Combat Training which consisted of three phases designed to train flight crew members to blend their individual skills together into a team as members of an aircrew and as a combat unit. Crew and unit indoctrination normally required about twelve weeks, after which the crews were then sent to staging areas to prepare for movement overseas.

Howard's future bombardier, Richard L. Daniels, from Cleveland Heights, Ohio, went through training at Salt Lake City, Utah, Galveston, Texas, and finally Bombardier School at Childress, Texas, where he received his commission to 2nd Lt. and bombardier wings on May 13, 1943. Bombardier School lasted 18 weeks. It consisted of 425 hours of ground instruction in the critical proficiencies of a bombardier. After three weeks this included 120 hours of air training in which the cadet began with practice runs and ended by performing

Richard and Virginia (Ginny) Daniels

bombing runs with live ordnance. Daniels was married to Virginia (Ginny) Ford on February 6, 1943.

Howard's future navigator, Robert Benninger, from Pittsburgh, Pennsylvania, went to Navigator School and received his commission to 2nd Lt. and navigator wings on July 15, 1943. Navigator School also lasted 18 weeks. It consisted of 500 hours of ground instruction in the duties of a navigator (charting, directional bearings, computed headings, airspeed, radio codes, celestial navigation, etc.). After four weeks, cadets acted as a navigator in both day and night flights.

Both bombardier training and navigator training included a flexible gunnery course and, upon completion of training, the graduates were assigned to crew and unit training. All of the enlisted members of bombardment crews, also referred to as non-commissioned officers or NCOs, were required to have flexible gunnery, some of whom were designated as career gunners with no other specialty. This specialized training was imperative because when a bomber was under attack by enemy fighters, it was the gunners who defended the plane and likely determined the fate of the crew.

Only the pilot and co-pilot were exempt from gunnery instruction on the Browning .50-caliber machine gun which was the standard equipment on American bombers. In addition to gunnery training, Roy Holbert, Howard's future flight engineer and top turret gunner, received his technical training at Amarillo Army Air Field in Texas. Although Amarillo was originally established for training mechanics to service B-17 bombers, it was later designated to train B-17 technicians and flight engineers.

Operational Unit Combat Training for pilots Howard Snyder and George Eike started in early July 1943 at Pyote, Texas. The First Phase was directed primarily toward checking out pilots and co-pilots and training individual crewmen for their designated positions. The first integrated crew training also took place during this phase. Combat crew #19-6-78 consisting of: pilot Howard Snyder, co-pilot George W. Eike, bombardier Richard L. Daniels, gunner John Pindroch, flight engineer Roy K. Holbert, radio operator Kenneth O. Blye, and gunner Richard W. Harper.

They were assigned to the 30th Bomb Squadron, 19th Bomb Group. Although each crew was assigned a number, the Army Air Forces always referred to a crew by the pilot's name; thus the men always referred to themselves as part of Howard Snyder's crew.

Marriage ... "on the Fly"

Pyote Air Force Base in Texas became the largest bomber installation in the country and was nicknamed "Rattlesnake Bomber Base" for the numerous rattlesnake dens that were uncovered during its construction. Despite morale problems caused by isolation, the lack of off-base recreation and the shortage of dependents' housing, Pyote achieved a distinguished record in molding inexperienced individuals into effective bomber crews. Ruth with her baby, Susan Ruth, and Helen Eike followed their husbands to Pyote. Being officer's wives, they were able to find housing and lived in nearby towns: Ruth and baby Susan in Kermit, Texas, and Helen in Monahans, Texas, where she rented a bedroom from a local couple. Pyote was located in West

Texas and very near the southeast corner of New Mexico. It was in the middle of nowhere. As George Eike wrote, "This post is next to a little one-horse, western town, and believe me, this country out here is desolate."

Susan Ruth Snyder at Kermit, Texas House

Because Howard and George had to live on base and flew training missions at all hours of the day and night, the young couples were only able to see each other about every other day. Nonetheless, they cherished their time together. Since Howard and Ruth were married while he was on leave from the Army, their time spent together in Kermit was the only time they were really "together" as a couple. As Howard wrote to Ruth,

> *I want to tell you how much I love you and how happy I am with you near. The last few days with you have been like a new world, sweetheart. It is such a comfort to know you and little Susan are so near and I will see you again soon. It is such a thrill to see you come to the door when I come back from the field. You would bring Susan with you and there you would be, the two that are my whole life.*

Both couples were trying their best to conceive. The Snyders were successful as Ruth became pregnant with their second child.

On July 30, 1943, Special Order #208 attached crew #19-6-78 to the 333rd Bomb Group, a B-17 Replacement Operational Training Unit under the command of the Second Air Force located at Dalhart Army Air Force Base, Texas. This was the Second Phase of Operational Unit Combat Training at the crew, flight, and squadron levels. This phase of training focused on bombing, gunnery and flying the aircraft under instrument flight conditions. The Second Air Force organized the personnel, aircraft and equipment into combat groups and squadrons.

The Third-Phase of Operational Unit Combat Training during September, also at Dalhart, Texas, included ground school study of intelligence and tactics, practice bombing, gunnery, instrument flying, formation flying, short-range navigation flights, and long-range navigation cross country flights. Specifically, third phase training emphasized squadron and group operations, especially with formation flying in the combat "box" which was developed by Eighth Air Force to maximize the firepower of the bomber aircraft and its defenses against attacking enemy fighters. In addition to long distance navigation, target identification was taught along with mock combat mission runs over practice target areas in the Texas Panhandle.

Nearly all new heavy bomb groups organized after Pearl Harbor were structured and trained at Dalhart by the Second Air Force, II Bomber Command. Once the newly formed crews finished their training, they received their combat assignments to either new combat groups or sent directly to the European Theater of Operations (ETO) for assignment as replacement crews for groups already in combat.

Ruth and Helen had followed their husbands again to Dalhart which was another desolate place in Northwest Texas, just east of New Mexico and south of Colorado. Howard called it a "God forsaken town," and Helen Eike wrote, "There isn't anything to do here in Dalhart, but George and I manage to keep very happy doing nothing. We only have about four more weeks left before he is shipped overseas." Knowing their husbands would soon be going off to war, the two couples treasured every minute they could be together.

When Howard's crew finally received orders to ship out, their young wives returned home; Helen to Rochester, New York, and Ruth driving herself and Susan in their Nash back to Pasadena, California. Howard would say,

I shall never forget the dance that last Saturday night at the club, the Sunday you spent with me at the post, the last good-bye in the dark that morning; how much easier you made it by being so brave and especially our last night (September 26) together.

5

SEPTEMBER 27, 1943 ... OFF TO ENGLAND

A B-17 had a ten-man crew comprised of a pilot, co-pilot, bombardier, navigator, flight engineer/top turret gunner, radio operator, ball turret gunner, two waist gunners, and a tail turret gunner.

The B-17

Departing on September 27, 1943, from Dalhart, Texas, the crew began their journey to Europe to join the war against Adolf Hitler and Nazi Germany. The first stop for Snyder's crew was Scott Field in Illinois where they were assigned a brand new B-17.

Built by The Boeing Aircraft Company in Seattle, Washington, the B-17 was a four-engine, heavy bomber aircraft first developed in the 1930s for the United States Army Air Corps. It was America's first four-engine, all metal bomber. Its main purpose during World War II was high altitude, daylight precision strategic bombing campaigns against German industrial and military targets. The B-17 was a potent long-range bomber. Through widely circulated stories and photos of B-17s returning home after surviving severe battle damage, its mythical and iconic status as a "Flying Fortress" flourished. Today, Boeing is headquartered in Chicago, Illinois, and is the world's largest aerospace company and manufacturer of commercial and military aircraft.

The B-17 underwent a number of improvements during its ten-year production run from the YB-17 model to the B-17G model. Throughout the war the B-17 was refined and improved based on data collected from combat missions during the war. The final B-17 production model, the B-17G, was produced in larger quantities (8,680) than any other previous model and was considered to be the definitive "Flying Fortress."

B-17 Flying Fortress

A B-17 had a ten-man crew comprised of a pilot, co-pilot, bombardier, navigator, flight engineer/top turret gunner, radio operator, ball turret gunner, two waist gunners, and a tail turret gunner. With its 11-13 .50-caliber machine guns (chin, cheek, top, ball, waist and tail), the B-17 earned respect from the German Air Force not only for its defensive firepower, but also for its ability to take and withstand heavy combat damage.

During World War II, the B-17 was deployed primarily by the Eighth Air Force in Europe, participating in countless missions from air bases in England. A typical B-17 mission often lasted for more than eight hours, striking targets deep within enemy territory. By the end of the war, B-17s dropped 640,036 tons of bombs on European targets in daylight raids, more than any other U.S. aircraft. A total of

12,732 B-17s were built between 1935 and May, 1945. Out of this total, approximately one-third, 4,735, were lost in combat.

The most famous B-17 was the *Memphis Belle*, a B-17F of the 91st Bomb Group and 324th Bomb Squadron. It became the first U.S. heavy bomber to complete 25 missions with her crew intact. Twenty-five missions were significant because at the time it was the number required for an airman to complete his combat tour and be able to return to the U.S.

For many, the story of the Memphis Belle became a timeless symbol of all the heroic United States Army Air Force (USAAF) bomber crews who flew against Nazi Germany in World War II. In 1944, a documentary film *Memphis Belle: a Boeing B-17 Flying Fortress* was made which depicted the last mission of the crew on May 15, 1943. It clearly illustrated the everyday courage of the men who manned the B-17 bombers and was used as a morale-building inspiration for the country. In 1990, a fictionalized version of the documentary was released as the theatrical film *Memphis Belle* starring Matthew Modine, Eric Stoltz, and Harry Connick Jr.

Scott Field—Final Flight Training

The primary purpose of Scott Field was to train radio operators, but it also was a major air terminal due to its centralized location in the United States. As a result of a major construction project, it provided the capability to give Advanced Flying School graduates instruction in instrument and night flying, navigation, and photography.

During their time at Scott, Howard Snyder's crew calibrated their navigation instruments, made a number of familiarization flights around the area, and were thoroughly briefed on the upcoming flight over the North Atlantic to England. On October 1, Howard passed the Second Air Force's test in Instrument Flying. He wrote to Ruth,

I found out at Scott at the last minute that we could have our ship named. I had so much to do that I sent Benny (navigator Robert Benninger) out to find a painter, but he was so busy that he didn't get around to the ship before we left so she still doesn't have her name painted on her.

On October 6, 1943, Howard Snyder and his crew finally completed their flight training and were assigned to the European Theater of Operations United States Army Air Forces—specifically to the Eighth Army Air Force. The crew then flew from Illinois to Dow Army Airfield in Bangor, Maine, which serviced long-range heavy bombers prior to their flight to England. On their flight from Illinois to Maine, the crew learned they would be flying right over George Eike's parents' house in Rochester, New York. George informed his father, Derwood, they would be flying over on a certain afternoon. George's father was so excited that he made a four foot sign out of a roll of paper that read "EIKE," and climbed up on the roof with his movie camera.

He waited there all day until, when in the early twilight, a B-17 came swooping out of the west so low he could almost count its rivets. The big bomber circled the house three times while Derwood gyrated wildly to keep his camera trained on the plane, while waving to George at the same time. About midnight, George called and said,

Hello Dad and Mother. I can't tell you where I am, but we landed all right. And say, tell me, what was our name doing on top of the house? My crew thought there was an "Eike Airport" nearby and started to prepare for a landing.

WC No. 15166

Name HOWARD JOHN SNYDER

Date of Birth 8/6/15

Weight 182

Height 6 ft 2 in.

Color Eyes Blue

Color Hair Blond

Date of Issue 4/12/43

Signature Howard J. Snyder

Ratings Held Pilot

1549—SANTA ANA—1-9-43—9,000

Howard Snyder
Pilot ID Card

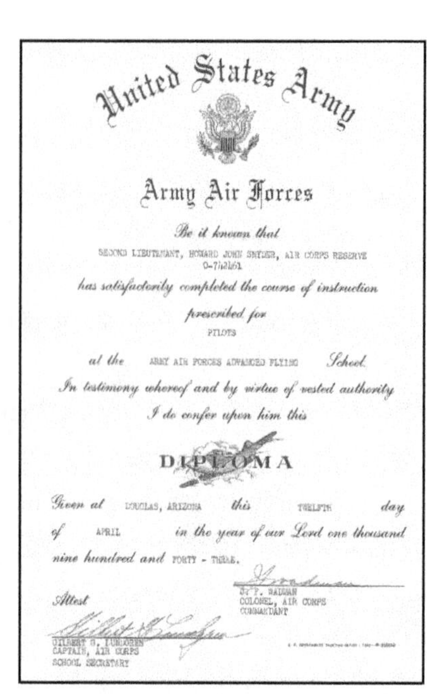

United States Army

Army Air Forces

Be it known that

SECOND LIEUTENANT, HOWARD JOHN SNYDER, AIR CORPS RESERVE
0-742161

has satisfactorily completed the course of instruction

prescribed for

PILOTS

at the ARMY AIR FORCES ADVANCED FLYING *School*

In testimony whereof and by virtue of vested authority
I do confer upon him this

DIPLOMA

Given at DOUGLAS, ARIZONA *this* TWELFTH *day*
of APRIL *in the year of our Lord one thousand*
nine hundred and FORTY - THREE.

[illegible]
COLONEL, AIR CORPS
COMMANDANT

Attest

GILBERT G. LUNDGREN
CAPTAIN, AIR CORPS
SCHOOL SECRETARY

Howard Snyder Advanced
Flying School Diploma

Ruth Snyder with
baby Susan Ruth

Susan Ruth Snyder

6

NEWFOUNDLAND

In Gander, flight crews worked feverishly on their planes to get them ready for the flight to England.

Beginning History of the Eighth Air Force

On 20 June 1941, the United States War Department granted autonomy to the Army Air Forces (AAF), and Major General Harold "Hap" Arnold assumed the title of Chief of the Army Air Forces. The Eighth Air Force under the command of Major General Carl Spaatz came into existence in January 1942, with its activation at Hunter Field in Savannah, Georgia. Shortly afterwards, its headquarters were established in England, and its first mission was flown on August 17 1942, to bomb the marshalling yards (railroad depot) at Rouen and Scotteville in northern France.

The main combat operations of the Eighth Air Force consisted of:

- The VIII Bomber Command overseeing strategic bombardment using heavy 4-engine bombers, the B-17 Flying Fortress and the B-24 Liberator (the B meaning bomber);
- The VIII Fighter Command providing fighter escort for the heavy bombers; and
- The VIII Air Support Command providing reconnaissance, troop transport, and tactical bombardment using 2-engine medium bombers (B-25 Mitchell and B-26 Marauder).

Its mission was to inflict strategic blows to Germany's economy and industry in order to destroy the enemy's will to fight, by means of "daylight precision bombing." Up to this point, bombing in Europe had been exclusively at night.

In response to Germany's sustained bombing of cities (particularly London) in England, the British Royal Air Force (RAF) strategy was one of "area bombardment" at night on German urban and industrial centers. The RAF experimented briefly in 1940 with daylight attacks on industrial targets in Germany but soon abandoned the effort when losses proved unbearably heavy. Area bombardment was laid out in a British Air Staff paper, dated September 23, 1941, and read:

> The ultimate aim of an attack on a town area is to break the morale of the population which occupies it. To ensure this, we must achieve two things: first, we must make the town physically uninhabitable and, secondly, we must make the people conscious of constant personal danger. The immediate aim is therefore twofold, namely, to produce (1) destruction and (2) fear of death.

In January 1943, at the Casablanca Conference, it was agreed that the RAF operations against Germany would be reinforced by the United States Army Air Force (USAAF) in a Combined Operations Offensive plan called "Operation Pointblank." The text of the "Casablanca Directive" read:

> Your (USAAF) primary objective will be the progressive destruction and dislocation of the German military, industrial and economic system and the undermining of the morale of the German people to a point where their capacity for armed resistance is fatally weakened.

That meant "precision bombing" of military targets, not simply bombing cities. Submarine construction facilities, aircraft factories, ball bearing production plants, and oil refineries were at the top of the list. In essence, the RAF and the Eighth Air Force planned a coordinated non-stop, night and day bombing offensive. British Prime Minister Winston Churchill had previously been skeptical of daylight bombing but changed his mind as a result of a comment made by Eighth Air Force General Ira Eaker who stated: "By bombing the devils around the clock, we can prevent the German defenses from getting any rest."

Casablanca

The Casablanca Conference took place in Casablanca, Morocco, then a French protectorate, from January 14 to 24, 1943. Its purpose was to plan the Allied European strategy for the next phase of World War II. In attendance were United States President Franklin Roosevelt, British Prime Minister Winston Churchill, and representing the Free French forces, General Charles de Gaulle and General Henri Giraud.

The meeting resulted in the "Casablanca Declaration" meaning that the Allies would accept nothing less than the "unconditional surrender" of the "Axis Powers" (Germany, Italy and Japan). Roosevelt had borrowed the term "unconditional surrender" from Union Army General Ulysses S. Grant who had communicated this stance to the Confederate Army during the American Civil War—from 1861 to 1865.

Premier Joseph Stalin of the Soviet Union had been invited to the Conference but declined to attend, citing the ongoing conflict in Stalingrad, Russia, required his presence in the Soviet Union. The Battle of Stalingrad took place from August 1942, to February 1943, and is considered by many historians as the turning point of the war. Marked by constant close quarters, hand-to-hand combat and disregard for civilian and military casualties by both sides, it was arguably the bloodiest battles in the history of warfare. It resulted in an estimated total of almost two million Axis and Soviet casualties.

The failure of the German Army at Stalingrad was a disaster. The entire German 6th Army was lost and more than 100,000 soldiers were taken prisoner with only 6,000 of them ever returning home. With such a massive loss of men and equipment, the Germans simply did not have enough firepower to cope with the Russian advance into Germany when it came. Stalingrad was Hitler's most fatal blunder. Even though control of the city was of no real strategic value, Hitler was determined to annihilate it simply because it was named after Stalin whom he despised.

The Mighty Eighth

The VIII Bomber Command (later renamed the Eighth Air Force in 1944), now under the command of Brigadier General Ira C. Eaker, was comprised of three divisions. The 1st Division had thirteen B-17 bomb groups; the 2nd Division had fourteen B-24 bomb groups; and the 3rd Division had fifteen B-17 bomb groups. When each group operated at full capacity, there were a total of 1,600 bombers and 1,200 fighters available for combat. Between airmen, ground crews, and support personnel, "The Mighty Eighth" consisted of 300,000 men.

By June 1944, the Eighth Air Force had forty-four heavy bomber bases and another fifteen fighter bases spread out through the East Anglia area of England, a province of just 1.7 million people, where Americans would come to outnumber the villagers by as many as a hundred to one. In an area about the size of Vermont, enough concrete for air fields was laid across cornfields and cow pastures to pave thousands of miles of highway in the broad peninsula of Suffolk, Norfolk, and Cambridgeshire that juts into the North Sea like a thumb.

Howard Snyder and his crew left Maine on October 7, 1943, with their next stop being Gander, Newfoundland, Canada. The United States used various Royal Canadian Air Force (RCAF) bases in Newfoundland as staging points and stepping stones for its buildup of a strategic air force in Great Britain. In Gander, flight crews worked feverishly on their planes to get them ready for the flight to England. The pilots and crewmen were busy test flying their planes and correcting any problems they discovered. Howard wrote,

> *Benny (navigator Robert Benninger) has been hitting his destinations right on the button. He has done a good job on the flights. This is really the first time he has had any flights that he has had to rely entirely upon himself. I propositioned a fellow here this afternoon to paint our ship. She is the* Susan Ruth *now! She's the sweetest little baby in the world! I will send you a picture when we get "over there."*
>
> *This is a barren and cold land way up here. The fields way up here from nowhere are better posts than the dumps we were at in Texas. The food is better, prices are lower, and the buildings are more comfortable. And they say the fishing is exceptionally good here. We are going fishing tomorrow and try our luck. This country is all forest and lakes. I remember when I was a little fellow, and dad used to tell me stories of the big North Woods and bear and moose. Well, this is it. The forests are full of wildlife.*

Civilians were often invited onto the Newfoundland bases to take part in various social activities, including softball games and movie nights. Many Newfoundland men resented the influx of thousands of young unmarried American servicemen, many of whom were away from home for the first time, and the attention they were receiving from local women. Howard said, "The boys call the local girls here 'Newfie Girls.' I had to laugh at the description one of the soldiers had for them, 'They either have no teeth and a figure or a figure and no teeth.'"

Gander also gave the crews a last opportunity to take advantage of shopping in North America. They filled their planes with cases of cigarettes, candy, liquor, and soap, with the more audacious and farsighted buying silk stockings. As Howard wrote,

> *Liquor is really cheap here. I got a fifth of Old Taylor for $1.75. I hope we get weathered in up here awhile. It is pretty nice, and we're getting extra overseas pay. We are having a good time. If it weren't for the fact that I am away from you, Princess, I would not miss this for the world. I suppose I will wish before long that I was back home, but right now it is pretty exciting, not knowing what kind of country we are going to fly over next. The suspense of the unknown is exhilarating. After being a home boy for so long and finally having something like this happen is like a book, only I wish it could have happened before I met you.*

7

ACROSS "THE POND"... ENGLAND AT LAST

Flying across the Atlantic was dangerous because it was done by recently trained, inexperienced combat crews in adverse weather.

Two Thousand Miles of Ocean

The combat air crews flew their own planes to Great Britain. However, the ground echelons were transported overseas by ships—usually on ocean liners like the *Queen Mary* and *Queen Elizabeth*. Leaving New York Harbor, the ships would carry four times the number of peacetime passengers, and staterooms were usually jammed with sixteen men to each compartment so they had to sleep in shifts. After leaving New York, the ships made a high-speed trip across the treacherous Atlantic Ocean in constant fear of attacks by German submarines. Even though large ocean liners, like one of the *Queens*, were fast enough to outrun any Nazi submarine or surface ship, as a precautionary measure, they still used automatic steering to follow a constantly changing zigzag course.

Flying across the Atlantic was dangerous because it was done by recently trained, inexperienced combat crews in adverse weather. Howard said, "We are ready to leave at any time. They say that very few planes are lost on the hop across the Atlantic which is good news. Do you remember Major Thomson at Pyote? He was lost about ten days ago on the way across. They haven't found him yet and probably won't."

From Canada, the *Susan Ruth* finally headed to Europe on October 13, flying to Prestwick, Scotland, which was the Eighth Air Force's destination for new aircrews and their planes. Howard wrote,

> *We left from Newfoundland for our long hop across. It was a long flight, over more than 2,000 miles of water. We had no trouble, and the ship flew beautifully. I can tell you that we are somewhere in England but not where.*
>
> *We had to take off on instruments, and off and on, must have flown about two or three hours on instruments. We picked up a bit of ice but nothing to become alarmed about. It was as cold as 20 degrees below but our heater worked well so we were comfortable. We flew over an under cast most of the way. The water looked cold and black, and I must confess I felt more comfortable when we were flying over the clouds. The sunshine looked beautiful, and we were glad to see the sun. I don't like flying at night very much. Benny knew where we were all the time, but when we hit weather and started flying instruments, we had to rely on our radio. Let me tell you, radio is a wonderful thing! It brought us right in. You put a lot of faith in that little needle when you follow it (meaning a radio beacon). Especially when you can't see a thing but clouds and snow and know that you are a thousand miles from the nearest land and that you can't last more than 24 hours at the most if you have to set down in the freezing water. It was quite an experience. As far as I know, we all got across. However, I have only seen a few of the boys over here.*

After landing at Prestwick, Howard's crew reported to the 2900 Combat Crew Replacement Center (CCRC) Group at RAF Bovington Airfield about 35 miles northwest of London. Replacement meaning to re-supply crews that had been injured, captured, or killed. For some reason, radio operator Kenneth O. Blye and gunner Richard W. Harper were taken off Snyder's crew and transferred to fill spots on other crews. Blye went to 94th Bomb Group stationed at Bury St. Edmunds.

At the CCRC, newly arriving crews received their introduction along with additional pre-combat training in gunnery, radio procedure, and high altitude formation work before moving on to their operational bases.

> *We have been moved from place to place very rapidly and haven't had a chance to settle down since we arrived. We will remain here for awhile and go to school, then be assigned to a combat unit. We hope to have some time off to go to London in a few days. They took our ship away from us. I was very disappointed as she was a good ship, and we were all very fond of her. We will get another, however, when we make our next move.*

B-17 *Susan Ruth* Crew Picture: Back Row, Roy Holbert, Louis Colwart, Ross Kahler, John Pindroch, Joe Musial, Bill Slenker; Front Row: Howard Snyder, George Eike, Robert Benninger, Richard Daniels

As a result, Howard and his crew had to take their crew picture in front of another plane. He said, "We went over the girl on the plane with ink and put a dress on her. We did that not to be embarrassed to show it. You should see the girls painted on the walls of the officers club. They are terrific! However, I would be embarrassed to bring you here."

The "Nose Art" on bombers was totally unique to the U.S. Air Forces. Neither the Germans nor the British did this, and the U.S. Marine Corps and Navy forbade it. However, during World War II almost anything was allowed by the Air Forces in an effort to boost morale and unit efficiency. But, as is the case with most things, a free hand led to some definite excesses.

The desire to personalize an object or machine, to make it unique among the multitude, was basic to the airmen's human nature. Separated from home, loved ones, and a familiar way of life, these men sought ways to personalize their situation and escape the harsh realities and uncertain future of the war. Thousands of B-17s, identical in every way, rolled off the assembly line and flew to an uncertain fate, but each one could be different. The difference was not in the tail number, but in the imagination and talent of the crew. Few, if any, crew members would ever talk about aircraft #247613 or #34356, but many tales would be told about the crews and their planes with names such as the *Farmer's Daughter, Hard to Get, Virgin on the Verge, Naughty Nancy, Impatient Virgin* and *Anytime Annie.*

Nose Art of B-17F *Impatient Virgin*

Painting Nose Art

The ideas for "Nose Art" came from everywhere: girlfriends, wives, posters, matchbook covers, calendars, the comics or some event related to the history of the aircraft. The majority of the "Nose Art" was inspired by the artwork in magazines and calendars of the time. Disney characters were prevalent, as well as the comic strips. But for the most part, the men thought about women and the most widely copied artist was Alberto Vargas, the famous pin-up artist for *Esquire* magazine. Years later in the 1960s, his "Vargas Girls" would also appear in *Playboy* magazine. Typically, "Nose Art" painters earned about $5.00 for their work.

Thurleigh, England ... and the 306th

On October 21 1943, Howard Snyder's crew was assigned to the Eighth Army Air Forces' 306th Bombardment Group (Bomb Group or BG) located at Thurleigh, England, and to the 369th Squadron of the 306th.

The 306th Bomb Group was activated in March 1942, and began training at Wendover Army Air Field in Utah. The following September, it moved operations and its 34 bomber crews to the RAF (Royal Air Force) Airfield, Station 111, built in 1941 at Thurleigh, Befordshire, in East Anglia. The Bomb Group was comprised of four squadrons—

367th "Clay Pigeons," 368th "Eager Beavers," 369th "Fightin' Bitin'," and 423rd "Grim Reapers." Over the next three years, these squadrons and their crews would fly 341 bombing missions over Western Europe.

The 306th was part of the 1st Air Division's, 40th Bomb Wing (which also included the 92nd Bomb Group and 305th Bomb Group) of the Eighth Air Force. It was the first operational bombardment group in the VIII Bomber Command, and was the longest continuously-serving bomb group of the Eighth Air Force during World War II, from September 1942 to December 1945. Not only was the 306th the first bombardment group to complete 300 missions over occupied Europe and Nazi Germany, it also had the significant distinction of being the first bomb group to attack a target located in Nazi Germany when it bombed Wilhelmshaven on January 27, 1943. Thus the 306th's motto became "First Over Germany," and their nickname was "Reich Wreckers."

As history has shown, the overriding obsession of Adolf Hitler and his National Socialist German Workers' Party (***Na**tionalso**zi**al-istische Deutsche Arbeiterpartei*) was to transform Germany into a totalitarian "*Nazi*" state, appropriately known as The Third Reich. (*Nazi* was shorthand for the first two syllables of the German word for national.)

The German word *Reich* means empire with the first major German *Reich* being the Holy Roman Empire which lasted from the coronation of Otto I as the Holy Roman Emperor in 962 until 1806 when it was dissolved during the Napoleonic Wars. The second *Reich* was the German Empire which lasted from the unification of Germany in 1871 until its collapse after World War I during the German Revolution of 1918–1919.

The 306th Bomb Group flew B-17 Flying Fortress bombers, which were identified by markings on the tail or vertical stabilizer. A "Triangle" denoted the 1st Air Division. A yellow horizontal band or stripe represented the 40th Combat Wing. The "H" inside the

Triangle stood for the 306th Bomb Group located at Thurleigh, England. The color of the band or stripe at the top of the tail designated the bomb squadron: the 369th was green. The aircraft's five digit serial number appeared below and came from the manufacturer's production lot. The "Letter" below the aircraft number was the squadron's designation of the plane. This letter was used on several different planes during the war, but never on two squadron planes at the same time.

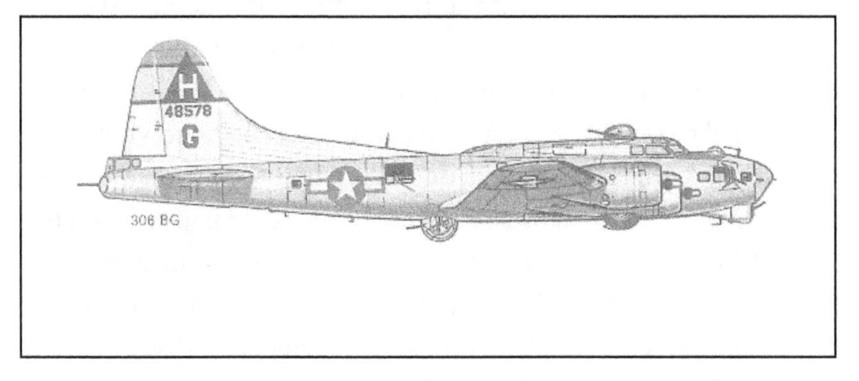

B-17G tail markings of the 306th Bomb Group 369th Squadron

During the early phases of the war, the Eighth Air Force suffered devastating high loss rates. The most significant reason for these losses was insufficient protection by U.S. fighter escorts which initially were only able to escort the bombers over the English Channel and were then forced to turn back after reaching mainland Europe because of inadequate fuel capacity. Inadequate training and tactical training were two other factors that adversely affected both losses and bombing accuracy.

In the latter part of 1942, the 306th Commander, Colonel Charles "Chip" Overacker, became very vocal about his belief that the training being conducted back in the States was poor, and that training in England was inefficient. Due to poor weather conditions in England, lack of adequate gunnery/bombing ranges, and limited airspace,

Overacker believed the answer was to enhance training in the U.S. After word of Colonel Overacker's criticism reached VIII Bomber Command Headquarters, its commanding officer, Major General Ira Eaker, removed Overacker. Unfortunately for Colonel Overacker, shortly after he was removed, the Air Force subsequently implemented his recommendations of increasing the amount of training in the U.S. and improving its quality.

General Eaker also had other reasons for replacing Overacker. Although the 369th "Fightin' Bitin'" Squadron had achieved an incredible record of completing 42 missions without a single aircraft loss (a record that was not surpassed until after D-Day), the 306th BG's overall record was poor. At the same time the 369th was achieving such success, the 367th Squadron had earned the nickname "Clay Pigeons," given to them by a reporter because they had suffered the highest losses of any unit in the Eighth Air Forces. In particular, General Eaker believed Colonel Overacker was too attached to his crews, and lacked necessary "military propriety and discipline." In order to allow the 306th to recuperate from the losses and focus on training, the Group was taken off combat status during December 1942. Following this brief rest, Colonel Overacker's successor arrived, Brigadier General Frank A. Armstrong, who was charged with the task of improving the 306th's performance.

Both the novel and 1949 film *Twelve O'Clock High* were roughly based on General Armstrong's (in the movie, General Frank Savage was played by Gregory Peck) efforts to successfully rejuvenate the 306th Bomb Group. The fictional 918th Bomb Group in the movie was conceived by multiplying each digit of the 306th by three. Colonel Overacker was portrayed as Colonel Keith Davenport by Gary Merrill, and General Eaker was portrayed as General Pritchard by Millard Mitchell.

The movie took its title from the clock position that the air crews used when describing the attack angle of German fighter planes.

German pilots had determined that the optimum angle of attack when approaching a U.S. bomber head-on was from ten degrees above the horizontal, which was what bomber crews came to call "12 O'clock High" (12 O'clock meaning straight ahead and High meaning above the horizon).

Beyond Hollywood's recreations of war time events were the real life and often heroic commitments of celebrities. For example, Clark Gable and Jimmy Stewart were both actual members of the Eighth Air Force, however, not with the 306th BG. Writing for the American newspaper, *Stars & Stripes*, located in *The Times* building in London, young Andy Rooney began his career as a war correspondent and flew on raids with the Eighth Air Force, in particular with the 306th Bomb Group in 1943. Rooney would later become famous for his weekly broadcast, *A Few Minutes with Andy Rooney*, part of the CBS television program *60 Minutes* from 1978 to 2011.

8

THE CREW OF THE *SUSAN RUTH*

An airplane's crew needed to develop a close rapport and camaraderie; the tone of which was largely determined by the pilot.

Replacements ... After the Disastrous Second Schweinfurt Raid

On October 21, 1943, the 10 man crew of the *Susan Ruth*, comprised of four officers and six non-commissioned officers (NCOs or enlisted men), reported to the 369th Bomb Squadron, 306th Bomb Group at Thurleigh, England.

Howard's crew along with 14 others came to England in the latter part of the month as much needed replacements following the disastrous second raid by the Eighth Air Force on October 14 to Schweinfurt, Germany. Located at Schweinfurt were five factories that manufactured nearly two-thirds of all Germany's ball bearings and roller bearings. Bearings were an extremely critical component to Germany's war effort because almost everything was dependent on them: cars, motorcycles, trucks, aircraft, ships, jet engines, rocket launchers, field guns, etc. The German aviation industry alone used 2.4 million of them a month.

Fifteen planes of the 306th BG carrying 150 men were among the Eighth Air Force formations that were met by more than 300 enemy aircraft. In addition, the anti-aircraft fire over the target "was thick enough to have walked on." Ten planes of the 306th did not come back, and of the 100 crew members, 35 died and 65 ended up in

German prison camps. It was one of the three worst days in the combat history of the 306th Bomb Group. The mission became known as "Black Thursday" because out of a total of 291 B-17s sent on the mission, 60 were lost outright, another 17 were damaged so heavily that they had to be scrapped, and another 121 had varying degrees of battle damage.

The crew of the *Susan Ruth*, like all bomber crews, was made up of men from all over the U.S. and from every walk of life. They were college graduates, farmers, lawyers, and coal miners, from all nationalities and all religious denominations. All that is, except African-Americans, who were prevented from flying on combat crews.

- 2nd Lt. Howard J. Snyder—pilot, age 28, Los Angeles, CA—serial # 0-742461
- 2nd Lt. George W. Eike—co-pilot, age 24, Rochester, NY—serial # 0-748164
- 2nd Lt. Robert J. Benninger—navigator, age 20, Pittsburgh, PA—serial # 0-685369
- 2nd Lt. Richard L. Daniels—bombardier, age 23, Cleveland Heights, OH—serial # 0-679378
- Staff Sergeant Roy K. Holbert—engineer and top turret gunner, age 22, Swannanoa, NC—serial # 34036012
- Technical Sergeant Ross L. Kahler—radio operator, age 30, Philadelphia, PA—serial # 33324107
- Staff Sergeant Joseph J. Musial—left waist gunner, age 25, Laurence Harbor, NJ—serial # 13025549
- Sergeant Louis L. Colwart—ball turret gunner, age 18, Houma, LA—serial # 18151729
- Sergeant John Pindroch—right waist gunner, age 19, Cleveland, OH—serial # 15329492
- Staff Sergeant William O. Slenker—tail gunner, age 20, Chicago, IL—serial # 16101156

Crew Positions

Every B-17 had a ten-man crew. There were four officers: pilot, co-pilot, bombardier and navigator. Five enlisted men manned the guns: one, who was also the flight engineer, in the top turret above and behind the cockpit; two waist gunners; the ball turret gunner crammed into a tiny rotating Plexiglas sphere that hung below the plane just behind the bomb bay doors; and the tail gunner looking to the rear. Another enlisted man was on the radio.

Crew Positions

1. Bombardier—Richard Daniels

The B-17 Pilot Training Manual stated:

> The accurate and effective bombing is the ultimate purpose of your entire airplane and crew. Every other function is preparatory to hitting and destroying the target. That's your bombardier's job. The success or failure of the mission depends upon what he accomplishes in that short interval of the bombing run. When the bombardier takes over the airplane for the run on the target, he is in absolute command. He will tell you what he wants done, and until he tells you "Bombs Away," his word is law.

Therefore, the basic principle of any bombing mission was to deliver 5,000 pounds of bombs accurately on the target. The bombardier's main tool was the Norden bombsight in the nose of the aircraft; a top secret piece of equipment the U.S. guarded throughout the war. The bombardier sat on a swiveling stool with the bombsight in front of him. On a mission, the bombardier's real job began at the I.P. (Initial Point). This was the point at which the bombing run on the target began, and from this point on, the bombardier would fly the airplane through the bombsight linked to the autopilot. The plane would have to be flown straight and level to the release point through anti-aircraft fire and enemy fighter attacks. Sitting on a small chair behind the bombsight in the Plexiglas nose of the plane gave him an unrestricted, bird's eye view. There was also a chin turret underneath the Plexiglas nose that the bombardier manned during enemy fighter attacks.

2. Navigator—Robert Benninger

The B-17 Pilot Training Manual stated:

> The navigator's job is to direct your flight from departure to destination and return. He must know the exact position of the airplane at all times. Navigation is the art of determining geographic positions by means of (a) pilotage, (b) dead reckoning, (c) radio, or (d) celestial navigation, or any combination of these four methods. By any one or combination of methods the navigator determines the position of the airplane in relation to the earth.

A navigator had to know the position of his aircraft at all times, for in war situations it could change rapidly, and a crew couldn't afford not to know where they were over enemy territory. Navigation was the key to avoiding heavily defended areas, reaching the target, and returning to base. The pilots flew the plane, but the navigator supplied the course they must fly. The navigator's table was fixed at the rear of the nose compartment, against the left side, behind the bombardier's station. They had the best views of the sky through the large Plexiglas nose. Throughout the mission, the navigator would inform the pilots of their position and time estimates to various check points. When the initial point (I.P.) was reached for the bomb run, the navigator would inform the pilot. The navigator also manned the cheek guns on either side of the plane when attacked by enemy fighters.

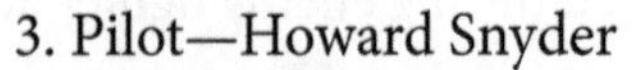
3. Pilot—Howard Snyder

The B-17 Pilot Training Manual stated:

> It is your airplane, and your crew. You are responsible for the safety and efficiency of the crew at all times—not just when you are flying and fighting, but for the full 24 hours of every day while you are in command. Your success as the airplane commander will depend in a large measure on the respect, confidence, and trust which the crew feels for you. It will depend also on how well you maintain crew discipline.

The pilot sat in the "left seat" of the cockpit, and it was his job to physically fly the aircraft while being assisted by his co-pilot. They sat on the flight deck above and behind the navigator's position with the pilot to the left and his co-pilot to the right with both having equal access to the controls and views of all four of the engines. The pilot was responsible for the operation of every flight. The nine other crew members fell under his command and the course of action in every situation was his decision to make. An airplane's crew needed to develop a close rapport and camaraderie, the tone of which was largely determined by the pilot.

The cockpit was actually the worst place to see anything because the pilot could only see straight ahead. He could not really look around or below and was told what was going on by either the navigator or bombardier who sat in the Plexiglas nose of the plane. Being 28-years-old, compared to the normal age of 21 for a pilot, Howard Snyder was consider "the old man" by most of his crew. He was only one of three crew members who was married and the only one with a child, so that added to his maturity.

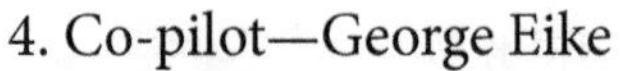

4. Co-pilot—George Eike

The B-17 Pilot Training Manual stated:

> The co-pilot is the executive officer—your chief assistant, understudy, and strong right arm. He must be familiar enough with every one of your duties—both as pilot and as airplane commander—to be able to take over and act in your place at any time. Always remember that the co-pilot is a fully trained, rated pilot just like yourself. He is subordinate to you only by virtue of your position as the airplane commander. The B-17 is a lot of airplane; more airplane than any one pilot can handle alone over a long period of time. Therefore, you have been provided with a second pilot who will share the duties of flight operation.

The co-pilot usually handled maneuvering the aircraft while it was on the ground before takeoff and after landing and spelled the pilot during combat missions. After takeoff and once in formation, the co-pilot normally flew the plane almost as much as the pilot. Both pilots and co-pilots received the same training and the only thing that separated the two was chance, which one got picked to be a pilot and which one was picked to be a co-pilot. The rigors of close formation flying for long periods of time placed tremendous physical and mental strain on a pilot. For that reason alone, the co-pilot, or "guy in the right seat," was essential. Working side by side, quite naturally the pilot and co-pilot became close friends.

Non-Commissioned Officers (NCOs or Enlisted Men)

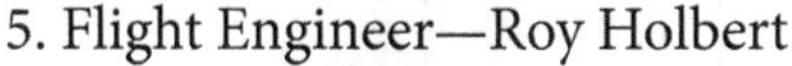

5. Flight Engineer—Roy Holbert

The Flight Engineer was specially trained to have a wide knowledge of the B-17 and its equipment. He stood right behind the pilots, peering over their shoulders and monitoring the gauges. He could perform most jobs of the ground crew and was a key figure in any emergency situation. As crew chief, he had working knowledge of all the aircraft systems, including the engines, guns, and bomb racks. When attacked by enemy fighters, his primary job became manning the B-17's top turret twin .50 caliber guns. With his head and shoulder inside the revolving Plexiglas dome, his view from the top turret covered a 360 radius over the aircraft.

6. Radio Operator—Ross Kahler

The radio operator was isolated from the rest of the crew in the mid-section of the bomber. The radio compartment was located between two bulkheads; one directly behind the bomb bay and the other just forward of the ball turret. He had a restricted view and usually had to sit at his receiver and sweat out the battle that raged outside. Yet he was a key member of the crew, handling the communication equipment. All messages received from or sent to headquarters were in Morse Code, originally developed in 1836 as a method of transmitting text information using dots and dashes. The radio operator was also trained as the first-aid man of the crew.

7. Ball Turret Gunner—Louis Colwart

Most crew members considered the Plexiglas ball turret the worst crew position on the aircraft. The confining sphere of only thirty inches in diameter was on the underside or "belly" of the aircraft and required an agile occupant; someone immune to claustrophobia and brave enough to be without a parachute close by. The turret revolved a full 360 degrees, providing an extraordinary vantage point and covering the aircraft against attackers from below. The turret was armed with the twin .50 caliber machine guns facing rearward for takeoff and landing. Once the aircraft was airborne, the turret would have to be cranked by hand to position the guns straight down, revolving the hatch inside the airplane. The ball gunner would then enter the turret, fasten his safety strap, turn on the power and operate the turret from inside.

8. Left Waist Gunner—
Joseph Musial

9. Right Waist Gunner—
John Pindroch

The waist windows of the B-17 provided excellent defense stations. However, great skill or good luck was required to hit an enemy fighter hurtling past. The single .50 caliber waist guns were an important defensive feature of the B-17 formations, combining the open lateral areas with a gauntlet of massive firepower. The waist gunners wore flak helmets, flak suits, and armor plate contoured to the curve of the fuselage below the open port windows as their only protection from shrapnel (exploded shell fragments) and bullets. Standing at their guns, their bodies filled a larger target area than the rest of the crew, who were sitting or kneeling.

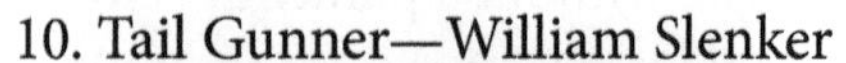
10. Tail Gunner—William Slenker

The twin .50 caliber tail guns of the Fortress were the most important defensive weapons of the bomber and inflicted severe damage on enemy fighters attacking from the rear. The tail gunner was well aware that the first objective of the attacking pilot was to eliminate him and his weapon. The tail gunner would be in the radio room for takeoff and once the aircraft was airborne, he would take his combat position in an extremely cramped compartment. Once seated, he would plug in his heated flying suit, oxygen and intercom. The gunner took a kneeling position with his knees resting on padded supports and his legs doubled back between a small seat.

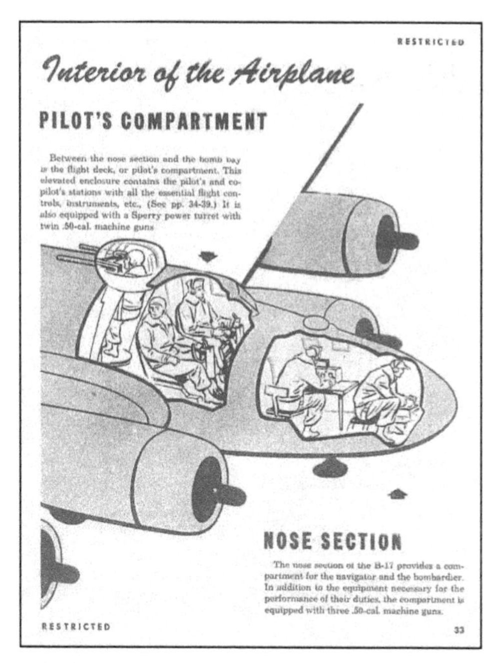

RESTRICTED

Interior of the Airplane

PILOT'S COMPARTMENT

Between the nose section and the bomb bay is the flight deck, or pilot's compartment. This elevated enclosure contains the pilot's and co-pilot's stations with all the essential flight controls, instruments, etc., (See pp. 34-39.) It is also equipped with a Sperry power turret with twin .50-cal. machine guns

NOSE SECTION

The nose section of the B-17 provides a compartment for the navigator and the bombardier. In addition to the equipment necessary for the performance of their duties, the compartment is equipped with three .50-cal. machine guns.

RESTRICTED 33

Pilot's Compartment and Nose Section

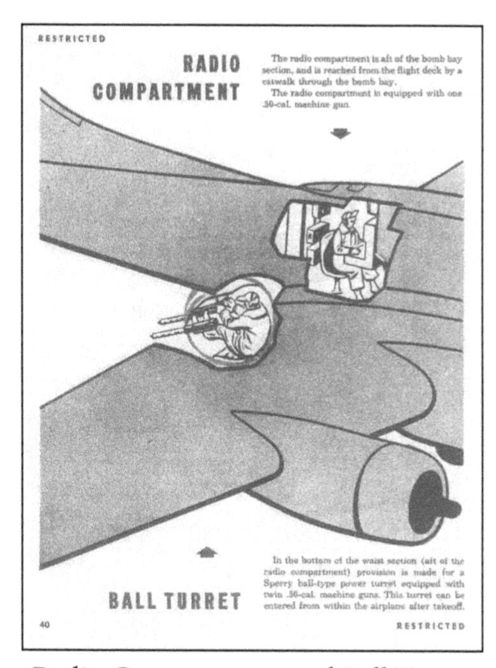

RESTRICTED

RADIO COMPARTMENT

The radio compartment is aft of the bomb bay section, and is reached from the flight deck by a catwalk through the bomb bay.

The radio compartment is equipped with one .50-cal. machine gun.

BALL TURRET

In the bottom of the waist section (aft of the radio compartment) provision is made for a Sperry ball-type power turret equipped with twin .50-cal. machine guns. This turret can be entered from within the airplane after takeoff.

40 RESTRICTED

Radio Compartment and Ball Turret

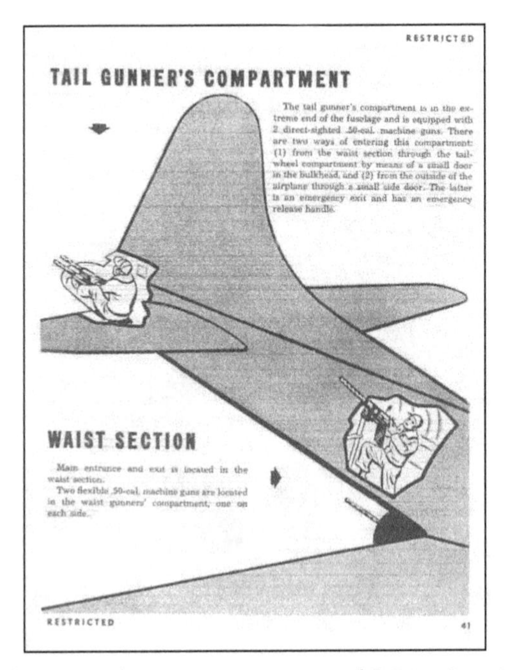

RESTRICTED

TAIL GUNNER'S COMPARTMENT

The tail gunner's compartment is in the extreme end of the fuselage and is equipped with 2 direct-sighted .50-cal. machine guns. There are two ways of entering this compartment: (1) from the waist section through the tail-wheel compartment by means of a small door in the bulkhead, and (2) from the outside of the airplane through a small side door. The latter is an emergency exit and has an emergency release handle.

WAIST SECTION

Main entrance and exit is located in the waist section.

Two flexible .50-cal. machine guns are located in the waist gunners' compartment, one on each side.

RESTRICTED 41

Tail Gunner's Compartment and Waist Section

9

THURLEIGH, ENGLAND

Vast fleets of four-engine monsters flying overhead, wave after wave, with their deep throbbing roar causing house items to tinkle and rattle from their vibrations.

Home of the 306th

During World War II, the Royal Air Force and the United States Army Air Forces constructed many air bases in the East Anglia region of England for their heavy bomber fleets of the Combined Bomber Offensive against Nazi occupied Europe. On average there was one American air base every eight miles with each bomber base home to about fifty B-17s or B-24s. By spring of 1944, there were 130 American and British airfields crowded into southeast England—an area no larger than the state of Vermont.

In the U.S., the air bases were usually located in areas dismally distant and remote from civilized life. However, in England the reverse was true. In essence, England was converted into a gigantic bomber field, a super aircraft carrier anchored off the shores of Europe. East Anglia, comprised of Norfolk, Suffolk, and Cambridgeshire counties in East England, was chosen because it had considerable open space and level terrain. It was also relatively close to mainland Europe, thus shortening flights and allowing for greater bomb loads.

Throughout East Anglia, little villages and quiet towns dotted the densely green landscape of the rural English countryside where tradition had remained undisturbed for generations. It was a 40 by 80 mile area where 500-year-old buildings were referred to as "new."

One of those little villages was Thurleigh, a small parish (village) in north Bedfordshire (County of Bedford), about six miles north of the borough (city) of Bedford and about 60 miles north of London. It was a peaceful landscape with winding country roads, small streams, hedgerows, and modest stone walls that formed a tapestry of farm land where herds of cattle and sheep grazed.

Then all of a sudden, the peace and serenity of the region was interrupted by streams of bomber groups making their way to and from bombing missions over Western Europe. Vast fleets of four-engine monsters flying overhead, wave after wave, with their deep throbbing roar causing house items to tinkle and rattle from their vibrations.

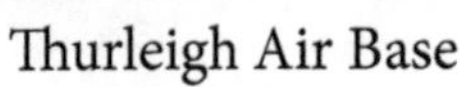
Thurleigh Air Base

East Anglia

Overnight, all over the region little hamlets like Thurleigh and nearby Bedford were transformed into bustling communities as the U.S. Army Air Forces arrived. Americans packed the trains, pubs, and movie houses, and by the end of the war, about three million U.S. soldiers would pass through Britain. For many G.I.s, it was the first time they had ever travelled away from their home towns, and they were the personification of America's diversified "melting pot" with peculiar accents from every state in the USA. The term G.I. originally referred to galvanized iron used to denote the equipment made from it for the U.S. Army. The term was later broadened to "Government

Issue" referring to all equipment of the Army and then further broadened to mean any member of the Army.

The British were startled by young men who were so breezy, chatty, friendly, generous, girl-crazy and self-assured. They were taken back by the G.I.'s unusually informal manners and their habit of approaching complete strangers which was a social taboo there. The villages had history and traditions from the past that were incomprehensible to the young boys from a still relatively new nation. However, despite the Americans loud and often brash behavior, the traditionally formal Brits were extremely grateful for what the G.I.s were doing. The U.S. servicemen also livened up the Brits' dreary lives and brought fun to the lives of the local people when they needed it most. Suffering greatly from the deprivations of the war, the locals were exposed to something totally new and exciting.

The Americans were all lonesome for home, and the townsfolk of Thurleigh and Bedford welcomed the Americans into their homes, shared their food, and offered a family life that the men missed so much. In turn, the Americans invited them to the base for movies or ice cream, acting as sons or brothers in place of those who were off at war. Many servicemen, especially ground personnel who were stationed there longer than combat airmen, developed close relationships with the British who lived around the base. Daughters dated them and many married them. The G.I.s also had a great liking for children who loved them back. The Americans brought with them a seemingly never-ending supply of chocolate, Coca-Cola, cigarettes and nylons. Children would flock around them and cry "got any gum, chum?"

The home for the 306th Bombardment Group was, in fact, a small city in itself, housing approximately 3,500 men and a small number of women. Thurleigh Air Field, just north of the village, became an independent, self-sufficient entity, including housing and various facilities such as a gymnasium, cinema, chapel, library, hospital and so on. The base included an elaborate and well-trained ground echelon which was the backbone of the bombardment group and without which, the 306th could not operate. The ground echelon included various detachments to assist in air operations, provide equipment, and give personnel support. Consequently, cinema operators, chaplains, librarians, medics, flight surgeons, quartermasters, aviation ordnance, weather squadrons, military police, maintenance and staff personnel for every task were needed.

306th Bomb Group Air Base at Thurleigh

306th Bomb Group Air Base at Thurleigh

More than half the men stationed at Thurleigh at any time were not part of the combat crews. They were the men who repaired, serviced and supported the combat operations; the men who "kept 'em flying." They were the men who maintained everything, supplied everything, fixed everything, and applied special talents to particular problems. Their contributions were made on the flight line and in the mechanical shops, in the administrative offices and staff areas across the base. They repaired the plane, loaded the bombs and munitions, policed the field, maintained the radios, cooked and fed the men, operated the laundry, worked in the PX, and handled the many other duties required to keep the planes flying and the field operating—all essential to the successful launching of the air strikes. They served with dedication and perseverance, contributing to the war effort, in jobs far less glorified, but equally as imperative as the combat crews.

On October 23, 1944, Howard wrote to Ruth,

> *Well here we are, Baby. We are finally in our permanent combat outfit. It seems to be a very good outfit and from the way it looks now we are lucky to be assigned to their Group (306th) and Squad (369th). It has a very good combat record with very few losses compared to other organizations.*

The 369th had achieved the incredible record of completing 42 missions without a single aircraft loss which ended on July 29, 1943, when two of its planes went down. The record was not surpassed until after D-Day on June 6, 1944. The 369th Squadron's "Fightin' Bitin'" nick-name, came from navigator Kermit Cavedo who had named his plane that because of the 369th numerical connection with the Civil War's "Fighting 69th."

Originally an Irish unit from New York City and the New York Army National Guard, the "Fighting 69th" was said to have been given its name by Robert E. Lee during the Civil War. The unit, also called the "Fighting Irish," was immortalized in Joyce Kilmer's poem *When the 69th Comes Home*. The name caught on as well as the emblem of a bumblebee wearing boxing gloves and became the squadron's nickname throughout the remainder of its life with the Eighth Air Force.

369th "Fightin' Bitin'" Squadron

369th Squadron "Fightin' Bitin'" patch

10

HOME AWAY FROM HOME

Although four officers and six NCOs or enlisted men comprised a B-17 ten-man crew and flew combat missions together, they basically lived separate lives while on base. The two groups lived separately, ate separately and socialized separately.

Quarters

Many of the buildings on the base were various sized Nissen Huts named after Canadian engineer Lt. Col. Peter N. Nissen, who designed them in World War I. The huts were made of corrugated metal bent into half a cylinder with a cement floor, a wooden door in the front, and two windows on either side. Despite being leaky and cold, they were cheap, quickly built and versatile. They made functional homes as well as offices and recreation spots for thousands of soldiers and airmen in WWII. The squadron operations office, where notices were tacked and orders handed out, was shared by the commanding major and the operations officer. There were a host of other offices and buildings for operations and maintenance.

Nissen Hut

At Thurleigh, the officers lived in relative comfort. Howard had his own 11' by 7' room with a bed, table and chair, stove, dresser, clothes rack, wash stand, and two windows. He papered the walls with large maps. To the right of the entrance, he put up a map of England between the door and the wash stand. To the left of the entrance on the other long wall and above his bed, he had a large map of Western Europe (England, France, Germany, Switzerland, Holland, Belgium and Denmark). He said, "They are big maps and take up the whole wall. It looks pretty good and is much more pleasant than bare walls." Opposite his bed and along the other long wall were the two windows with the stove in between them.

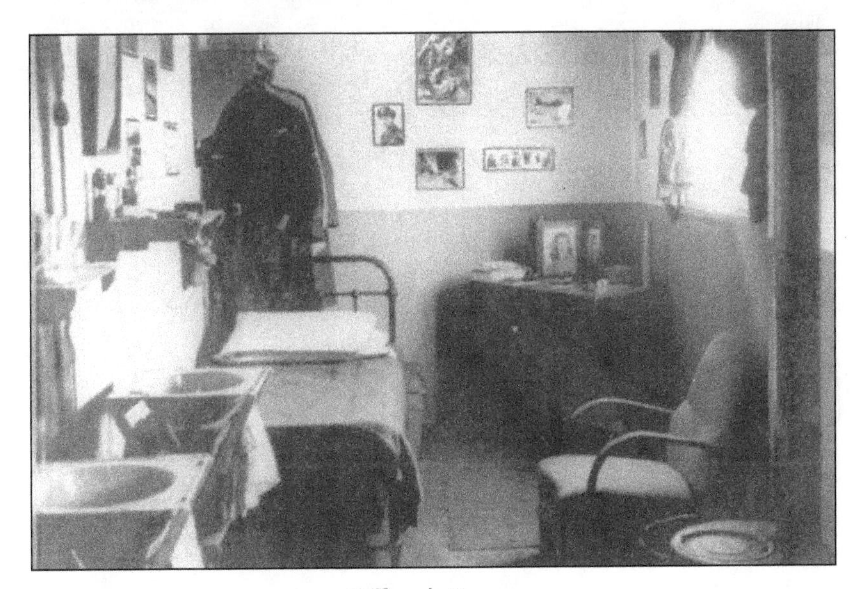

Officer's Room

The three other officers (Eike, Daniels, and Benninger) shared a room next to Howard's, but it was larger. The only problem was that they all had to walk a long way to take a shower and had to carry water back to their rooms to shave. They then could heat the water on the little stoves in their rooms. They had the luxury of an orderly (an attendant who performed various tasks for superior officers) who cleaned their rooms, made their beds, brought in coal and wood for the fire, and did just about anything they wished for which they each paid him 10 shillings a month ($2.00).

The enlisted men (NCOs Holbert, Kahler, Musial, Pindroch, Colwart, and Slenker) lived separately from the officers, and their quarters were not as spacious. There were rows of cots along each wall and a pot-bellied, coal burning stove in the middle. Each airman's space consisted of a metal cot with a footlocker underneath. It was a small army trunk in which the men kept a change of clothes, books, photographs, letters, writing paper and other cherished mementos.

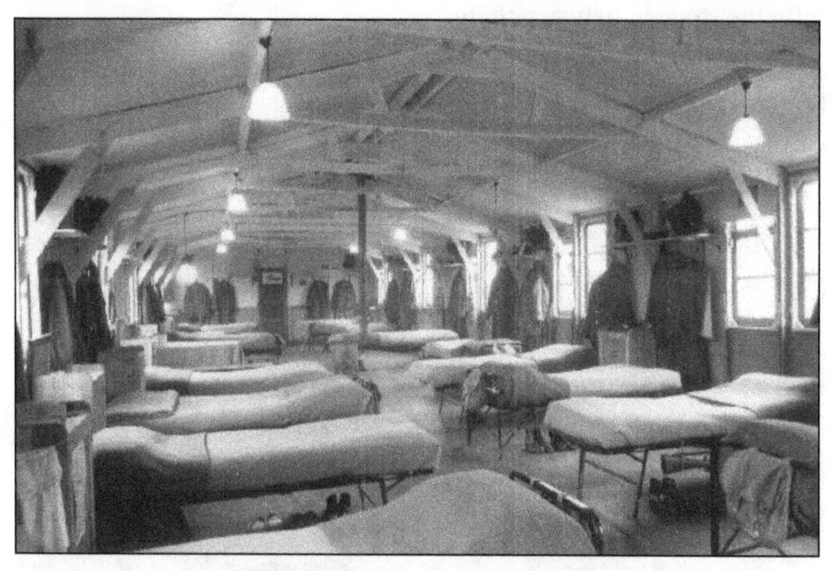

Barracks Ready for Inspection

Although four officers and six NCOs or enlisted men comprised a B-17 ten-man crew and flew combat missions together, they basically lived separate lives while on base. The two groups lived separately, ate separately and socialized separately. The Red Cross Aero Clubs were for the enlisted men and were like the Officer's Clubs except they only had beer while the Officers' Club had a bar with hard liquor. On the base, each squadron had its own Officers Club and NCO Club.

Relaxing in the Barracks

Both officers and enlisted men could go into town every evening if they wished. However, the enlisted men had to be back by midnight while the officers only had to be back in time for the 8:30 morning meetings the next day. The NCOs ate outside on picnic tables and washed their own dishes in garbage cans while the Officers had an indoor Mess Hall. The exception being after flying combat missions, the NCOs did get to go to the Officers' Club for a shot of whiskey and a good meal.

While the officers and enlisted men might have lived separately while on the ground, when flying combat missions the ten men became a close-knit team and as close as brothers. Every member of a combat crew knew the feeling of teamwork and the confidence each had in the other. When in combat, the only thing that really mattered was the safety and well-being of each other. Although under extreme stress, each man had a strong sense of holding it together because they didn't want to fail their buddies no matter what happened.

One of the first things all servicemen soon did after arriving in England was to buy a bicycle which became their primary source of

Red Cross Aero Club

Officers' Mess Hall

transportation to the mess hall, the PX, or into the numerous villages surrounding each base. The barracks were located far from duty stations so the bicycles became essential for transportation. Actually, the entire base was spread out over a large area—not only the buildings, but all the aircraft as well, so in case of a German attack damage would be minimal. After the Americans arrived, Thurleigh became littered with bicycles. As Howard wrote, "I went into Bedford which is about five miles from the base and got a bicycle today. They help out a great deal and save a lot of time for the base is spread out, and we have to walk a great deal. I was getting tired of walking so far every day. Everyone rides a bicycle here."

11

TRAINING ... AND MORE TRAINING

I get up about 7:15 every morning and go to a meeting at 8:30. We have school and trainers, or fly if the weather is good. We eat at 12:00, another meeting at 1:15 and the same thing in the afternoon. School never lasts later than 4:00.

Co-Pilot at First

The men were kept busy with training and more training. Newly arriving air crews needed additional training before being allowed on bombing missions. They worked on assembly skills, formation flying, navigation, simulated bomb runs and the unique radio customs and procedures used over England. The air crews were kept so busy they didn't have time to worry much about anything except what was coming up the next day. Howard wrote,

> *I have flown every day that we have been here. Some of it is the same training we had in the States that we keep practicing on, but a lot is new. We attend classes, air crew training, and practice flying, especially formation flying and being able to fly "tight" to other planes. Although the formations we fly here are tighter than we flew in the states, I am not having any trouble. I overheard a major talking to the colonel about our crew. He was really laying it on; he thought we were a good crew. A captain told me that the Group Operations Officer thought I would be leading the Group on their missions before long. I was at a big party we had, and he was pretty high, otherwise, I don't think he would*

have told me. I don't know what he formed his opinion on, but I hope I can live up to it.

I get up about 7:15 every morning and go to a meeting at 8:30. We have school and trainers, or fly if the weather is good. We eat at 12:00, another meeting at 1:15 and the same thing in the afternoon. School never lasts later than 4:00. We eat dinner at 5:30. I usually listen to the radio in the club or go to my room and write or read after building a fire in the evening.

I will fly as co-pilot for four or five missions and then fly as pilot again. Eike will fly with another experienced pilot until I fly as pilot, and then he will come back to me. I have all my other crew with me, and they will continue to be my crew. The officers are very friendly and all seem to be very good fellows. It is a lot different here than in the States. All the big shots call you by name and are quite chummy. I think I will like it here fine.

Unlike the infantry that had many long term soldiers, almost everyone who flew in a bomber had volunteered within the last two years. In addition, everyone who flew in a bomber had the rank of sergeant or higher. Therefore, officers and non-commissioned officers were closer than in the Army. At the time Snyder and his crew arrived, Colonel George Robinson, who would complete 26 combat missions, was the Commander of the 306th Bomb Group.

Major Robert "Rip" Riordan was Commanding Officer (CO) of the 369th Squadron. An original member of the 306th when it arrived in England, Major Riordan was an exceptional combat pilot. Even after completing his twenty-five mission tour requirement, he still flew voluntarily, completing an astounding forty-one, not only as lead pilot for the 369th Squadron but frequently as lead pilot for the 306th Bomb Group as well. He was an extremely disciplined individual who didn't smoke, drink, or swear.

Major John Stanko was the 369th Executive Officer in charge of administrative functions and day-to-day activities. He did not fly combat missions, but was considered "one tough cookie" and had the nickname of "Stinko Stanko" due to his abrasive personality. Major Charles "Charlie" Flannagan, an Irishman from Indiana, was the Operations Officer in charge of training and combat and did fly combat missions, completing thirty-one. Captain Charles "Pop" McKim was the 369th Squadron Flight Surgeon and a "bosom drinking buddy" with Stanko.

When the 306th arrived in England in August 1942, the British countryside was war torn having suffered from two years of war, the loss of loved ones, heavy German bombing in the cities and extensive rationing. After overwhelming Western Europe, Nazi Germany had turned its attention to Great Britain in September 1940. The German air force, the *Luftwaffe* (meaning air weapon), initiated a sustained bombing crusade which became the first major war campaign, referred to as The Battle of Britain, that was fought entirely by air forces. The failure of Germany to achieve its objectives of destroying Britain's air defenses and forcing Britain to negotiate an armistice or an outright surrender is considered Germany's first major defeat and a crucial turning point in the war. Much of the credit for turning back Germany's air offensive must go the RAF's highly maneuverable fighter plane, the Spitfire. Because the offensive failed, Adolf Hitler could not implement his plan, Operation Sea Lion, to invade Britain.

The Blitz

Germany's prolonged air bombardment of England, referred to as the *Blitz* (the German word for "lightning"), began on September 7, 1940. London was bombed by the *Luftwaffe* for 57 consecutive nights. During the Blitz, which lasted almost 37 weeks, more than one million London houses were destroyed or damaged, and more than 40,000 civilians were killed, almost half of them in London.

In an attempt to save civilian lives, Britain developed "Operation Pied Piper," the evacuation of civilians, particularly children, from London and other main cities to rural towns and villages in designated areas thought to be less at risk. It began on September 1, 1939, and officially relocated more than 3.5 million people. East Anglia received many children evacuated from Dagenham, a large suburb of East London. Around a third of the entire population experienced some effects of the evacuation with towns in Kent and East Anglia receiving more than 40 percent of the population. The movement of urban children to unfamiliar rural locations, without their parents, had a major impact.

Although England suffered terribly, Germany lost almost 2,400 planes, and more importantly, their sustained bombing did not achieve its intended goal of demoralizing the British into surrender. By May 1941, the threat of an invasion of Britain had passed. Instead Hitler proceeded with Operation Barbarossa, the invasion of the Soviet Union beginning on June 22, 1941.

Howard Snyder to Ruth,

> *You have no idea how four years of war has affected England. Luxuries are taxed at 100 percent of cost so everything is terribly high. No one can buy clothing without ration slips. It is practically impossible to get anything. There just isn't anything made here that isn't used in the war effort. Eike and I went to a dozen different places looking for Wedgwood, but it isn't being made any more due to the labor shortage. It is very hard to get, and the only place to get any is in London.*

Wedgwood was founded in 1759 by Josiah Wedgwood, known as "the father of English Pottery." He invented Jasper ware (a white, unglazed type of porcelain) which was often painted light blue-gray using metallic oxide pigments. The trademark color of this world-famous pottery became known as Wedgwood Blue.

About the only way you can buy bottles of liquor is on the Black Market and then you pay $12 to $16 for a fifth of Scotch. I priced a linen table cloth the other day. They are very hard to get, and the shop only had one and a small one at that. They wanted $40 for it. You can easily see why the English prices prohibit inflation. People just can't buy anything with the high tax on all unnecessary items.

The town (Bedford) is a good sized place, but there isn't anything to do unless you are on the lookout for girls. We had dinner and Eike wanted to go to a dance. I went along and sat in the corner all evening watching him and the rest dance. Most of the girls are quite "icky" as you would say. This damp climate gives them beautiful completions though. When I see the English women and think of you, I can't believe there is that much difference. How fortunate I am that I was blessed with you for a wife. We are not allowed to say anything detrimental about the English, not that there is much to say. They are very fine people, but the four years of war they have gone through must have done something to their morale.

Bedford

It has rained every day that we have been in England. Our cleaning bill will be high for we are always getting wet and dirty. We are getting over here at the worst time of the year. From what

> *they tell us, I will get promoted to 1st (Lt.) after I have had three or four raids. However, that might take a month or two the way the weather is. With the fog and rain, we will be grounded most of the time so it will take us longer to get our missions in. Musial, the fellow that had been in combat before, was in an automobile accident yesterday. The night was very foggy, and the car he was riding in ran off the road and overturned. He only had a little cut on his head and is OK.*

Joe Musial was on his second combat tour having already flown 72 missions with the 13th Air Force in the South Pacific. He was a nephew of the great Hall of Fame St. Louis Cardinals major league baseball player, Stan Musial. Joe enlisted on April 2, 1941, and after basic and advanced training was stationed at Hickham Field, Hawaii, where he went through gunnery school while learning aircraft maintenance at the same time. On December 7, 1941, when Pearl Harbor was bombed, he recalled,

> *I was on the barracks second floor thinking, Man, they sure are shooting those coastal guns close today. Then I heard the planes. I came out with just a towel wrapped around me, and here comes this plane right down the street. I looked into the pilot's face and then saw the rising sun on the tail.*

As part of the 4th Reconnaissance Squadron, Musial was on a B-17 crew, *Gill's Gulls*, flying missions as a ball turret gunner in the Pacific. He flew his first combat missions during the Battle of Midway in June 1942, and won the Distinguished Flying Cross for a series of missions he flew in November 1942, during the Battle of Guadalcanal. Although Joe saw plenty of action aiding invasion landings and bombing Japanese installations and ships at the Marshall Islands, Wake Island, and others, B-17s were used mostly in a reconnaissance role in the Pacific rather than in their intended purpose of bombing.

This was because of the bomber's limited ability to hit the moving targets of Japanese naval ships, and because land combat took place on islands far from air bases and out of range of the B-17's fuel supply. By the end of 1943, B-17s were phased out of the Pacific Theater.

In July 1943, a flight surgeon finally determined Musial had seen enough action and sent him back home to be an instructor. However, after a couple months, Musial asked for and received a new assignment to the European Theater of Operations. Prior to entering the service, Joe had been living with his older sister, Sophie Vachitis, in Laurence Harbor, New Jersey, for 15 years after their mother died. She was quite a bit older and had a 22-year-old daughter, only three years younger than Joe. As a result, he called his sister "Mom." In a letter to his sister, he wrote,

> *Dear Mom, This is going to be quite a jolt to you but ... I just can't take it here in the States. I know you will have a hard time understanding just why I should want to go again. It's just something that's in me, I guess. Maybe it's because I lost so many of my best friends. Or maybe I just can't stand staying on the ground and watching these new boys going over into combat. They are so blame young. They really don't know what they're going into. Now don't take it too hard. And try to understand that it is what I've got to do to be able to live with myself ... even though I know of what horror is ahead. Whether I come back or not is not important. Cause when you realize all the suffering, bloodshed and horror other people have already gone through in the occupied countries, even if I do give my life trying to help, it will be meager in comparison.*

On October 8, Joe reported to the Eighth Air Force and was then assigned to Howard Snyder's B-17 crew. After spending his early war days on an island in the Pacific, he was now in the rain and cold of England.

Since Musial had experience as a ball turret gunner in the Pacific, Snyder was going to have him and Louis Colwart switch positions, but Colwart loved the ball turret and talked Howard out of it. Colwart was a very good natured guy and liked by the entire crew. He always had a smile on his face and liked to joke around. Musial said later, "Even in the thick of everything, he was always laughing and getting a great kick out of it all." Musial also became good friends with Ross Kahler, and they often played Ping-Pong together. However, Kahler, being a skilled and passionate competitor in not only Ping-Pong but also tennis, badminton, squash, handball, archery and fencing, would always win.

Ross Kahler, who wore a Charlie Chaplin mustache, had gone through gunnery school at Tyndall Field in Florida, and as a Staff Sergeant, was originally a waist gunner with another crew. There was a comic strip in the paper at that time called *Smilin' Jack* who was a dare-devil pilot of a single engine bi-plane with an open cockpit and his trademark was a white silk scarf which always streamed out from his neck when he flew.

As a result, Kahler bought himself a white silk scarf which he wore when at his waist gun position and enjoyed how it flapped in the breeze like Smilin' Jack's. He described standing at the opening in the plane firing the gun as "the greatest thrill of my life," and said he felt like a bird up there but hoped that he "didn't get his tail feathers shot off." He subsequently took training courses to become a radio operator, resulting in his promotion to Technical Sergeant. He was made part of Howard Snyder's crew because the 306th CO Major Riordan felt Kahler, being 30-years-old, could add some age and experience to the young enlisted men in the crew.

12

RECREATION

Not all time was spent eating, sleeping, flying, and working. There was also time for an extensive recreation program which included basketball, football, baseball and handball.

Mixing with the Locals

The numerous English pubs (short for public houses) became an irresistible attraction for the American soldiers. Pubs were very different than bars back in the United States, and the members of the 306th discovered that pubs were the center of all social activity in England. Many of them, such as The Falcon in Bletsoe and The Swan in Bedford, dated back to the 17th and 18th centuries and both are still in operation today. The pubs around the area became frequent social destinations for the men until closing time or until the beer ran out.

The Americans were not used to the warm English beer, and many times they rode their bikes into ditches on the way back to the base from a pub. One serviceman commented after the war that his favorite pastime was to go to the mess hall late at night and watch all the men who had too much to drink attempt to ride their bicycles back to the base. Howard commented, "We joined a little club in town called the Key Club (the building still stands today on High Street in Thurleigh). It is very small but somewhere to go to have a beer. It is for officers only. It cost us $1.20 to join and is fixed up nice. They give every member a key and keep the doors locked."

Bedford Officers Club

Not all time was spent eating, sleeping, flying, and working. There was also time for participating in an extensive recreation program which included basketball, football, baseball and handball. Team sports became increasingly organized and a great deal of competition developed between the four squadrons in the 306th. Major Riordan was a basketball player and in charge of the 369th Squadron team. After Howard arrived at Thurleigh, Major Riordan quickly found out that Snyder had played AAU ball and told Howard he wanted him on the team. Howard wrote,

> *We had a basketball game tonight, and right now I feel like an old man. I ache all over. Our Squadron was tied for first place for the first round of the league, and we had the playoff. It so happened that the team (367th Squadron) we played is our big rival for everything. I was thrown out on fouls in the second half, but we won 32-31, and everyone was happy. It is surprising how basketball helps a fellow. Everyone treats me like an old pal just because I can play a little. Oh well, I don't mind at all.*

London

In addition to being the capital of England and Britain's largest city, London was also the capital of the British Empire, one of the largest in history. Prior to World War II, the British Empire comprised one-fifth of the world's population and almost a quarter of the earth's land. London was one of the most significant financial and cultural capitals of the world, and with the European continent being under Nazi occupation, the only free one in Europe. During the middle war years, London was one of the most sensational places on earth and a major attraction and distraction for the airmen.

To the G.I.s, most of whom had never even been to a large city, let alone a place like London, it was wonderment. There was a multitude of historical places and sites to see, innumerable bars and pubs in which to socialize and party, and plenty of women. Although blacked out and bombed out, it was still a spectacular place with throngs of people from all over the world. Its streets were filled with uniformed military personnel from all over the Empire (such as the fierce looking Indian Sikhs in their turbans and Nepalese Gurkhas with their curved daggers) as well as from all the countries occupied by Nazi Germany.

Because of "The Blitz," man-made lights on the ground were extinguished to make it more difficult for the *Luftwaffe* to navigate and locate targets. Blackouts required that all windows and doors be covered at night with suitable material such as heavy curtains, cardboard or paint to prevent the escape of any glimmer of light that might aid enemy aircraft. External lights such as street lights, traffic lights and vehicle headlights were either switched off, or dimmed and shielded to deflect light downward.

Most men went into London to drink and forget about the war for a night or two, hopefully in the company of women. London was expensive, and liquor was hard to get, but U.S. service men were paid three to five times what a British soldier was paid so they were able to get what they wanted in terms of both women and booze. English pubs closed early, but private clubs stayed open late; they were hot, noisy and filled with sultry women. After a two-day "superbender" in London, many flyboys staggered back to their bases with hangovers and empty pockets. However, having a blast and forgetting the war for a few hours was well worth it.

On Howard's first visit to London he wasn't able to see much, saying,

> *We had dinner and then walked around in the blackout trying to find a place to go. Lord, is the blackout black. We walked by the place we were trying to find a half dozen times before seeing it. It will take several days to see much of the place.*

At the end of October back in Pasadena, California, a pregnant Ruth and little Susan moved into a small house at 211 South Roosevelt Avenue, Pasadena. Ruth's mother, Hulda, didn't want a baby in her home, so she advanced Ruth the money for a down payment on the house. Howard wrote, "I am so glad to hear that you are happy in our new house. I am very glad you went ahead and bought it. It was swell of your parents to let us have the down payment."

13
FLYING COMBAT

A combat Wing of 108 B-17G aircraft, each carrying about 5,000 rounds of ammunition, could in combat bring to bear over 1,000 machine guns firing 14 rounds a second with an effective range of 600 yards.

Preparation

During the preparation for and execution of bombing missions, every day began and ended with the work of the ground crews. In performing the critical tasks that were absolutely essential to a successful mission, the crews were exposed to England's cold weather which reflected their relentless dedication and commitment to duty under all conditions.

It was the job of the ground crews to maintain the B-17s and to ensure that each bomber was ready for combat. Despite the fact crews often worked extraordinarily long hours to accomplish these goals, at any given time only 37 to 50 percent of the planes were ready for another mission because of mechanical problems, shortage of parts, and combat damage. Relying on feats of great ingenuity, they frequently returned many seemingly ruined bombers to combat.

On the day of a mission, the ground crews checked the engines, tires, wings, controls, wiring, oxygen systems, radio systems, fueling systems, brakes, and gun turrets to make sure they were all operational. They loaded the bombs, generally 500 lb. general purpose bombs into the bomb bay racks, set their fuses, loaded the .50 caliber shells for the machine guns (usually not less than 5,000 rounds), and made sure every plane had full tanks of gas (typically 2,800 gallons representing one fourth of the plane's gross weight at take-off). Tanks, called Tokyo Tanks, were in the plane's wings and comprised of a rubber composite divided up into 18 small cells.

Ground Crew

Each night, the combat air crews waited anxiously around the squadron bulletin board for the posting of the pilots' names that would be flying the next day. If the name of their pilot was posted, the next thing for the crew members to do was try to get some sleep, but usually no one got much. Instead, there would be chatter and lots of silent prayers. For crews that weren't scheduled to fly the next day, the nights were ones of relief and relaxation.

If crews had men who were sick or injured, men from other crews were pulled at random to fill in. Usually, men were apprehensive about flying with another crew and in a plane they didn't know. Substitute crew members found themselves in airplanes about which they were unfamiliar with the idiosyncrasies and potential malfunctions that the plane's regular crew had learned to correct.

On the day of a mission and way before sun up, an orderly would go from barracks to barracks calling out the names of the pilots who were flying that day to arouse the crews. The crews then had about a half hour before breakfast to wash up, shave (shaving was essential to avoid the discomfort of wearing an oxygen mask), go to the latrine, and get dressed. The crewmen would walk, ride their bikes, or take a truck to the mess halls and have an hour to eat breakfast consisting of non-flatulent foods. From there, they would go to the Briefing Room for an hour to receive information and instructions on the day's mission.

Briefing and Preflight

The main briefing began when the Commanding Officer (CO) entered the room. "Tenn-Hut!" would be called out, and the men would rise and remain standing until the CO said, "Be seated, gentlemen." For many men, it wasn't too long ago that they were sitting like this in a high school or college classroom. During the briefing, the crews would learn what target they would be bombing and be shown a map of Western Europe with red woolen yarn attached, indicating the route the bombers would fly. Once the crews saw what target they would be flying to, the room would always be filled with lots of murmuring and often times with gasps and groans.

In addition, aerial pictures of the target with objects such as roads, lakes, rivers, woods, and towns would also be identified. The crews would receive information on the time to start engines, taxi and take-off position, assembly point, position in the formation, the I.P. location, and the rally point. I.P. stood for Initial Point and was some identifiable landmark approximately 20 miles from the target. When the formation reached the I.P., the bombers had to fly straight and level to the target without taking any evasive action. That was sweating time.

The crews would learn what weather conditions to expect at takeoff, along the route, over the target, and on the return; their bomb load; the amount of flak and enemy fighter opposition that could be expected; what U.S. fighter escort support would be with them; and given radio instructions. If they were shot down and taken prisoner, the crews were told not to give any information except name, rank, and serial number. The last instruction was for the crews to synchronize their watches with the CO's.

Briefing Room

After the general briefing, many crews would pause for a moment of prayer or short religious service with the group chaplains. Pilots, bombardiers, and navigators would have their own individual meetings to receive additional specific instructions and advice. While the ground crews were still working to get the planes ready, the crews would put on their flying clothes, receive their escape kits (in case they were shot down), turn in valuables and identification, and pick up their oxygen masks, electric suits, parachutes, and machine guns (each one weighing 64 pounds).

After picking up their gear, the crews were driven to their planes in trucks or jeeps a minimum of an hour before takeoff. Once in their planes, the crews went through preflight procedures and then waited for the signal from the control tower to take their stations. From this point on, the men ceased to be individuals and became a cohesive team. The tower would give the signal to start engines which took 10 to 15 minutes. The sound of the engines would slowly begin with first one or two starting up. Then all four engines on all of the B-17s comprising the bomb group for that day's mission would start up resulting in a deafening roar. The control tower would shoot off a green flare if the mission was "a go" or white flare if the mission was "scrubbed" because of bad weather. It took another 10 to 15 minutes for marshalling and taxiing, and as the B-17s started moving into position, each pilot would watch for the tail number of the plane he was to follow on takeoff. Finally, it was "zero hour"—takeoff.

Taxing

Takeoff and Forming Up

Every takeoff was packed with anxiety due to a number of factors:

- The planes were usually overloaded and would exceed their maximum weight limit of 33 tons;

- The length of the runways were relatively short; and
- The usual English weather of fog, low cloud cover, and rain always had to be contended with.

In addition, there were certain critical speeds that needed to be reached for a successful take-off. The first was the speed beyond which the pilot could no longer stop the airplane on the runway. Next was stalling speed, the speed above which the airplane will fly once it's in the air but below which it will drop like a stone. Finally, there was takeoff speed which needed to be well above stalling speed. Once the plane lifted off, the pilot would immediately call to the co-pilot "Wheels Up!"

Taking Off

Bombers would take off at 30 second intervals in clear weather and at one minute intervals in poor weather. Each plane would climb according to a preset flight pattern to the assigned assembly altitude and then home in on the radio beacon of their bomb group where squadron leaders would shoot off colored flares. Getting into formation took up a lot of time (at least an hour) and effort, used up a significant percentage of valuable fuel, and increased the possibility of pilot fatigue.

Takeoff was bad enough, but it only got worse as hundreds of airplanes occupied the same clouds at the same time in close proximity to each other. Any deviation in course, rate of climb, or airspeed could put them in the path of others.

The whole process of getting into formation was very slow because every plane had to keep up with every other plane. It was very dangerous, especially in bad weather. While assembling into formation, every member of the crew had the responsibility to watch out for other aircraft to avoid mid-air collisions. Visibility could be terrible while the sky was full of planes circling around like a flock of geese over a feeding area.

Within East Anglia, there were 44 bomber bases and 15 fighter bases with each airfield just three to five miles apart. Just imagine hundreds of heavy bombers, all taking off at the same time, under radio silence and no air traffic control. Pilots did their best to stay together without the advantage of today's navigation technology. It was not uncommon for planes to collide during this process. Tragically, about five percent of the aircraft lost during the war resulted from in-flight accidents during formation assembly.

Combat Formations

The heavy bombers assembled into a "combat box formation" because it was the most effective tactic against enemy flak and fighter attacks. The building blocks of the combat boxes were *Elements*—three ships formed into a tight "V." The Element's lead plane was responsible for maintaining its Element's position relative to the Squadron's lead plane at all times. One plane flew off the lead plane's left wing and the other off its right wing. Those flying the left and right wing positions were responsible for staying in "tight formation". When a fourth plane was included, it flew in the "slot," a position a little below and behind the others, thus converting the "V" into a diamond.

The configuration of bomber formations changed several times, but in mid-October 1943, when the crew of the *Susan Ruth* arrived, it had settled into one that was comprised of four Elements of three aircraft each, forming up a 12 plane Squadron, three Squadrons forming up a 36 plane Group and three Groups forming up to make a 108 plane Wing. Each Group formation occupied a stretch of sky 600 yards long, about a mile wide, and a half mile deep; Combat Wings would form up at four to six mile intervals to create a Divisional Column; and finally Division Columns would form up.

For an example, three of the four 306th squadrons (367th, 368th, 369th, and 423rd) would rotate to form the Bomb Group of the 306th. The 306th Bomb Group would then form up with planes from the 305th Bomb Group and 92nd Bomb Group to form the 40th Combat Wing formation. The 40th Bomb Wing would then join up with the 1st Bomb Wing, 41st Bomb Wing, and 94th Bomb Wing to form the 1st Division Bomb Column. Finally, the 1st Division Column would then form up with the Eighth Air Force's other two Bomb Divisions, the 2nd and 3rd. On any given mission, the total number of planes in the strike force varied a great deal but could be in the hundreds and into the thousands, including fighter escorts.

The formation, whether it be Squadron, Group or Wing, was three dimensional with a Lead Group, a High Group to the right and behind the Lead Group, and a Low Group to the left and behind the Lead Group. This configuration was designed to take full advantage of the B-17's combined defensive fire power. However, the Low Group was the most dangerous position in the formation and was the main target of enemy fighter attacks. In particular, the rear-most plane in the Low Group was the last to bomb and thus nicknamed "Tail-end Charlie" and its position referred to as "Purple Heart Corner."

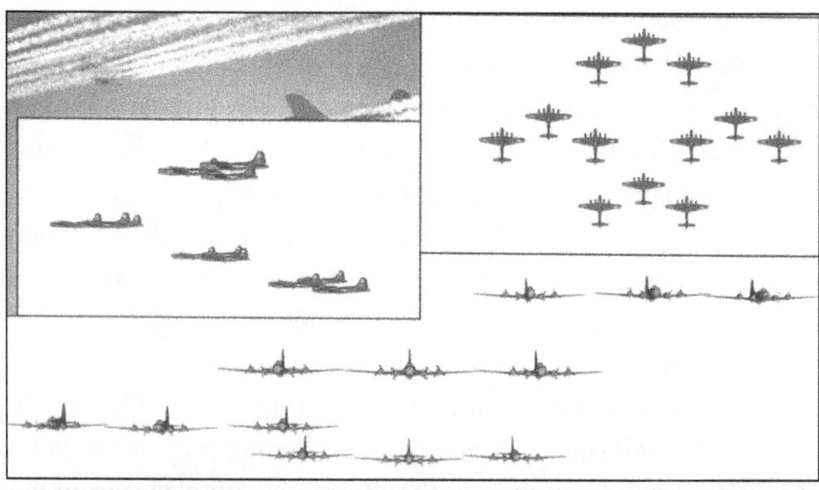

Formation Diagram; B-17 Formation

Once a Group was assembled, it homed in on the radio beacon of its Wing, and the Group took its assigned place in the formation. Finally, the Wings homed in on yet another beacon and the entire armada was ready to depart on their mission. It was quite a sight to see squadron after squadron of B-17s directed by the "lead-ships" rise and circle to pre-determined points where they would organize themselves into Group and Wing attack formations and then set out for their journey across the English Channel or North Sea to their target.

The B-17

The inside of a B-17 was like a cigar tube, held in place by thousands of rivets. The aluminum "skin" was very thin and easily penetrated. The plane smelled of sweat, grease, cordite (basically smokeless gunpowder from the .50 caliber shells the machine guns fired), cigarette smoke (airmen who had never smoked before found relief in tobacco) and often urine and dried blood. The ten-man crew was enclosed in a space tighter than a submarine. This was especially true for the tail gunner and ball turret gunner who were enclosed in extremely cramped locations—so much so that they could not wear their parachutes.

The bombardier, navigator, pilot, co-pilot, and engineer/top turret gunner were separated from radio operator, ball turret gunner, two waist gunners, and tail gunner by the bomb bay. The bombs, typical ten 500 pound, general purpose (GP) bombs, were stacked in racks from floor to ceiling on both sides of the plane, five to a side. In between was a catwalk only eight inches wide, and when the bomb bay doors were open, the view was five miles straight down to the earth below.

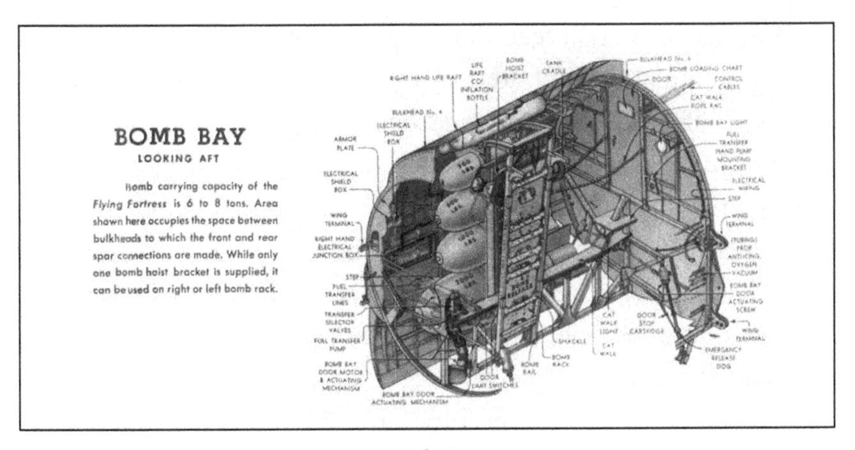

Bomb Bay

To defend themselves, B-17s were equipped with .50 caliber Browning machine guns. Once in formation and over the English Channel, the gunners cleared their guns shaking the entire plane with ear-splitting noise and filling the plane with the smell of cordite. Then everything became quiet with the only sound being the monotonous drone of the engines as the planes made their way to the target.

The B-17's dedicated gunners were the ball turret underneath the plane with twin .50 caliber guns having about 500-650 rounds of ammunition; the tail gunner with twin .50 caliber guns in the tail; the top turret gunner (flight engineer) with twin .50 caliber guns, and two waist gunners each with a single .50 caliber gun on either side of the plane. There was also the chin turret with twin .50 caliber guns that the bombardier could fire and the two cheek guns for the navigator.

A combat Wing of 108 B-17G aircraft, each carrying about 5,000 rounds of ammunition, could in combat bring to bear over 1,000 machine guns firing 14 rounds a second with an effective range of 600 yards. However, the amount of ammunition was limited and the guns would get too hot for the gunners to just hold the trigger down and fire relentlessly when engaging enemy fighters. To be most effective, the gunners shot in bursts of four or five rounds at a time.

Once above 10,000 feet, the crew donned oxygen masks as the planes continued to climb to their operational level that could be as high as 30,000 feet. At that altitude, one minute without oxygen and a man would lose consciousness, after 20 minutes he would die. The strain on the men and the plane would mount as they climbed higher and higher at 300 feet per minute. To say the least, it was very strenuous on the pilots to keep a 30 ton Flying Fortress in tight formation on missions that lasted eight to ten hours, but it was necessary; the formation was the bombers' best defense against enemy fighters.

It took every ounce of concentration and physical strength to hold the aircraft steady, and the pilot flying the ship had to have his eyes glued on his lead aircraft, even during enemy fighter attacks and flak.

While one pilot was flying the plane, the other would be monitoring all the instruments and gadgets, for there were more than 150 different switches, dials, cranks, handles, and gauges to keep track of, all of which measured vital elements of the flight: engine revolutions, manifold and fuel pressures, aerodynamics, barometric pressure, altitude, wind drift, airspeed, position and direction.

Cockpit Controls

Europe—Engaging the Enemy

The B-17G aluminum silver planes would shimmer in the blue sky leaving contrails streaming behind them. "Contrails" is an abbreviation for condensation trails which are linear cloud-like water vapor formations caused by hot engine exhaust gases coming into contact with cold moist air at high altitude. Far from beautiful, contrails were bad news to the bomber formations. They not only tended to obscure visibility of the target and the formation for those aircraft following behind, but they acted as giant "pointers" to German fighter interceptors, leading them directly to the bombers.

Contrails

Each crew member would don a 30-pound flak suit (a body armor combat vest made of overlapping steel plates inside of aprons), and a steel helmet designed to protect against anti-aircraft fire. They reduced casualties from flak fragments and enemy fighter shell splinters but would not protect a man if hit straight on by cannon fire or bursting flak. The suits were cumbersome but could be shed quickly in an emergency by pulling on a cord. Parachutes were too bulky to be worn all the time, but crewmen did wear a harness that allowed them to quickly clip on their parachute when needed. As the plane climbed higher, the temperature got colder reaching 40 to 60 degrees below zero. If a man took off a glove, he could lose fingers to frostbite. Each crew position had "relief tubes" except for the ball turret gunner, who, if he had "to go," just "went," let it freeze, and then pushed it out the ammo chute.

As the planes approached the coast of mainland Europe, pilots would give instructions saying things such as,

- "Stay on the ball."

- "Keep your eyes peeled."
- "Save your ammunition and make your shots count."
- "Don't get excited and yell when you talk on the intercom."

Combat Gear

Crossing the enemy coast, steel helmets went on and tense gunners became alert. Pilots would change course every 15 seconds in evasive action to confuse the German flak batteries.

The Germans had erected radar stations all across continental Europe and knew the U.S. bombers were coming from the time they took off from England. As the bombers neared the target, they would begin to run into anti-aircraft fire called "flak" from the Germans 88 mm anti-aircraft guns. Flak accounted for far more air crew casualties than German fighters and took down more American planes than the fighters.

The word flak was a contraction of the German word ***Fl***_ugzeug_***a***_bwehr_***k***_anone_ meaning "aircraft-defense cannon." It was estimated that the German air defense involved 900,000 men and 10,000 pieces of anti-aircraft artillery. The guns, which could fire up to 20 shells per minute, were set so that the shells exploded at a certain height to correspond to the altitude that the bombers were flying. When the shells exploded, they broke up into all shapes and sizes of metal pieces or shrapnel; jagged shell splinters able to rip through aircraft hundreds of feet from the burst.

Approaching the target area, the B-17s could see ahead of them the ominous black clouds of exploding flak filling the sky. From a distance, the small clouds looked like a cluster of polka-dots, harmless looking silent puffs of smoke, except that each puff was a shell exploding. As hundreds of anti-aircraft shells began exploding, they formed a dense carpet that hovered in the air. Upon reaching them, the sky seemed to be painted black with flak, an "iron cumulus."

German 88 mm anti-aircraft gun – *Flugzeugabwehrkanone (Flak)*

When flak was close enough that the crews could see and distinguish the orange and red centers of the bursting shells, they knew they were in serious trouble. When among the bursts of exploding shells, close ones violently rocked the ships

Flak

Flak

and everything would momentarily go black. The planes would shudder and shake from the vicious exploding metal; shrapnel of steel splinters that could rip through a B-17's thin-skinned fuselage. Flak had a devastating psychological effect on the crews as all they could do was just sit and take it, dripping sweat even though it was 40 to 60 degrees below zero at the altitude they were flying. As the late Dr. Stephen Ambrose wrote, "It was said that there were more soldiers converted to Christianity by the 88 than by Peter and Paul."

The Bombing Run

Besides flak, the B-17 bombers also had to contend with the German Air Force, called the *Luftwaffe* which was part of the *Wehrmacht* (meaning defense force) the unified armed forces of Germany. When World War II began, the *Luftwaffe* was one of the most technologically advanced air forces in the world with the Messerschmitt 109 and the heavily armed Focke-Wulf 190 (nicknamed "Butcherbird" because it was so lethal) comprising the backbone of its fighter aircraft.

Messerschmitt 109

Focke-Wulf 190

During the early years of the war, the *Luftwaffe* quickly established air supremacy over the skies of mainland Europe. To address this threat, the USAAF had developed the bomb group box formation. A B-17 on its own stood little chance of survival; a 1943 study clearly showed that about half of the B-17s lost in combat had left the formation. Staying in formation was literally a matter of life and death. The staggered combat box wing formation was designed to give the B-17s full coverage of the sky. Tiered up and down and lined up left and right, the planes were deployed to uncover every gun and to avoid gunners firing into other B-17s. They were arranged so that concentrated cones of fire from their .50 caliber machine guns covered the sky for 1,000 yards in every direction. All the B-17s could cover the other bombers in their formation, thus theoretically making the formation a dangerous one for enemy fighters to engage. However, if a bomber fell out of the formation, it became easy pickings for the faster, more maneuverable enemy fighters.

Norden Bombsight

As the bomber formation drew closer to their target, they reached the "I.P." (Initial Point) usually a prominent landmark. The formation would make a 30-45 degree turn towards the target and begin their bombing run which could be 20 to 50 miles long. From this point on, the bombardier would fly the airplane through the Norden bombsight linked to the plane's autopilot. The Norden bombsight simplified the bombardier's job considerably by taking into account factors of altitude,

Bombardier

airspeed, ground speed and drift to automatically calculate the bomb release point. The plane would have to be flown straight and level through the exploding flak to the bomb release point. Once committed to the bomb run, aircraft could not engage in evasive maneuvers to dodge flak. Thus during the final bomb run, the bombers were extremely vulnerable.

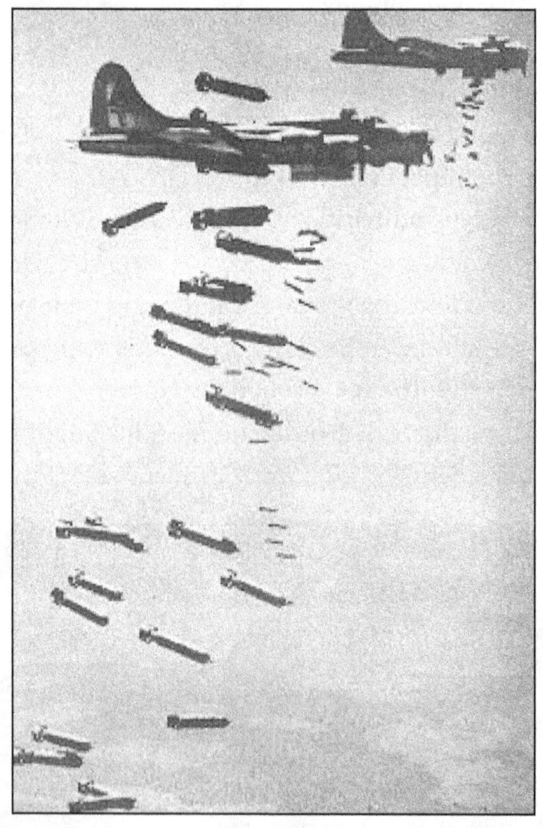

Bombs Away

Bombers were torn apart by flak, and if hit directly would explode instantly, disappearing from sight. Some bombers would break apart and plunge straight down in pieces. When wings were badly damaged or broken off, a B-17 might start a slow decent, out of control, trailing smoke. Others limped along smoking, burning, and with engines out.

Bombs Away

Shot Down

Shot Down

Ideally, the formation would bomb a compact area 500 by 250 yards. After all the planes had dropped their bombs, they would make a wide sweeping turn and proceed to the "rallying point" which would be a location out of range of known flak batteries and where the bombers would form back up again. With some planes shot down and with others damaged, the bombers tried as best they could to pull themselves back into some semblance of a defensive wing formation for their return flight to England.

14
MAKING IT BACK TO BASE

Crippled B-17s staggered back towards England with lacerated tails, gaping holes in fuselages, wing damage, and engines out or on fire. The crew of a bomber lagging behind and no longer able to keep up with the formation knew they were sitting ducks for the German fighters.

The Return

At this point, the first half of the mission over, but now the B-17s needed to get home. When the flak stopped, it meant enemy fighters were lurking. The crews braced themselves to run the gauntlet of enemy fighters they could expect to find between themselves and home. Sometimes the trips home could be the worst part.

At first German fighters would appear as specks in the sky, each looking like an inch of silver. Quickly they would grow to two or three inches and start to give off little sparklers, indicating their guns were firing. Then suddenly, all hell would break loose with the sound of the enemy planes' engines roaring, their machine guns and cannons firing, and their shells exploding.

The German fighters would be spitting fire, flipping over, and then zooming down below and away from the B-17 formation. They would be continuously twisting, turning, climbing, and diving. The enemy planes would zoom out of the dazzling sunlight, riddling the bombers at 2,300 rounds a minute. They would wheel in the air like hornets and close in with incredible speed, ripping through the formation. When approaching head on, it was like an incredible game of "chicken" until the German planes would suddenly veer off seconds from impact.

The bombers themselves were filled with the deafening noise of their own guns drilling the air like electric sledgehammers. Inside the bombers, one of the most important instruments became the interphone as crew members called out enemy fighter locations. Enemy aircraft were called "bandits" and was an alert word that commanded immediate attention. For example, a crewman might call out, "Bandit at 4'clock!" Conversely, the U.S. escort fighters were referred to as "little friends."

Waist Gunner firing .50 caliber machine gun

Whether bombers were hit by anti-aircraft fire or shredded by German fighters, as they went down, their crews would be fumbling for their parachutes and praying for survival. Sometimes the men were able to bail out of their falling planes and parachutes were seen opening up, but many times not.

Crippled B-17s staggered back towards England with lacerated tails, gaping holes in fuselages, wing damage, and engines out or on fire. The crew of a bomber lagging behind and no longer able to keep up with the formation knew they were sitting ducks for the German fighters. It was a forlorn feeling seeing their formation slowly disappearing from view. Losing airspeed and altitude, drifting alone and helpless, they became stragglers as Nazi fighters swarmed like a pack of wolves, circling for the kill. All the bomber could do was try to fight back if they could and to set off flares in a cry for help in the hope U.S. fighters would come to rescue them and escort them home. The other B-17s couldn't go to their aid. They had to stay in formation.

Battle damaged planes had tough decisions to make. If they crash landed or bailed out in Europe, they would most likely be captured. If they ditched in the sea, they had to be rescued quickly or they would freeze to death in the icy waters. (4,361 Eighth Air Force crewmen ditched in the North Sea but only 1,538 or 38 percent were rescued.) The other and most palatable option was to try and make it back to England safely. Some did and some didn't.

Back at the base, the mission was also being flown, and it was none less real. There was drama there too, waiting to see who came back. Gathered in clusters around the control tower, apprehensive and somber, the men on the ground were tense and plenty worried. They called it "sweating it out." They knew the flight plan; they knew when the planes crossed the enemy coast, when they would encounter flak, be over the target, and when they should be nearing the field coming back. When the B-17s starting returning to the base in mid-afternoon or early evening, everyone on the ground would rush out to the runway. They would anxiously wait and watch; every ear straining to hear the first sound of the engines.

Control Tower

Initially, the planes appeared as faint dots in the distant sky and then a distant rumble could be heard. Men on the ground would count the planes and try to read the tail numbers on the ships. If there were wounded on board, the ship would set off a red flare to alert the medical personnel on the ground and get priority to land first. Those wounded had to endure great pain being bounced around in their plane for hundreds of miles through the frozen stratosphere. There were no medics on board the planes. Crewmen had to try as best they could to help the wounded survive until they could get proper medical attention at the base hospital. The trauma that took place inside of battle damaged planes was immense.

No landing was complete until the engines were shut down, and the crew had safely disembarked. The final moments of flight, gently settling to the ground, were comforting with the promise of rest and relief after an exhausting, nerve-racking mission. After landing, the crews were picked up by truck and driven to a building for debriefing and interrogation by the Group Intelligence Officer. First, however, they were given a double shot of whiskey.

Some ships that appeared to suffer little apparent damage actually carried wounded or dead men on board while others which appeared so battered they were incapable of flying brought home crews without a scratch. Each B-17 had an assigned ground crew (mechanics, electricians, prop specialists, sheet metal repairmen) run by a crew chief whose job it was to keep the airplane flying. At the end of each mission, battle and mechanical damage was assessed and the time to make the necessary repairs was estimated. Many times they worked around the clock to ready planes for the next raid. In cases where a plane was so severely damaged that it could not be repaired by the ground crew at Thurleigh, it was turned over to the VIII Air Force Service Command for repairs.

Battle Damage

On some days, tragedy would not only strike the bombers and their crews but also the quiet English countryside as well. Villagers would be going about their normal daily activities when suddenly a bomber would come crashing down on top of them. This could occur on takeoff or landing as a result of a number of factors such as mid-air collisions, mechanical failures, adverse weather conditions, or battle damage. Fields, orchards, dwellings, cottages, livestock, and civilian lives (grandparents, husbands and wives, children) were lost when an entire aircraft or large chunks of it fell out of the sky. Bombs intended for German targets would explode, machine gun shells would start firing off in every direction, and fireballs raged from unused fuel.

Crashed

15

1943 PROBLEMS

The crews kept flying combat missions until one of three things occurred: 1) they were killed in action; 2) they were shot down captured and became prisoners of war (POWs); or 3) the war ended.

Devastating Losses

The men who made up the crew of a B-17 Flying Fortress were each specially trained for their position. Nonetheless, on every combat mission they faced possible death and destruction.

The challenges each crew member faced on every mission was formidable: enduring the physical strain of using oxygen in an unpressurized aircraft at an altitude where the temperature dropped to minus 60 degrees; suffering the heartache of watching a buddy's aircraft suddenly blow up and instantly disappear in a cloud of grey smoke; seeing the tail, wing, or engines break off and the plane then drop like a stone; witnessing a bomber slowly rolling over and begin its slow plunge to the earth below; and watching for parachutes to see how many men got out, if any. If a plane went down too fast, the crew would be sealed into what would become their coffin.

Worse yet was the sudden horror when a crew's aircraft was hit by flak or enemy fighters five miles above the earth. Many men would be reported missing or killed after only one or two missions, while others might survive only to be killed on their final mission.

As a result of high numbers of casualties, the 306th and Eighth Air Force began facing a severe morale problem. The aircrews who were going up on missions felt that "there was no light at the end of the tunnel" because initially there was no limit on the number of missions they could fly. The crews kept flying combat missions until one of three things occurred: 1) they were killed in action; 2) they were shot down, captured and became prisoners of war (POWs); or 3) the war ended.

By the early weeks of 1943, the 306th had lost nearly 80 percent of its original combat crews. As a result, morale spiraled downward as the apparent odds of surviving grew smaller and smaller. The physical and mental stress being endured by combat aircrews was recognized by the 306th Group Surgeon, Major Thurman Shuller, and in March, he expressed his concerns in a letter that made its way up the chain of command to General Ira Eaker. Thankfully, the Eighth Air Force set a twenty-five mission limit giving the airmen some hope. However, even with the twenty-five mission mark, less than one in four crew members could expect to complete their tour (in other words, 75 percent failed to complete 25 missions) during the remainder of 1943.

Inadequate Fighter Support

Incredibly, prior to April 1943, there was only one fighter group assigned to provide the B-17s with escort support. The VIII Bomber Command was under the false belief that bombers could adequately defend themselves against air attack and that the heavily gunned bombers flying in their well designed formations could penetrate deeply over the Reich unescorted. Even after the Bomber Command finally identified the necessity of escort protection, the U.S. fighters escorting the B-17s on their bombing missions weren't very effective. Because of their limited fuel capacity, range was miserably insufficient and the fighters had to turn back to England before the B-17s reached their targets over Germany.

The P-38 Lightning, nick-named "fork-tailed devil" by *Luftwaffe* pilots, was a twin-engine U.S. fighter plane easily identified by the U.S.

bomber gunners. The "P" stood for Pursuit. Unfortunately, they were only available in small numbers in the European theater. Furthermore, its engines were difficult to maintain, and it lacked sufficient maneuverability to successfully take on the *Luftwaffe* fighters.

P-38 Lightnings

The other U.S. fighter plane at the time was the P-47 Thunderbolt. It was the largest, heaviest, and most expensive fighter aircraft in history to be powered by a single piston engine. It gained the nickname "The Jug" because its profile was similar to that of the common milk jug of the time. Although it was capable of meeting the *Luftwaffe* on more than even terms, it also did not have sufficient range. The *Luftwaffe* fighters simply waited for the incoming bombers just beyond the point where the Thunderbolts had to turn back to refuel.

P-47 Thunderbolts

Unescorted, the bomber formations were no match for the German fighters. Uninhibited, the German fighters could pounce on the lumbering, heavy B-17 bombers and inflict a deadly toll. An example was the August 17, 1943, Schweinfurt–Regensburg mission during which 376 bombers from 16 bomb groups were dispatched into Germany well beyond the range of escort fighters. Tragically, 60 aircraft were lost: 600 airmen killed in action (KIA), wounded in action (WIA) or missing in action (MIA) with an additional 55 to 95 aircraft badly damaged.

Overwhelming Casualties

Casualties in the Eighth Air Force were never higher than during the autumn of 1943. The month of October, in particular one seven day period referred to as "Black Week," was especially bloody. On the October 8 raid to Bremen, Germany, known as "Flak City," 30 aircraft were lost with the 100th Bomb Group, nicknamed the "Bloody

100th," losing nine out of eighteen. The flak was so heavy that one pilot joked that, "If we put wheels down, we could taxi on it." The following day a raid was made to Anklam and Marienburg, Germany. It was almost to Poland, a prodigious 15 hour round trip, on which 28 bombers went down (280 men).

Then on October 10, the third mission in three days was flown to Munster, Germany, and another 30 planes went down. Because of the previous two days' losses, the 100th Bomb Group could only put up a 13 plane group instead of the normal 18 to 21 aircraft. Fewer planes meant less defensive firepower and an easier target for German fighters. As a result, the 100th BG almost lost its entire group; only one of the 13 planes made it back.

In three consecutive days, the Eighth Air Force had almost 900 men fail to return to England from these missions. The men were exhausted, morale was in the tank, and the German *Luftwaffe* was handily winning the air war. Crewmen felt they were living on borrowed time. It was said that to hold rank in 1943 was like having a ticket to a funeral—your own. After Munster, the Eighth Air Force had to stand down as they did not have enough men or planes to mount another raid for several days.

Making things worse was the fact that the raid to Munster was the first time that the U.S. specifically went out to bomb civilians; targeting the front steps of the cathedral on a Sunday during Mass. Many crews, especially Catholics, had serious problems bombing a house of God and questioned their orders. Although the British RAF bombed towns, doing so for the U.S. was a shockingly different concept for many crew members.

The next raid the Eighth Air Force undertook was on October 14; it was a second visit to the Kugelfischer ball bearing factory at Schweinfurt, and 306th pilot John Noack said he was "scared shitless to go back." As usual the P-47s were unable to escort the bombers to the target, and things were made even worse when the 305th Bomb Group didn't show up as Low Group in the 40th Combat Wing formation because of thick cloud cover. It ended up flying with the 1st Combat Wing formation so the 92nd BG and 306th BG were left vulnerable.

Furthering their trouble was the fact that the 92nd and 306th were both short the normal number of 21 aircraft, only able to put up 13 and 18 respectively, and of the 306th's number, three turned back to England for various reasons leaving only 15 to actually reach the objective. Hundreds of German fighters attacked the Eighth Air Force that day in what was the biggest air engagement between the U.S. and Germany up to that time. The horrific result was that the 92nd BG lost six aircraft, the 306th, 10 out of 15, and the 305th, 13 out of 16.

Of the 291 B-17s sent out by the Eighth Air Force, 60 were lost outright and another 17 damaged so heavily that they had to be scrapped. Some crews reported that the scene looked like a parachute invasion because so many men were forced to bail out. No one could believe what had happened. Demoralized by sharing barracks with so many empty beds, the combat crews were physically and mentally exhausted, needing rest and consolation.

Excerpts from the 369th Squadron Combat Diary read, "This was the most disappointing day the 306th has known. Sixty Fortresses from the First Division were lost to the greatest resistance yet encountered. Ten out of the fifteen Fortresses representing the 306th were knocked out. There's no way to gloss over such a loss, no way to show how the whole group has been jarred. We look forward to the inevitable replacement crews. May they be the equal of these good fellows who have gone down. And may their luck be better."

The Eighth Air Force had lost 148 B-17s (1,480 men) in a matter of seven days; resulting in it being "grounded." Due to the shortage of airplanes and airmen, it needed to take time to repair the damaged bombers and return the number of crews to full combat status. With less than one third of B-17 crews expected to survive, the Eighth Air Force realized that this loss rate was unsustainable, and for the remainder of 1943, daylight penetrations beyond the range of fighter escorts were sharply reduced.

The heavy losses of "Black Week" finally resulted in the 8th Air Force revising its tactics of daylight bombing. The defensive firepower of the combat box formation was not enough. The B-17s could not protect themselves on their own. They needed long-range fighter support to and from the target. Although the P-38s and P-47s were fitted with auxiliary fuel tanks to increase their range, the bombers would not enjoy the full advantage of escorts until the beginning of 1944 with the introduction of the P-51 Mustang.

P-51 Mustangs

A Long-Range Fighter ... Finally

The Mustang was specifically designed as an anti-fighter combat plane with capabilities that allowed it to hunt down both of the German fighters (ME-109 and FW-190) with relative ease. Not only was it superior to the German fighters in the combat arena, it could also escort the B-17s on their long-range penetration raids deep into Germany. The 2,000 mile range of the Mustang when equipped with extra drop tanks was far in excess of what was available to other fighters of the day. This, plus the Air Force's ability to mount escorts in force (with 3-to-1 and later 4-to-1 odds) proved devastating to the *Luftwaffe*. P-51 pilots achieved many of their victories simply because of overwhelming numerical superiority.

The P-51 Mustang was the solution to the obvious need for an effective bomber escort and shifted the air war to the Allies' favor. With this plane augmenting the P-47 Thunderbolt escorts which had increased their range by adding auxiliary fuel tanks, daylight operations in depth could once again be resumed. Meanwhile, the U.S. heavy bomber force had been increased substantially in strength, both by replacement aircraft and by new combat crews of which Howard Snyder and the crew of the *Susan Ruth* were a part. Although the Eighth Air Force had teetered on defeat, the German *Luftwaffe* would never again come close to victory in the skies over Europe.

16

NOVEMBER 1943 ... FIRST MISSION

In response to the B-17's "Bombs Away," 20 to 25 single engine and twin engine German fighters broke through the overcast and started climbing toward the B-17 formation. Just as the German fighters were closing in, P-47 escorts followed by P-38s penetrated the enemy formation, attacking and dispersing the German aircraft.

A New Technology

On November 3, 1943, the Eighth Air Force flew only its second mission following "Black Thursday," the Second Schweinfurt Raid. As the 369th Combat Diary stated, "A few successful raids in early November will do wicked wonders to restore confidence and fighting spirit." It was also the first combat mission for Howard Snyder flying as co-pilot to Lt. Bill Hilton.

306th Bomb Group B-17s

Significantly, this was the Eighth Air Force's first combat operation of more than 500 bombers, including 25 from the 306th. The mission was to the seaport city of Wilhelmshaven, one of Germany's largest and most important naval bases and shipbuilding works, constructing submarines. In addition to the bombers, 45 P-38s and 333 P-47s provided escort.

On the day of the mission, Wilhelmshaven was completely obscured by clouds, or in Air Force vernacular 10/10ths. The Air Force always expressed the ground area obscured by clouds in "tenths." Therefore, 1/10ths coverage meant only one-tenth of the ground area was obscured by clouds, while 10/10ths coverage meant a solid layer of clouds completely obscured the ground.

10/10ths Cloud Cover

Despite the thick cloud cover over the target area, a new technology enabled the mission to proceed. The "Pathfinder Force" (PFF) were specially equipped B-17s of the 482nd Bomb Group, into which a new form of air-to-ground radar (H2X) was installed; it was a system originally devised by the British that could locate targets through thick overcast. For the first time, PFF planes led the formation and dropped parachute flares to guide the bombers to the potentially invisible target. The H2X was encased in an electronics dome which replaced the ball turret in the B-17s. This state-of-the-art configuration had the secret code name "Mickey," which was coined by Major Fred Rabo, Commanding Officer of the 482nd, because the first time he saw it, he thought the radar dome looked like Mickey Mouse.

At Wilhelmshaven, the PFF ships performed exactly as planned, opening their bomb bay doors at the I.P. ("Initial Point" which was the point on the flight plan that the PFF bombers began their bombing run), first releasing their parachute flares and then their bomb loads. Although the 1,450 tons of bombs that day were not dropped with perfect precision, it was nonetheless clear that the new technology was very promising.

In response to the B-17's "Bombs Away," 20 to 25 single-engine and twin-engine German fighters broke through the overcast and started climbing toward the B-17 formation. Just as the German fighters were closing in, P-47 escorts followed by P-38s penetrated the enemy formation, attacking and dispersing the German aircraft. Because of the life-saving protection they received from the escort planes, B-17 crews held fighter support in very high regard.

The same day that Howard Snyder flew his first mission, a young 20-year-old German fighter pilot, Hans Berger, and his very good friend, Johannes Rathenow, were also in the sky. Berger reported that while he was maneuvering into position to attack a box of B-17s, Rathenow's plane took a direct hit and exploded only a few meters away. Lt. Berger was a member of *Jagdgeschwader I*, a *Luftwaffe* fighter unit; the name derived from *Jagd*, meaning "hunt," and *Geschwader*, meaning "wing." It would not be the last time Berger engaged a B-17 formation.

Even though the 369th Squadron didn't receive so much as a scratch, two B-17s from the 368th Squadron, piloted by Lt. George Goris and Lt. Donald Wadley, tragically collided in midair over the

North Sea on their way to Germany. Both planes went down killing all 20 crewmen. As was often the case, midair collisions in tight combat formations were not uncommon with planes flying so close together, often through heavy overcast.

First Mission

Howard wrote to Ruth,

> *I've been on my first mission! They call the fellows "virgins" until they have their first mission in, so we have had our "cherries popped" if you'll pardon the expression. Twenty-Four more to go. They won't all be as easy as this one. It gives one an awful, sickening sensation in one's stomach to see a big Fort (Flying Fortress) go down like a great, stricken monster. I must admit I was a little nervous even though it was exceptionally easy. I guess because it was my first raid. You get used to it after awhile. When you think of the damage we do, it is a very cheap price to pay.*

The air war over Europe was a new kind of battle front in which the U.S. heavy bombers sought out the enemy's infrastructure, but not its infantry, artillery, or tanks. Instead, the U.S. bombers attacked the industrial heart of Germany, the foundation on which the Nazi Empire and its army relied. The targets to be destroyed were steel mills and refineries, shipyards and submarine pens, factories and munitions plants; points on the map of Western Europe which produced rubber, guns, ball bearings, shells, engines, planes and tanks.

The nature of this type of combat from a distance made it a more impersonal war for air crews. They didn't see the enemy down below and tended to view their targets as hardware to be destroyed rather than people to be killed. They knew people were down there, but they couldn't think about that. It helped the crews to feel like they were bombing things, and not human beings; assessing damage below as simply pillars of smoke and fire, not as human anguish and death.

Even so, it was war after all. The Germans were building things to kill British and Americans. You reap what you sow; payback.

All of Howard's crew went on the mission with him, with the exception of Joe Musial and Ross Kahler who were sick. Their positions were filled by Harold Maron as waist gunner and James Hobbs as radio operator. Eike didn't go either, but he was technically on another crew. Howard said, "Eike was very disappointed. He has been all set to go several times, but the missions have always been called off because of bad weather. One pilot and two enlisted men from our squadron finished up on the raid and will be leaving for the States soon. The boys painted them all up. They were a mess. All the boys were out waving when we took off. It certainly felt good to see them cheering us off! They gave us a big feed when we got back. I got the first fresh eggs I've had since we were over here."

The following year, waist gunner Harold Maron, a member of Lt. Gerald Haywood's crew, would be shot down on March 29, 1944. After a bombing run on the Waggum Airfield near Brunswick, Germany, their escort fighters suddenly disappeared for twenty minutes and during that time, Haywood's plane and that of Alvin Schuering were attacked by Focke-Wulf 190s. Both B-17s were knocked out of the formation and finished off as they drifted behind the other bombers. Six members of Haywood's crew were killed in action. Harold Maron and three others were captured and taken prisoner. All ten members of Schuering's crew bailed out safely but spent the remainder of the war in German prison camps. Both Haywood and Schuering were on their 25th and final mission, and their two planes were the only two B-17s of the 306th shot down by enemy fighters during the entire month of March.

War and Faith

During the war, many Americans turned to the church for spiritual and emotional support during a time of great uncertainty. This was especially true of soldiers who were often in harm's way. The expression, "There are no atheists in foxholes" was coined during World War II, because almost universally in times of extreme stress and fear during war, people will believe in, or hope for, a higher power. Nearly eight thousand clergy enrolled as chaplains in the military, and churches provided Bibles and devotional literature for the troops. In addition to their regular ministerial functions, chaplains also assumed the role of psychological counselors to battle-stressed and battle-fatigued soldiers, providing important emotional support for all service personnel.

While many servicemen might have turned to religion and God only to keep them safe during the war, Howard and his wife Ruth had both been raised in strong Christian families and had a strong faith in Jesus Christ as their Savior. Howard told Ruth, "I read the Bible nearly every evening before I go to bed, and I always pray that God watches over you, the baby (Ruth was now four months pregnant), and Susan."

During his youth, Howard grew up around other Christians and most all his friends were Christians. One night in the barracks while he and his three fellow officers were chatting, he was absolutely shocked to learn that Robert Benninger was not a Christian. He wrote to Ruth,

> *I have been trying to write, but we have been arguing with Benninger about religion. Can you imagine the crazy little fool thinks he needs no help from God! In other words, he is an atheist! He doesn't believe in creation or anything. Maybe I can settle down to continue to write, but there have been a good many interruptions. It is midnight so you can see how much talking we have been doing.*

On November 5, Eike finally went on his first raid as co-pilot on Captain David Wheeler's crew. It was to Gelsenkirchen, Germany, which was a center of coal production and oil refining. Although it was a rough trip, all of the 306th planes got back safely, and no one was wounded. Escort support from the P-38s and P-47s was good. However, flak was intense and persistent from the start of the bomb run throughout the Ruhr Valley. Most of the bombers from the 306th had holes in them, but only Eike's plane was badly damaged.

During November, Howard and his crew flew many practice missions, during which he began flying as first pilot again which pleased him. In addition, Howard was flying with his entire crew except for Eike. He stated,

> *We took a short cross-country hop today over to the field where we went to school for a few days after first arriving in England. Dan (bombardier Richard Daniels) had some laundry to pick up, and I got the yardage I wanted for my blazer. We were over and back in an hour. It sure seemed good to fly from the left side (pilot's seat) of the cockpit again. If I do a good job, I will probably get a ship and be in line for a promotion to 1st Lt. Don't think that I'm in on every "Fort" raid that you read about in the paper. Several raids were cancelled that I was not scheduled to go on. The crews are sometimes alternated and then sometimes they go on several in succession. One never knows when he is going.*

Some Shopping and the Flu

On another venture into London in early November, Howard reported, "I went to London the other day with Benny and Dan, but Eike wasn't able to go because of being on another crew. I shouldn't have gone because I didn't feel well, but I wanted to get you something for Christmas and also wanted to get my battle jacket made. I played basketball the other night and probably shouldn't have because I had a bad cold which I guess developed into the flu. You might as well forget about Wedgwood. You just can't get it except for little novelty pieces."

The battle jacket Howard referred to was the type A-2 leather flight jacket, also called a bomber jacket. It was a military flight jacket worn by officers, who typically decorated their jackets with squadron patches and artwork. Its original designation was "Jacket, Pilot's (summer)," and its construction was "seal brown horsehide leather, knitted wristlets and waistband." It became a symbol of the American pilot and a treasured item, worn with as much pride as his wings. In mid-1943 General "Hap" Arnold cancelled any further leather jacket contracts in favor of newer cloth-shell jackets which was a very unpopular decision with the flyers. As a result, a small cottage industry arose in England making the A-2 style jackets for airmen.

369th Squadron A-2 jacket

Although he couldn't find any Wedgwood, Howard did buy some china tea cups and plates from Thomas Goode in London. Thomas Goode was established in 1827, ten years before Queen Victoria took the throne, and Howard had been told that it was one of the finest bone china, crystal, and silverware stores in the world.

You have no idea how beautiful and expensive their merchandise is. It is all handwork, but the pieces I bought were made before the war so I didn't have to pay luxury tax.

We stayed at the Red Cross Club, and I spent most of the time in bed. We arrived in town about 10:30. It is very nice. We had three big beds, a bath, and hot water. I went to bed at 2:30 p.m., got up at 11:00 the next morning and shopped some more. I didn't look around much because I felt too punk. There are a lot of devastated buildings from the blitz. All the rubble is cleared away, but the skeletons still stand.

Beautiful Westminster Abbey and Cathedral were destroyed, but they are now practically rebuilt. We had tickets to a musical comedy, and Dan and Benny went. They said it was very good and didn't get in until 6:00 a.m. They ran into a French paratrooper and went to a French speakeasy. They sat around drinking and talking until morning, so they say. We went back to the field at 6:00 p.m., and I went to bed as soon as I got back.

17
LOSSES

Scudder's plane blew up and completely disintegrated when it hit the ground near Great Haseley in Oxfordshire.

Bad Weather

On November 13, Snyder's entire crew headed out on a raid to Bremen, Germany, with Lt. Morris Reed as their pilot, but they and more than 100 other planes had to abort the mission and return to their bases because of bad weather. Bremen was Germany's greatest inland port and a major shipbuilding center. Two ships of the 368th piloted by Lt. Floyd Scudder and Lt. Clyde Cosper encountered extreme turbulence and icing and crashed in England. Icing was always a real danger. The combination of high humidity and freezing temperatures could cause "clear ice" to form rapidly on a B-17's surfaces and could make the plane too heavy to fly. If this extreme icing occurred, the plane would start to spin out of control until it broke apart.

Scudder's plane blew up and completely disintegrated when it hit the ground near Great Haseley in Oxfordshire. Seven members of the crew had only just arrived on October 31 and only eight bodies were immediately identified in the wreckage. Lt. Cosper fought the controls and succeeded leveling out long enough for his crew to bail out. In a heroic effort to prevent his plane, which still carried a full bomb load, from crashing in an English village, Cosper chose a clearing near the town of Princess Risborough in Buckinghamshire to crash land his almost uncontrollable plane. When the aircraft came down in the open field, it immediately caught fire and exploded within a few seconds, instantly killing Cosper. Through Cosper's valiant efforts, not only did he save the lives of his crew but also, without a doubt, the lives and property of many British civilians.

On November 16, Howard flew as co-pilot again with Lt. Morris Reed. The rest of Howard's crew with the exception of Eike also flew with him on a mission to Kaben, Norway, where the only molybdenum mines (a vital element in hardening steel) still in operation in Europe were located. He reported,

> *What a day! We started out on a mission but had to drop out because of an engine failure. Then this damn weather gets bad, and we had to land at another field. We waited all day for some-one to fly over and bring some parts and a mechanic. They finally came in the afternoon, and by the time we took off to go back to our field, the weather was bad again.*
>
> *We took off anyway and had a h--- of a time finding the field. You can't see a thing when the weather fogs up here. A whole day wasted; a lot of bad flying and nothing to show for it. The boys had an easy mission and really smashed the target. They said there wasn't a thing left of it when they got through. Eike went with Lt. Howard Sharkey's crew, and they couldn't get their landing gear down so they had to make a wheels up landing at another field. I drove over and saw them come in. There was nothing to it. No one even had a scratch although the plane is all banged up.*

Lts. Howard Sharkey and George Eike's wheels up landing

The success of the mission to Kaben did much to restore the confidence and morale of the crews, because a series of earlier accidents and questionable bombing strategy were having a profound negative effect. Aircraft accidents occurred frequently, and unfortunately, resulted in many non-combat deaths. Usually overburdened with bombs, fuel, flight crews and armament, the B-17s often barely managed to take off. Even after successfully bombing a target, returning back to base could be a very stressful time.

During their long trips back to England, combat crews continually fought against the possibility of being intercepted by enemy fighters, the unrelenting necessity of monitoring the aircraft systems (especially if battle damage had occurred), and the ever present danger of bad weather. The harsh reality was that the crews were never really safe from the moment they took off to the time they shut the engines down after landing.

Based on a paper submitted by Charles J. Westgate III, Major, USAF, in 1998 to the faculty of the Air Command and Air College at Maxwell Air Force Base in Alabama, the following statistics concerning aircraft accidents were presented:

- 3 per cent approximately, occurred while parked,
- 16 per cent taxiing for takeoff,
- 12 per cent during takeoff,
- 29 per cent in flight, and
- 40 per cent during landing.

The most common forms of pilot error were: improper taxiing, leveling off too high, hitting too hard, overshooting the landing, and misuse of landing gear or flaps.

The Human Price of Flying Combat

Carrying the battle to the enemy flying combat missions, the crews paid a price both physically and mentally. Fear and anxiety were always there. No one felt gallant or heroic. They flew combat because they were assigned to a mission and did what they were asked to do. They didn't think about the future. There was only the present for the crews to worry about, hoping they'd survive another day, until the next mission when the worry would start all over again. Most crew members had a feeling of euphoria when they touched down after a long mission. For many, even if their bombs had fallen well wide of any target, just making it back made it a successful mission. For a high percentage of the men, it was go to the bar, get drunk, and go to bed.

As Howard reported,

They had a big party at the club last night. Everyone proceeded to get good and drunk and everyone seemed to have good time. This is the most free and easy crowd I have ever been around. I can see how they feel, "Let us make merry today for tomorrow we …." It goes something like that. A good many simply use that as an excuse though, but then the poor fellows are not as fortunate as me. They don't have a beloved wife and darling little girl waiting for them. I don't think I need anything to remind me to behave, but if I did, you and Susan are more than enough.

During the month Howard commented,

We flew for several hours this morning. I am flying as co-pilot again. I don't know what the deal is. I guess as soon as Capt. Wheeler gets his 25th raid in, I may get a ship. Wheeler has 24 raids in with one to go. I don't mind co-pilot in a way. It is an easy life, but I want to get somewhere. That is the curse of ambition. I have been here nearly a month now and don't seem to be getting anywhere. I don't have my own plane yet and am still as far from 1st Lt. as ever. Only one raid in too. The most I could have gotten in would have been three. Oh well, I guess it will all work out. Awhile back another captain had 25 in and was on his 28th raid when he crashed on return because of no gas. Reed, the pilot I have been flying with, was co-pilot. You should see the pictures of that plane! It is a mess! The captain was hurt and also the navigator. Reed was in the hospital for two to three weeks but wasn't hurt much.

We flew this morning and again this afternoon on practice missions. Some days we don't have anything to do and other days they push us to death. The Operations Officer (Flannagan) told me I will get my crew back tomorrow so I am a first pilot again! When I get my ship, she will certainly be named Susan Ruth.

R & R

The American Red Cross was asked by the U.S. Armed Forces to provide recreational services to the servicemen in the various theatres of operation. Red Cross American girls ran the NCO Aero Clubs which were located in Nissen huts like most buildings on the base and consisting of a living room, library, game room, dance area, and snack bar. Each club became a source of recreation, entertainment, and relaxation. The snack bars were extremely important, providing sandwiches, coffee, tea, and sweets as well as stationery and cigarettes. The Clubs also served coffee, donuts, and sandwiches from vans called Clubmobiles that drove around the base. They were remodeled London Green Line buses driven by an English driver with three American girls assigned to each Clubmobile. Each one consisted of a good-sized kitchen with a built-in doughnut machine, staffed by the three girls nicknamed "Donut Dollies."

The Aero Clubs were centers of normalcy for the men during a time of harsh reality. They afforded the soldiers a place to write letters, watch motion pictures, read, play cards, or simply talk with the Red Cross women who worked there. The volunteers and staff of the Clubs were a source of comfort, compassion, and a little bit of home in faraway England. Ball turret gunner Louis Colwart met an English girl who worked at one of the clubs and spent all his free days at her and her mother's (Mrs. Ansler) home in Bedford.

Red Cross Clubmobile

Although the Aero Clubs were specifically for the use of the enlisted personnel on the base, officers were welcome to use the library facilities anytime, and on occasion the rest of the club, as guests of the enlisted men. As Howard confirmed, "The Red Cross does a great deal of good. Everywhere we have been over here they have clubs, shows, traveling trucks that serve food or something. There is a Red Cross representative at every field or post just like in the States. You can't go wrong giving to them. We had a Red Cross show at the field tonight. It was pretty poor, but the girls were cute and they didn't have much on so the boys seemed to enjoy it."

World War II was the first conflict to take place in the age of electronically mass distributed music, and the airmen had regular access to their favorite songs on Armed Forces Radio established by the War Department in May 1942. The first actual transmission to U.S. troops began in July 1943 when the Army began broadcasting from London using equipment and studio facilities borrowed from the British Broadcasting Company (BBC). Its audience was the vast air armada carrying out the great offensive against Hitler's Germany along with

Red Cross Aero Club

the many thousands of American troops pouring into Britain in preparation for the invasion of Nazi-occupied Europe. From 70 broadcasting stations in the United Kingdom, the American Forces Network (AFN) continued transmitting programs until December 31, 1945, when it moved to Germany.

Being able to listen to special songs reminded the men of home and their loved ones. It was a great comfort, but could also cause sadness and heartache. Howard reported, "They have an American network here. The music is very good." And in various letters to Ruth wrote, "Frances Langford is singing *You'll Never Know How Much I Miss You.* How true that is! Oh Lord, now Bing Crosby is singing *Won't you tell me when we will meet again Sunday, Monday or Always.* The most popular record shows were Johnny Kerr's *Duffle Bag* and George Monaghan's *On the Record.* AFN London gave pleasure to many thousands of American servicemen and women during the war, as well as five million Britons who tuned in regularly, as eavesdroppers. The Armed Forces Network popped up overnight and then vanished almost without a trace when the war ended.

Captain McKim, the Squadron Flight Surgeon, had a radio in his room next door to Howard's and Howard was able to rig up a speaker and connect it saying, "It works very well. I have the speaker on my dresser and enjoy it very much. Fred Waring is on the radio. It is good to listen to all the old programs. The American Network over here plays transcriptions of all the best programs." Fred Waring was a popular musician, band leader and radio-television personality, sometimes referred to as "America's Singing Master" and "The Man Who Taught America How to Sing." He was also the promoter and financial backer of the Waring Blendor, the first modern electric blender on the market and which was named after him.

On November 21, Howard went into London to get fitted for his battle jacket and trousers, saw a show, Betty Grable in *Sweet Rosie O'Grady,* and then went back to camp.

> *It seemed good to sit in a comfortable seat and see a show for a change. The underground railway in London is very good. You go down several very steep escalators and wind around through a lot of tunnels to the train. They make very good time, are comfortable riding, and inexpensive. The steam trains are very good also. You travel either 1st or 3rd class here. Officers are expected to travel in 1st although sometimes you may buy a 1st class ticket and sit in 3rd because of the crowded trains.*
>
> *The meals here keep one alive and healthy but are nearly all the same and getting awful tiresome. I would love something like fried shrimp or chicken for a change. Breakfasts are pretty much the same every day: powdered eggs, greasy corn beef, toast, juice, and coffee. Any time you or mother want to send me cookies, go right ahead. Sugar is so scarce here that the Army doesn't bake much, and of course when they do, it isn't too good. We do get candy too and one package of gum each week, and I could never use all the tobacco we are allowed each week.*

18

THE AMERICANS

Three millions G.I.s would serve in or at least pass through Britain during the war; and not only were Americans plentiful, they were also attractive.

Being an American in England

The Americans had shown up in England almost overnight. With British men away serving in the war, there had been a shortage of eligible bachelors until the streams of incoming U.S. airmen and American G.I.s came over in preparation for the Normandy invasion. As in the United States, with the absence of men in the workplace there became a great need for women to fill the void. Britain had been fighting for its survival with hundreds of thousands of families being displaced and thousands killed as a result of the Nazi air raids. The entire country had been mobilized, and every able-bodied person between eighteen and sixty performed some type of national service. Approximately eighty thousand women were employed in the Women's Land Army where they worked on farms, cultivating crops and caring for livestock.

Three million G.I.s would serve in or at least pass through Britain during the war; and not only were Americans plentiful, they were also attractive. The Yanks for the most part were sharply dressed and carried with them a certain amount of confidence. As one woman described it, "The Americans were very smart in their uniforms, quite dashing in comparison to the typical British soldier in his rustic and ill-fitting tunic."

The girls saw the U.S. as a magic country, and "real" Americans were everything they'd ever dreamed of. Confident, outgoing, and friendly (many excessively so), they were something of a blow between the eyes for many in quiet, rural East Anglia. British women often found that American men paid them more attention than British men, were quicker to give compliments, and made them feel special. They were captivated, looking at the G.I.s as movie stars. They were Tyrone Power and Cary Grant personified to the mass of English girls "in love" with the originals.

Many Americans had entered the service just out of high school or college and had never had a paying job before. Suddenly, they became well fed and well paid. Moral restraints of family, church, and friends disappeared and everything seemed to be available for the buying, asking or taking. With average salaries more than five times that of a British soldier and no living expenses to worry about, the G.I.s were very generous and "prone to spoil a girl." One woman said, "The girls went mad. They never had such a good time. They had never been with fellows who had so much money."

Socializing

The British men often complained about the G.I.s and described the Americans as being "overpaid, oversexed and over here." British women simply had no experience dealing with men as glamorous, bold, and testosterone filled as the "Yanks." They were bowled off their feet. So much so that 70,000 British women became G.I. brides. One British war bride commented, "Even if you weren't a very good looking woman, you could get a man. We had so many darn men—it was fantastic!"

Attending dances was another popular form of entertainment for young British women and American G.I.s. The Red Cross Aero Club dances were closely chaperoned and considered a suitable way for girls to associate with servicemen. Trucks would be sent out to pick up the girls who loved to jitter-bug and bring them to the club. However, because the clubs were alcohol free, the Aero dances had a lot of competition from the local pubs and dance halls in the villages. The American Red Cross Club in Bedford was on Goldington Road. The Bedford Corn Exchange on St. Paul's Square was a very popular spot.

Red Cross Dance

The Corn Exchange was constructed in 1874 and designed to be a concert venue and meeting space, as well as a place of business. It played host to many famous stars during the war such as Bing Crosby, Bob Hope, and in particular Glenn Miller whose notable recordings include *Chattanooga Choo Choo, String of Pearls, Moonlight Serenade, At Last, Pennsylvania 6-500, In the Mood*, and many others. In fact, there is a bronze bust of Glenn Miller and plaque beneath it in an alcove on the front of the Corn Exchange.

At the peak of his civilian career, Miller decided to join the war effort in 1942. At 38, Miller was too old to be drafted so he volunteered and served as assistant special services officer for the Army Air Forces. He formed a 50-piece Army Air Force Band and took it to England in the summer of 1944, where he gave 800 performances at various venues and airfields all over the area. The band's first performance was at Thurleigh on July 14, on a makeshift stage that was built inside one of the 306th BG hangars. People were sitting on the floor, perched on the wings of the planes, and literally hanging from the rafters.

Glenn Miller at Thurleigh

Miller spent his last night in England at the Hall in Milton Ernest, a village and civil parish in Bedfordshire and about five miles north of Bedford itself. On December 15, 1944, Miller departed for Paris in a Canadian built Norseman C64 from the RAF Twinwood Farm Airfield at Clapham on the outskirts of Bedford. He was going to play for U.S. troops there, but the plane disappeared while flying over the English Channel. Tragically, no trace of the aircrew, passengers or plane was ever found. A couple of theories were that Miller's plane might have been hit by British Royal Air Force "friendly fire" or that Miller had actually arrived safely in Paris, but had a heart attack while consorting with a French prostitute, and the American military covered it up.

R & R

Although Snyder and his fellow officers went to dances, he wasn't really into them. It only made him homesick for Ruth. He commented,

> *I hung around the party for awhile last night. Daniels played the piano in the band for a while. He used to have one of his own, you know. Eike had a girl there. He must have met her in town the other day, I guess. When I watch Eike and the others dance, I don't care about it at all. All I did was think how I wished I were with you and what a sorry lot all the girls are compared with you. I go to the dances once in awhile and sit around with a drink watching them. Daniels has been very good too. He and I usually sit together with our beers while the rest play around.*

Howard reported to Ruth,

> *Daniels is very true to his wife. He doesn't have anything to do with other women. I'm not 100% sure about Eike. I think he might have messed around before he met Helen. He met a*

little blond in a bicycle shop in town and took her out to dinner and a dance. He also went to London earlier this week and spent the day with a little French girl. However, he swears everything is all on the up and up and that he doesn't do anything so I believe he is telling the truth. Benninger is on the lookout for anything that comes his way. Either he picked some gal up or perhaps she picked him up and they had a "quick job" on a park bench in town. That happened two nights in a row. Most of the fellows are very free, and they have no trouble finding what they want.

Later in November on another trip into London, Howard and Robert Benninger were fitted for and ordered their battle dress jackets and then decided to go to a show before going back to Thurleigh. However, when they got to the railroad station, they found that they had missed the last train by five minutes. Howard recalled,

We were madly worried and tried every way to get back. The next train didn't leave until 4:30 the next morning. We finally called the Operations Officer (Flannagan) and told him our sad story and asked him if he wouldn't send some transportation to meet us, but he wouldn't. He told us that we were scheduled to go on a raid the next day, but he would have to send someone else to fly in our place. We really felt bad about it, but he said to get the morning train, so we went back up town.

There was no use trying to get a room so we went to several clubs, but they were all closing. Public bars and clubs close about 11:00. There are a lot of private clubs that stay open late, but you have to have a membership card, and we haven't been here long enough to get one. We finally found a speakeasy and stayed there drinking and watching the crowd until train time. We met two English naval officers, and the time passed very pleasantly talking to them. One had lost an arm in a P.T. boat engagement. We got back in time for the 8:30 a.m. meeting to find out that it had been cancelled. We were very glad to hear that. The Operations Officer (Flannagan) told us the major (Riordan) wanted to see us; so, very meekly, we went in to see him. He was very nice about it and asked what had happened. He didn't say much but remarked that we would probably be restricted the next time our two-day pass came up. So that was that.

Bedford Train Station

The boys kidded me about it a great deal for you know it isn't often I do anything like that and they thought it was very funny that something like that happened to me. They told me I had better play some good basketball to get in the major's good graces again.

19

SECOND MISSION ... AND PROMOTION

All the crew bailed out, but four were killed, possibly by German fighters while they were in their parachutes. Jefferies and five others survived. Fortunately, all the planes from the 369th Squadron came back.

Howard's Second Mission

On Howard Snyder's second combat mission, he flew as pilot on November 26 to a Focke-Wulf aircraft manufacturing factory at Bremen, Germany. The 306th supplied 29 planes for this mission out of a total of 390 B-17s that went on the raid. Lt. Bill Grisham from Long Beach, California, flew as co-pilot, and Paul Christensen subbed in as radio operator for Ross Kahler who was still sick. Once again, the target was completely covered by clouds (10/10ths overcast). Flak from the German 88 mm guns was intense, and enemy fighter opposition was strong. More than 100 enemy aircraft were encountered, but U.S. P-47s and P-38s gave splendid support. The 56th Fighter Group had a field day, and shot down 25 percent of the German force.

Two planes of the 306th did not return: those of pilots Lt. Francis Hoey of the 368th and Virgil Jeffries of the 423rd who was on his 25th mission. Near Oldenburg, Germany, Hoey's plane, damaged by enemy fighters or flak, peeled off seemingly under control. Fortunately, all the crew bailed out and survived, becoming POWs. About 40 miles west of the target, Jeffries' B-17 *Las Vegas Avenger* peeled off from the formation after having two engines knocked out, and with his controls shot out, eventually crashed in the Netherlands. All the crew bailed out, but four were killed, possibly by German fighters while they were in their parachutes. Jefferies and five others survived. Fortunately, all the planes from the 369th Squadron came back.

Howard wrote,

> *It was a little chilly up there today, about 52 degrees below. Pindroch passed out from lack of oxygen when his connection parted and froze his face. He is in the hospital and probably won't be able to fly for months. He is a good lad too. I am sorry to lose him. It was a lot rougher today than the last time. The last time was too easy. Colwart was knocked off his feet while I was taking some rather abrupt evasive action to mess up a fighter attack. He hit his tail bone, and it was quite badly swollen today. He is going to the hospital tomorrow to have an x-ray taken. I hope it is nothing serious.*

The B-17s routinely operated above 20,000 feet during their long missions, where temperatures could plunge way below zero. Exposed skin would freeze to metal on contact. Only the front part of the plane (cockpit, nose, and radio room) was heated, albeit inadequately. The gunners did wear electrically heated suits, but these occasionally malfunctioned. Frostbite made suitable flight clothing essential with the typical combat dress for a B-17 gunner consisting of: heavy woolen underwear, two pairs of lined wool socks, electric suit, electric gloves and socks, boots, overalls and helmet. Additionally, some men wore their leather jacket over their overalls. Also part of their flight gear was an inflatable

Flying Gear

life preserver called a "Mae West" so-named because someone wearing it appeared to be as physically endowed as actress and sex symbol Mae West, as well as rhyming slang for breast. All this clothing became cumbersome for the crew.

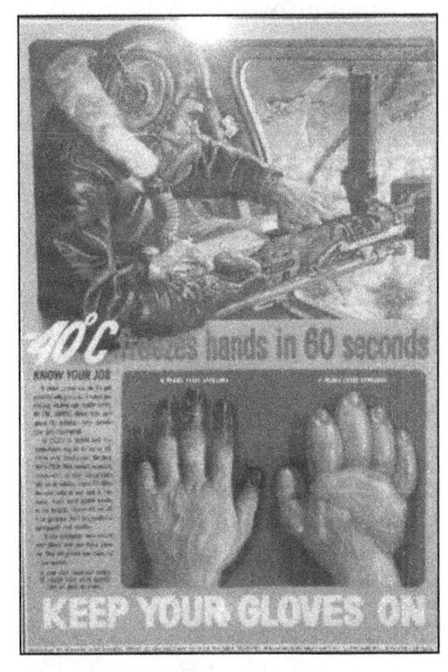

Frostbite Poster

The probability of suffering from frostbite was highest in the isolated gunner positions, such as the waist gunners who were stationed at open windows of the B-17F and subject to the howling winds. Wounded men were particularly susceptible to frostbite. The subzero temperatures inside the planes sometimes froze oxygen lines, leading to anoxia (the lack of breathable oxygen above 10,000 feet) for unsuspecting crew members who quickly died if the problem was not caught. Saliva or vomit would turn to ice and clog oxygen tubes which could suffocate the men.

Captain David Wheeler, one of the 369th flight leaders, finished his 25-mission tour on the Bremen raid. Howard commented,

> *He is a swell fellow, and Eike has flown with him a good deal. He has given me a lot of pointers. He has had some really rough times too so we were all glad to see him finish. He is married but wants to stay here. You would be surprised at the number of fellows who want to stay until it is all over. Some, very few, are made squadron commanders and are forced to stay, but most have a choice.*

The following day Howard wrote,

> *Colwart's x-rays only showed a sprained back, so he will be all right. Pindroch, however, will not be able to fly for a long time because of his frostbite. We were going to have a basketball game tonight, but I guess the Major thought we were too tired to play so he cancelled it. There is a big party here tonight. I will go over and watch the boys get drunk. They usually have a pretty good meal too after a raid.*

As an athlete, Howard was a competitor and an achiever, with a strong desire to advance in rank and responsibility. He said,

> *My promotion to 1st Lt. was finally put through. It will be a nice Christmas present, and we can use the extra money that goes with it. After my 1st Lt. goes through, I will have to wait at least three months before I can get my captaincy. Major Stanko, the executive officer of our Squadron, told me today that I would be a flight leader before I knew it, and that means captain.*
>
> *We played basketball the last few nights and won our games. The Major (Riordan) plays forward and he has me playing center. He really takes basketball seriously and plays to win. It seems like the games are as important to him as the raids. He is a young fellow about 25 and came over with the group (the 306th in September 1942) and has been flying for a long time. He has 25 raids in and volunteered for five more. He doesn't fly much, just takes care of the Squadron.*
>
> *I'm in pretty good shape now, and the last two games I played rather well. He is quite pleased. It pays to play I guess. He made the remark that he was going to give me one of the new ships (B-17G) they expect to get. The one I have now isn't too good. I don't want to put Susan's name on her. Anything that is connected with my little girl has to be exceptional, so I will wait until I get a new ship and name her.*

The B-17G

In September 1943, the B-17F version of the bomber in use during the early years of the war gradually began to be replaced by the B-17G with the first big influx coming in October to replace the bombers lost on Black Thursday at Schweinfurt. The biggest problem with the model F was that it had no defense against enemy fighters at the nose of the aircraft which left it extremely vulnerable to head-on attacks. In light of this deficiency, a chin turret was added under the Plexiglas nose of the G model.

In all, there were more than 400 engineering changes between the F model and G model with the other most significant modifications being the addition of cheek guns, installation of Plexiglas waist windows to protect the gunners from the ice cold air, and staggering the waist guns to give the gunners more room. The F models were painted a dull green color, which required 500 gallons of paint, as camouflage in case of German *Luftwaffe* attacks on the U.S. air bases in England. However, it was concluded that such attacks were unfounded and there was no value in camouflaging planes for combat missions when flying at altitudes of 20,000 feet or more. Therefore, the B-17G's aluminum silver skin was left unpainted.

B-17Fs (shaded) and B-17Gs (silver)

A couple days later on the 29th, Howard and the 306th started out on another raid to Bremen and got within a few minutes of Germany but had to return because of weather, saying, "The thick clouds and heavy vapor trails obscured everything except the planes right next to you." Pilots often said that they would have almost preferred flak rather than flying through that type of weather. Although Howard wasn't involved in combat that day, *Luftwaffe* pilot Lt. Hans Berger was. In fact, Berger was shot down, and although wounded, was able to bail out, coming down nearby at Delmenhorst, Germany.

The German Perspective of Air Combat

Hans Berger commented about air combat saying,

> *When we approached the bomber formations, usually at a flight level of 8,000 m (25,000 ft), we tried to attack them from the front. In the early days without the presence of U.S. fighters, we used to attack from the rear, but in view of the massive defensive fire of the B-17s, our losses had been so severe that this had to be given up. When you attack from the rear, your speed is only slightly higher than that of the bombers, so the gunners have plenty of time to sight at you and to calmly fire half an ammunition belt at you. Attacking from the rear (which would give you time to aim carefully) was more or less equivalent to suicide.*

Therefore, he said, the *Luftwaffe* fighter pilots quickly "converted from half-kamikaze rear attacks to frontal attacks with (not really fair, but anyway better) chance of survival."

Attacking from the front was no picnic either as Berger went on to say,

> *And when you attacked head-on, you were lucky if you (1) got close to them in the first place; (2) got one of them into your reflector sight with an adequate (and correct) amount of lead;*

(3) hit him with a few of your highly effective bullets within those tiny fractions of a second; (4) managed to dive under or hop over him instead of crashing right into him; (5) had not yet been hit by a burst of cannon and machine gun fire; (6) did not have a Thunderbolt or Mustang in your back; (7) had not been hit by a fragment of iron fired off by a brave German AA gunner way down underneath; (8) still had enough fuel to reach some small airfield somewhere at the back of beyond where you were the only one and thus not compelled to take off again with some unknown fellow for another try; (9) got something decent to eat and drink, and (10) were still alive ...

Sometimes we managed to score a few hits, sometimes even enough to shoot one of them down, but usually we were engaged in fighter attacks before we could do the bombers any harm. In such air fights it was very soon a case of everyone vs. everyone, a huge turmoil of planes where you tried to fire at any enemy plane that happened to turn up somewhere in your sight line, but then always had to watch out for the "big bad wolf" (enemy fighters) coming from behind, you were frightened to hell anyway, and at some time or other, if you had been lucky enough not to have been hit or wounded or even shot down yourself, you managed to get out of this nightmare, fly off sideways, hopefully to find some airbase or airfield to land for refueling; again always looking behind to make sure there wasn't any "big bad wolf" again to shoot you down with your landing gear out for landing. That was the reality of air fighting over Germany in those days.

Berger stated that flying against the U.S. air armadas had become difficult because the *Luftwaffe* fighter planes had to go up against bomber formations comprised of hundreds of B-17s and accompanied by hundreds more P-51 Mustangs and P-47 Thunderbolts. He said the *Luftwaffe* did not have many encounters with P-38 Lightnings, and the problem with the P-47s and P-51s "was that there were so many of them."

He continued:

In dogfight combats, the Mustang was an equal match to the Focke-Wulf, FW-190, maybe even slightly superior whereas the Thunderbolt was heavier and therefore less easily maneuverable and thus slightly inferior to the FW-190. The real problem was that they outnumbered us by far. Their planes were good, no doubt about that; their pilots knew their business and were fair (most of them, except for that one s.o.b. who fired at me on a parachute).

He said,

They found themselves chased like hares by greyhounds in each sortie, in view of the 10:1 U.S. supremacy. We suffered severe losses in each sortie. The majority of us had no chance of rising above the level of mediocrity; they were either in the hospital or dead before they could.

Hans Berger; Hans Berger with mechanic Konrad (Karl) Ell

English Weather

On November 30, Howard and other crews flew out on a raid to Solingen, renowned as the "City of Blades" for its manufacturing of fine swords, knives, scissors and razors. Even today, Solingen remains the knife-centre of Germany. Unfortunately, once again Snyder and his crew had to turn back because of bad weather and towering cumulus clouds. It was very disappointing for him after flying all those hours and not having accomplished anything, but said, "It is just the breaks in the game I guess. I wish I had more raids than two but perhaps we will speed up a bit. I hope so! I am tired tonight and could sleep for a week."

The weather in England would often be freezing rain, fog, sleet, and snow; one dark gray day after another. Northern European weather was difficult to predict and had to be favorable at takeoff, on assembly, on the way to the target, over the target, and on returning to base. Even when the weather permitted flying, there were usually very few days when visual bombing was possible. Pathfinder (PFF) bombers had to lead most raids, and radar bombing became the normal procedure.

Scrubbed and aborted missions were a festering morale problem, especially because they did not count towards the mission requirement needed to go back home. The pre-flight trauma and tension of scrubbed missions was just as bad as or worse than actual combat missions due to the letdown and depression the men suffered when they occurred which was quite frequently. There was nothing worse than waiting, with all kinds of negative thoughts running through their heads, and then having the mission canceled. Aborted missions caused by bad weather or mechanical problems that occurred after takeoff not only included the burden of preparation and the agony of anticipation, but also all the hazards associated with takeoff, assembly, and landing as well.

The crews had come to England to fight, not to sit around and continually train as a result of raids being canceled. If they couldn't get their planes up, they couldn't bomb the Germans. Furthermore, the inclement weather was no friend to the health of the air crew either. The damp chill would get under the airmen's skin, right down to the bone, which added to their irritability and depression. Howard wrote, "I am getting as used to the cold as I ever will, but you just can't accustom yourself to the dampness. My radio man, Kahler, is in the hospital with a case of the flu. Everyone seems to have a cold. The hospital is full."

306th Base Hospital

Overall, November 1943 was a very unremarkable month for the 306th. Out of fourteen mission briefings, one of which was for a futile air sea rescue search, only five raids were actually flown. However, Major Riordan's 369th Fightin' Bitin' Squadron flew the highest percentage of sorties, dropped the most bombs, had the most flying time, and lowest percentage of missions aborted.

During November, Howard made Joe Musial assistant engineer to regular engineer, Roy Holbert. Unfortunately, Howard received the sad news that someone has poisoned his dog "Fritz" that, somewhat ironically, was a Belgian Shepherd.

20

DECEMBER 1943 ... THIRD MISSION

I finally got my third raid in, and we all got back safe and sound. I was very tired afterwards and slept 12 hours. A few holes in the ship, but then that happens on every raid.

The Third Combat Mission

Howard flew his third combat mission on December 1, one of 22 planes from the 306th. The original target was Leverkusen, however, the mission was diverted because of violent cumulus clouds to the secondary target of Solingen, Germany, to hit the aircraft component and machine tools factories located there. Every mission had a primary and secondary target. If the lead pilot decided that the primary target was a bad risk due to weather or adverse conditions, he could elect to attack the secondary target.

The weather was bad everywhere and a close tragedy was averted when the B-17 of Captain George Reese of the 423rd was spun down from 7,200 feet to 3,000 feet over England by the violent currents of a thunderhead. Reese climbed back up to 5,500 feet but was tossed around again. The left wing started to buckle, and the plane began to fall apart. Reese ordered the crew to abandon ship, headed the plane to an open space, cut the switches, and jumped through the forward hatch. Unfortunately, the chute of the ball turret gunner Staff Sergeant Kenneth Rood didn't open and he was killed.

The bombardier, Woodrow Ellertson, with his parachute shrouds in front of his face so he could not see to pick out a landing place, hit the only obstacle in a large field, a harrow, and broke his ankle. Afterwards, his buddies kidded him that he was one hell of a farmer not to handle such equipment better than that! Reese's plane crashed in the woods two and a half miles north of Lapham with a full bomb load, and exploded on impact. Luckily, no damage was done to British citizens or their property other than the trees.

Once again, Lt. Bill Grisham flew as Howard's co-pilot, and filling in as radio operator for Ross Kahler (still sick) was Staff Sergeant O.L. Need. Filling John Pindroch's waist gunner position was Sergeant Patrick Gaynor, and filling in for Louis Colwart in the ball turret was Corporal Phillip Mundell who was just 18-years-old and flying his first mission. Mundell, said later in life, "I really don't remember what happened on the mission. It was so exciting and thrilling to be in combat, I was just wide-eyed looking at everything that was going on around me." The following year, Mundell was shot down over France on his 28th mission on August 8, 1944, as part of Andy Kata's B-17 *Dam Yankee* crew. Fortunately, he was able to bail out safely over neutral territory and made it back to the American lines.

One of Howard's friends from Advanced Pilot School, George Hale, was flying in the Low Squadron of the 92nd Bomb Group during the raid. His plane was hit by flak and caught fire causing the tail to twist and fall off. In an example of sheer courage, Hale held the blazing plane steady for four and a half minutes trying to give his crew time to bail out, however, only his tail gunner Sgt. Donald Wilson survived.

There was confusion and crowding at the target, and Lt. J.P. Toombs' ship from the 423rd had incendiary bombs dropped on top of it by a B-17 flying overhead with another group. The aileron on the left wing was completely destroyed, holes were burned in the left wing and in the nose, the #3 engine was hit, and the chin turret was badly damaged. All this happened so violently and suddenly that the right waist gunner, Staff Sergeant Guy Aubrey, thought the ship had "had it" and bailed out. Toombs performed quite a feat bringing his plane back to base. The 369th was fortunate in having no such accidents or bad breaks.

Pilot Lt. Robert "Junior" Fallow of the 369th, with whom Eike was flying as co-pilot, gave everybody some anxious moments when his ship did not come back to Thurleigh with the other 306th BG aircraft. Later, they found out he got back safely, landing 140 miles away at Manston Field.

Snyder wrote,

I finally got my third raid in, and we all got back safe and sound. I was very tired afterwards and slept 12 hours. A few holes in the ship, but then that happens on every raid. My co-pilot (Grisham) is just a kid, only 19, but he is a good lad. I kept him on the ball up there and he is very eager to do what I tell him. He was pretty scared up there, but you can't blame him. I am so busy I don't have time to get frightened.

Slenker, my tail gunner, had some of his equipment about two feet behind his position, and when he came back up from the tail after we were over England, he found it all shot to shreds. He didn't know about it until then although he could hear the shells hitting the ship. He would have had a fit if he had known it was that close. They won't give me Eike back. Robert Fallow, the pilot he is flying with, evidently isn't too good in their estimation, and they want Eike to fly with him as he is a good co-pilot. They try to balance the pilot and co-pilot up.

Benny has a bad cold and is in the hospital. Kahler is out of the hospital but still grounded. Colwart is OK for flying duty again, but Pindroch will not be able to fly for months because of his frostbite. It makes the effected parts very sensitive to cold after it is healed and only time will enable him to stand cold again. I have another gunner (Mundell) in his place who is very good. Ice coated the entire cockpit yesterday, but I was perspiring so much, steam was coming up in a cloud all around me. The throttles were coated with ice under my hand.

Movies were very popular and a frequent form of relaxation. It was a way to escape the war for a couple of hours and a connection to home. Theaters were located on the base and in the local villages. The main cinema in Bedford was the Granada, but there was also the Plaza and the Bridge Hotel. Before every show began, the words to the British National Anthem and the Star-Spangled Banner were put on the screen, and everybody stood and sang. Howard said, "George (Eike) and I went to a show at the post theater this evening. It was *Keeper of the Flame* staring Katharine Hepburn and Spencer Tracy. Remember when you saw it at Douglas (Arizona)? I thought of you all the way through it. They have a show about three or four times a week. The theater (on the base) is an old building with benches without any backs and the light and sound is not good, but we enjoy it." Other movies Howard mentioned seeing were *Presenting Lily Mars* with Judy Garland and *Arsenic and Old Lace* with Cary Grant and Pricilla Lane which he thought was very good, "about the funniest show I have seen."

On December 5, Kahler, Holbert, Colwart, and Musial flew with Lt. Robert Fallow on a mission to La Rochelle, France, where Germany had established a submarine base. The weather was very bad, and the formation ran into a solid wall of cirrus clouds over the target. No bombs could be dropped, and the planes headed back to their bases. To avoid the danger of landing with full bomb loads, the planes released their bombs over the English Channel. Lt. William Kirk lost a propeller on landing and narrowly averted a serious crash. The raid was considered a flop, but because the "flakgauntlet" was run near the French towns of Rennes and Nantes, mission credit was given. That helped everybody's feelings but did little toward furthering the war effort.

Letters

V-Mail, short for Victory Mail, was the process used as the primary and secure method to correspond with soldiers stationed abroad. To reduce the logistics of transferring an original letter across the military postal system, a V-mail letter would be censored, copied to film, and printed back to paper upon arrival at its destination. V-mail correspondence was on small letter sheets (7" by 9 1/8") that would go through mail censors before being photographed and transported as thumbnail-sized image in negative microfilm. Upon arrival to their destination, the negatives would be blown up to 60 percent their original size and printed.

V-Mail ensured that thousands of tons of shipping space could be reserved for war materials. The 37 mail bags required to carry 150,000 one-page letters could be replaced by a single mail sack. The weight of that same amount of mail was reduced dramatically from 2,575 pounds to a mere 45 pounds. This saved considerable weight and bulk in a time in which both were hard to manage in a combat zone. In addition to postal censorship, V-Mail also deterred espionage communications by foiling the use of invisible ink, microdots, and micro-printing, none of which could be reproduced in a photocopy.

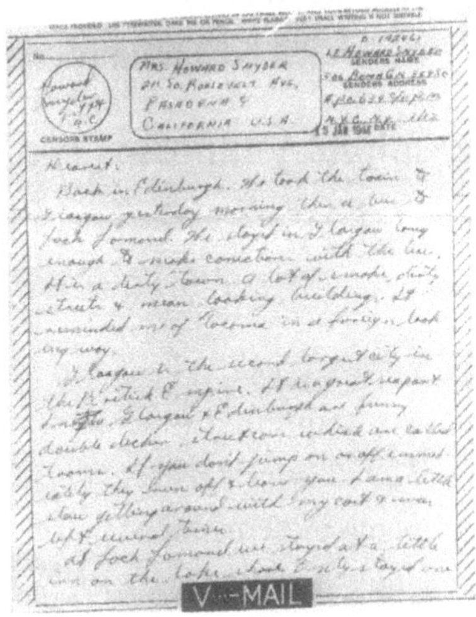
Mrs. Howard Snyder
211 So. Roosevelt Ave.,
Pasadena 4
California U.S.A.

Sender's name
Sender's address
Date
Censor's stamp

Dearest:
Back in Edinburgh. We took the train to Glasgow yesterday morning then a bus to Loch Lomond. We stayed in Glasgow long enough to make connection with the bus. It's a dirty town. A lot of smoke, dirty streets & mean looking buildings. It reminded me of Tacoma in a foreign look any way.
Glasgow is the second largest city in the British Empire. It is a great seaport. [illegible] Glasgow & Edinburgh are funny [illegible] double decker streetcars which are called trams. If you don't jump on or off [illegible] quickly they leave off & leave you. I am a little slow getting around with my coat & [illegible]
At Loch Lomond we stayed at a little inn on the lake [illegible]

V-MAIL

V-Mail Letter

V-Mail Envelope

All mail from military personnel was censored during the war. Officers could censor their own mail; enlisted men had to have their superior officers read their mail for any "sensitive" material—things that if the letter were intercepted by the enemy would give clues as to location, military strength, and upcoming military engagements.

Letters from "girls back home" were the highlight of mail call. That is, unless it was a "Dear John" letter telling the recipient that she had found someone else. Howard wrote, "Mail! We finally received some and was it wonderful to hear from you. It seems to come in bunches. George received nine letters from his wife today and was he happy. You should see the faces of the boys when they receive mail! They're the happiest fellows in the world and their faces beam. I had a dream of you last night, Baby. If I told you about it, the letter would be censored, but it was terrific."

Respiratory Illnesses and Worse

Both Howard and George Eike ended up getting sick and were hospitalized. Wrote Howard,

> *I wasn't feeling well and started chilling so they stuck me in the hospital. It is very comfortable here, nice and warm, and I don't mind the rest. The only trouble is I missed our mission being in here and our two-day pass starts today so I will miss going into London with the boys. Eike is in here too. He came down to see me, and seemed to think I had a pretty good deal. He had a cold and when they found out he had a temperature, put him right in. We have been playing knock rummy nearly all day.*

In the morning of December 10, Howard and George both got out of the hospital. At one time or another, his entire crew had been in the hospital with the flu, a common cold, or slight case of pneumonia. Daniels and Benninger had come back from their two-day pass in London and said they saw Earl Houston's co-pilot (Henry Hainline). "He was drunk as a lord and had some cheap looking wench with him. He was so drunk he could hardly talk." Lt. Earl Houston was another pilot that Howard had gone through Advanced Pilot's School with at Douglas, Arizona.

Plenty of British and French prostitutes nicknamed "Piccadilly Commandos" roamed the streets of London and were readily available.

They were so named because of Piccadilly Circus, a major traffic intersection in London's West End close to major shopping and entertainment areas. It was a busy meeting place and tourist attraction and with its video displays and neon signs was much like Times Square in New York City.

Piccadilly Circus

With the "Blackouts" in London, often times a G.I. would meet a girl, not knowing what he was picking up until the two of them got into a room. By that time, even if she wasn't anything to look at, the G.I. would think, "What the heck? I'm here now, so we might as well go on with it." By the end of 1943, there was a venereal disease epidemic with most contracted around Piccadilly Circus. The Red Cross and the Army could hardly keep up with the demand for condoms. Flight surgeons only half joked about treating VD as much as or more than battle wounds.

We won the basketball championship the other night but I was in the hospital when we played the last game. The major (Riordan) was very happy, of course. I was chosen for the all-star team so will probably have to keep on playing. I was hoping I was through. It is too much bother, and I think that is how I got my cold too. We are having a squadron party this evening and it should be a good one. It is costing us eight dollars each! However, I have to go to mix with the boys. Everyone has a good time.

One day, Howard flew over to the 379th Bomb Group, part of the 1st Air Division like the 306th, located at Kimbolton and about eight miles from Thurleigh. Howard went to visit his friend Lt. Earl Houston.

He (Houston) was very surprised to see me. Easton (Thomas E., another friend from Advanced Pilot Training) was there too. We have a much better field and many more privileges than they. They cannot go to town any night they please as we can. I watched one of their formations flying around, and it was pretty sad. Yes, I am quite satisfied where I am.

Eaton's bombardier (Melvin Henroid) lost his left kneecap in a raid. He will be sent back to the States and can no longer fly. Conley's ship (James W., another Advanced Pilot Training school buddy) was pretty well shot up the other day, and some of his enlisted men were wounded. I heard that Hale (George C.) was shot down, but I don't know how true it is." Howard learned that one other friend from Advanced Pilot School, Ray M. Spofford, almost lost his hand when he accidently walked into a propeller.

On a December 11 mission to the seaport town of Emden in northwest Germany, anti-aircraft fire was extremely accurate and mortally wounded the B-17 of the 369th's Lt. John Noack. All the crew were combat veterans, except the co-pilot who had only been with the group for three weeks. All bailed out and became POWs. Their loss kept down the natural feeling of elation following a successful job. Leading the 306th Bomb Group and 369th Squadron were 306th BG CO, Colonel George Robinson and 369th SQ CO, Major Robert Riordan, flying as pilot and co-pilot.

On December 16, Eike flew with Lt. Fallow on an uneventful raid to Bremen. Once again, with 10/10th cloud cover over the target, the Group bombed on PFF. Only one plane from the 306th received battle damage and all returned safely. However, visibility at Thurleigh was very poor, and six planes from the 306th had to land at other bases making for some uneasy moments until they were accounted for.

21

WOUNDED ... IN BASKETBALL!

While in the hospital, Howard said, "I suppose I would get the Purple Heart for my ankle if the major (Riordan) had anything to do with it."

Wounded on a Basketball Mission

While playing basketball on December 16, Howard tore the ligaments in his left ankle when he came down on the side of his foot and turned his ankle underneath. Howard wrote,

> *Some good and some bad news tonight, sweetheart. I am in the hospital again (Diddington) about ten miles from my base where they took x-rays. This time with the ligaments of my left ankle torn, and the swelling is quite a sight. I will be in the hospital several days and after the swelling goes down, they will put a "walking cast" for a couple months. Most of the boys in this ward have been wounded. One received an invitation to call at Buckingham Palace, but he didn't see any royalty. He had written home that he was going to meet the King, and all the boys have been kidding him.*
>
> *Remember the fellow (Melvin Henroid) I wrote you about who had the kneecap shot off? He was in the same bed I am in. He is in a different hospital now and will be going back to the States in a few weeks. The nurses are very sweet. Very considerate and do everything possible to make us comfortable. It is a treat to talk to American girls. All the English girls I have seen the Americans with are a cheap sort. Naturally, you can't pick*

up a decent English girl, and the only girls these fellows run around with are that type. You need not worry about me being good, Baby. I get tight now and then. It does us good to relax and get our mind off things.

While in the hospital, Howard said, "I suppose I would get the Purple Heart for my ankle if the major (Riordan) had anything to do with it." The Purple Heart was awarded to those who have been wounded or killed while serving with the U.S. military and is the oldest decoration that is still given to members of the military.

He is really a nut about basketball. Eike is back in the hospital with a cold, and Musial, my assistant engineer, is over here with pneumonia, only a slight case. The fellows usually tell jokes for awhile after the lights go out at night. Yesterday afternoon several new patients arrived, and they brought a fellow in who had just had his appendix removed. I thought they should be considerate of his condition and quiet down, but a new voice seemed to be telling all the jokes. Suddenly, someone asked who it was, and I'll be damned if it wasn't the appendectomy patient. We had quite a laugh over it.

I saw a pilot today who was in George Hale's outfit. I was surprised to hear that Hale's ship was the one that was hit directly in front of me on one of my raids (December 1 to Solingen). Flak knocked off the ball turret and set Hale's #2 engine on fire. The ship then exploded and crashed (near Frauenberg, Germany). The group (92nd BG based at Podington) Hale was in flies with us (as part of the 40th Combat Wing) on our missions. There was one ship lost in their group that day, and it was Hale's because I saw it go down.

During a mission, the sky was a busy place, and any one man was only able to see only a small part of the action taking place around him. The times they did witness planes going down from their own squadron, group, or of men they knew, crews were definitely affected. Whenever men went missing in action or were killed, clean-out crews would come into the barracks and gather up their belongings to ship back to the States. Watching friends go down and seeing the empty bunks of fallen comrades would often cause a sinking feeling in the stomachs of the ones who made it back.

Regardless, most men were able to keep a relatively detached attitude, centered on self-survival and the common belief that it only happened to someone else. Most men never thought about their own death as it didn't occur to them that "they" might die. During missions, the crews might be filled with anxiety, excitement, churning stomachs, and pounding hearts, but they were not afraid. This was especially true while under attack because everyone was so busy. They were young and believed things would work out OK. Demonstrating an attitude of invincibility and a warrior mentality, Howard wrote while in the hospital,

> *I can hear the "Forts" go over in the morning on their way "over there." I don't envy them, but yet I wish I was up there with them. I am not heroic, but if it weren't for you and Susan with the great desire in my heart to be with you, I would stay here after I had completed my raids and volunteer for more.*

Finally ... the Promotion Comes Through

On December 22, Howard left the hospital and wrote,

> *It is good to get back and about again. The little thatched roof farm houses, the two wheeled carts with their sturdy horses, the neatly kept patchwork of the fields, the rolling hills and all the rest that goes to make up the traditional English countryside looking good, but how I would love to see the palms, flowers, the stucco houses and green hills of California.*

I wore silver bars (his promotion to 1st Lt. had come through on December 15) for the first time today. I will keep the gold bars (2nd Lt.) you pinned on my shoulders at Douglas (AFB, Arizona) as a keepsake. They won't let me fly combat until my cast is off. My crew will fly with another pilot. It wouldn't be fair to hold them back.

After leaving the hospital, Howard wore a walking brace over a plaster cast on his leg. He couldn't fly because the brace was too long for him to get a flying boot on to protect his foot from the extreme cold of high altitude. Major Flannagan had him check out some of the newer co-pilots so he could fly enough to keep in practice. Flannagan had him "stooge" around the operations office, and appointed him deputy assistant flight leader to keep him busy. Howard also started playing cribbage with Flannagan every afternoon and usually won, saying, "He owes me $12.00. I started teaching Benny, Dan, and Eike the game too. We played in my room until 1:30 a.m. this morning. I have now won about $100 so far."

Howard wrote,

I feel sorry for Daniels. He is very worried about his wife's pregnancy. She has only gained two pounds, and he thinks she is afraid of the delivery. I know how much he wants to get back to his wife and my flu and now my ankle has prevented us from getting our raids in. Of course it means as much to me or more to get home too, but I'm holding myself back. I feel guilty holding him back too. Perhaps they will fly with another pilot until I get well.

Soon it was Christmas but Howard reported,

It is very little like Christmas here, but we had a little party in our room on Christmas Eve. Drank some of the bourbon we have been saving. We toasted some bread over our fire and had a can of salmon. Benny passed out and was pretty sick later on. We went to the club and played poker. Had a very good dinner with turkey, baked potatoes, corn, peas, cranberries, dressing, orange juice, coffee, ice cream and pie, candy and cigarettes. There are two Christmas trees up in the club with some red and green paper stars and figurines, and the lounge room is hung with red and green crepe paper. Don't know what we'd do without the American Radio Network. Having all the old familiar programs makes us seem a little closer to home. The British radio programs are so very corny, and their sense of humor is flat.

Doc McKim, the squadron doctor, and I were kidding Eike about oxygen and high altitude making a person sterile. Eike was worried for awhile. "What would my wife say if she heard that," he said. "After I talked her out of having a baby back at Dalhart (AFB, Texas), if we can't have one when I get back, she never will forgive me!"

McKim says that it is a lot of bunk. There are too many of the fellows getting girls pregnant over here to bear out that story."

Ruthie responded by saying,

Don't let Eike kid you. I think they tried in Dalhart but just weren't successful. The last day we were there, Helen was practically crying because she had just got sick so she knew she wasn't pregnant. If that sterile rumor is true, I'm glad we already have Susan and Stevie in the hanger.

Even though Ruth and Howard did not know the sex of their baby on the way, they were hoping for a boy and so usually referred to the baby as Stevie or Steve. If a girl, her name would be Nancy. The following excerpts from various letters from Howard prove the point:

"That would be something if Steve was born on Dad's birthday. He really would be proud."

"Can you feel any life yet? I don't think I will be home by the time he is born. Nancy or Steve, whomever it may be."

"You and Susan, and Steve have all my love."

"Give Susan a kiss and Steve a pat for me."

"When I see you and Susan and ? for the first time after all these months, it will probably be the biggest day of my life."

"Steve will be walking by the time I get home at this rate."

"Hope Steve or Nancy is not giving you any trouble."

"It would be nice to have a boy. To be truthful, when I think of the baby, I always think of a boy, but I wouldn't be all that disappointed if we had another girl."

On December 30, Eike flew as co-pilot once again with Lt. Fallow to Ludwigshaven, Germany, to bomb the giant chemical plant, I.G. Farbenindustrie, stretching along the Rhine River for three miles. German radio reported that the plant was severely damaged, and poison gas that was manufactured and stored there had been released to the detriment of the civilians in the vicinity. More than 700 planes from the Eighth Air Force were sent on the mission, dropping over 1,300 tons of bombs.

1943 ... Wins and Losses ... New Leadership

The year 1943 came to a close with Howard Snyder having three combat missions to his credit. About New Year's Eve, he said, "Everyone was pretty high last night. I felt pretty good myself."

For the year, the 306th Bomb Group led the Eighth Air Force in the number of missions completed, credited with 1,886 sorties against the enemy. It had dropped more than 4,000 tons of bombs and fired almost three million rounds of ammunition. The 306th was credited with destroying 315 enemy planes and 109 probables. However, all this was at a cost of 87 downed B-17s, with the 367th Squadron suffering 40 percent of the losses.

Under the direction of General Dwight D. Eisenhower, Commanding General of European Theater of Operations and Supreme Allied Commander of the Allied Expeditionary Forces (SHAEF), Harold "Hap" Arnold, Commanding General of the United States Air Forces, decided to replace Lt. General Ira Eaker as Commander of the Eighth Air Force with Major General James "Jimmy" Doolittle and appointed Lt. General Carl Spaatz to have overall responsibility for strategic bombing operations in Continental Europe.

Doolittle was famous for leading the first retaliatory air raid on the Japanese homeland on April 18, 1942. After Japan's sneak attack on Pearl Harbor, the United States was reeling and wounded. Something dramatic was needed to turn the war effort around. With no airfields close enough to Japan for the United States to launch an attack, a daring plan was devised. Sixteen B-25s were modified so that they could take off from the deck of the aircraft carrier, *USS Hornet*. Sending such big, heavy bombers from a carrier had never been tried before. The all volunteer five-man crews, nicknamed "Doolittle's Raiders," under the command of Lt. Col. James Doolittle who flew the lead plane, knew that they would not be able to return to the carrier because of lack of fuel. They would have to hit Japan and then hope to make it to Japanese occupied China.

After bombing Japan, all the planes flew as far as they could. Four planes crash-landed, 11 crews bailed out, and one made it to Russia. Two crewmen drowned while crash-landing in the ocean. One man fell off a cliff after landing and died. Eight were captured of which three were executed, and another died of starvation in a Japanese prison camp. The majority of the crews were able to escape with the help of Chinese guerillas and a Baptist missionary, John Birch.

Jimmy Doolittle received the Medal of Honor for this feat which was a huge morale-building victory for the United States after the devastating attack on Pearl Harbor. The raid demonstrated that Japan itself was vulnerable to American air attack, and back in the

U.S., "Doolittle's Raiders" were celebrated as national heroes and models of bravery. Metro-Goldwyn-Mayer produced a 1944 motion picture based on the raid called *Thirty Seconds Over Tokyo,* starring Spencer Tracy as Jimmy Doolittle and Van Johnson as Captain Ted Dawson. It was a patriotic and emotional box office hit.

It was Doolittle's job with the Eighth Air Force to kill the *Luftwaffe*, and under his command the P-51 Mustangs would do just that in 1944. Expanding the fighter's role from one of simply trying to protect the bombers, Doolittle unleashed the Mustangs to not only pursue and destroy the enemy, but to also go after any target of opportunity on the ground. The effects were devastating to German troops, transport, and communications. In the spring of 1944 as the U.S. fighters were achieving air superiority, and the *Luftwaffe* was taking massive casualties, Doolittle increased the minimum combat tour from twenty-five missions to thirty. Eventually, the tour limit was raised to thirty-five.

22

JANUARY 1944 ... NEW YEAR'S AND CONTINUING LOSSES

Nineteen B-17s were in the formation when the attack started, and seven and one-half minutes later just eleven ships remained. Five of the planes that went down were from the 306th with 43 men killed.

Death and Life in the New Year

Life at Thurleigh went on. While the combat crews of the 306th came and went (either completing their tour, being shot down, or being killed), there was a core ground element that came over at the beginning in September 1942 and remained. Some or those men, mostly enlisted ground personnel, found a home at Thurleigh and the surrounding areas. Many American servicemen and British women dated, some casually but some seriously resulting in marriages. Therefore, weddings were a common occurrence. In addition, estimates suggest around 9,000 war babies were born out of wedlock.

The 306th Commanding Officer, Colonel Robinson said, "The chaplain and I had an agreement: all applications for marriage to English girls were turned down on first submission. We felt this helped some men who found themselves in an untenable position and could then say, 'The Colonel says I can't get married!' We also just as quickly approved the second application by the same couple." Ironically, Robinson ended up marrying Mim Smith who was in charge of the Red Cross at Thurleigh.

Howard wrote Ruth, "One of the bombardiers in our squad married the nurse he had while he was in the hospital. She comes over when she can get away. They manage to see each other quite often. I am very envious of him, but our day will come, Darling."

The new year began with a two day pass and a trip into London for Daniels, Benninger and Snyder. Lt. Bill Grisham who was flying as Snyder's co-pilot in place of Eike also joined them, but Daniels stayed at the Red Cross Rainbow Club while the rest of them went sightseeing. The Rainbow Club, whose official name was Rainbow Corner, was the most famous American Red Cross Club in Europe and was located at the corner of Shaftesbury Avenue and Denman Street, a short distance from Piccadilly Circus. In addition to extensive recreation facilities and programs, the club offered excellent food. It was a fairly inconspicuous building in peace time, operated as part of a chain of Lyons Corner Houses and the Monico Restaurant, built to accommodate a few thousand people.

Red Cross Rainbow Corner in London

Howard reported,

We went through Westminster Abbey where all England's greats are buried. It was practically destroyed but has been restored and quite impressive. Also saw Buckingham Palace with the beautiful parks around it. We then went to Parliament and the House of Lords. We took a taxi to London Bridge and over to the Tower of London which was by far the most interesting. It was built way back in the 12th century by William the Conqueror and was where Henry the Eighth had two of his wives beheaded. We saw two shows, Sahara *with Humphrey Bogart and* Jane Eyre *staring Orson Welles and Joan Fontaine.*

The First Mission of 1944

The 306th BG's first mission in January was on the Fourth. George Eike flying with Lt. Robert Fallow, was among 33 planes from the 306th and over 500 from the 8th Air Force that went to Kiel, Germany, to bomb the naval base there and the Friederich Krupp *Germaniawerft*, a shipbuilding company producing German U-boats. U-boat was the English version of the German word *U-Boot*, a shortening of ***U**nterseeboot*, which means "undersea boat."

No aircraft were reported hit, but Lt. Charles Tucker of the 367th mysteriously failed to return and was reported to have gone down under control in the target area. Even though he had engine problems at takeoff, Tucker did not want to abort the mission and struggled all the way across the North Sea. After an engine finally caught fire, he decided to head back to England when flak hit his plane, the *El Diablo*. Even though this caused his ship to go into a spin, Tucker was able to gain control and landed on a sandbar on the Isle of Sylt in the North Frisian Islands. All the crew survived but were taken prisoner.

The next day, January 5th, Kiel was bombed again, and again Eike was flying as co-pilot with Lt. Fallow. Unfortunately, Lt. Ian Elliott from the 367th crashed on takeoff, killing eight crew members and injuring the two survivors. Flak was moderate and one crewman commented, "Must have been good bombing yesterday because we didn't get half the flak today with much better visibility." However, escort fighter support did not show up, and all hell broke loose. The B-17s from the 306th engaged in a fierce battle with about 30 Focke-Wulf 190s and Messerschmitt (ME) 109s near the target area.

On only their second raid, the 369th's Lt. Sidney Wolfe and his crew went down under the attack. Wolfe came through the target area OK, but German fighters knocked the tail off his plane, and it went into a spin. Only the co-pilot Alvin Enos and navigator Fremont

Jewell were able to bail out and could only watch as their B-17 exploded when it hit the ground killing the rest of the crew. Enos and Jewell were both captured by the Germans. The B-17F, aircraft 42-30794, that Wolfe was flying was the plane that Howard Snyder had flown on the December 1 mission to Solingen, Germany.

On the mission, 379th BG's Lt. Thomas Eaton whom Howard had visited about a month earlier, was also shot down. Both Eaton and his co-pilot Henry Hainline were killed in action along with six other crew members. His plane, *Deacon's Sinners*, was attacked by Messerschmitt 109 fighters just after leaving the target. One of the ME 109s rammed Eaton's B-17, breaking a wing in half and causing the plane to disintegrate. Eaton's ship was right behind that of Earl Houston's, the Tenny Belle, named after Houston's wife. Houston was another friend of Howard's from Pilot School.

Deacon's Sinners B-17 Crew Picture: Top Row - left to right: pilot Tom E. Eaton, co-pilot Henry L. Hainline, navigator Robert S. Doty, bombardier Melvin D. Henroid plus the enlisted crew members

On the same day, radio operator Kenneth Blye who had been a part of Howard Snyder's crew during Operational Unit Combat Training at Dalhart, Texas, flew on a mission with the 3rd Air Division. Blye was now a Technical Sergeant and a crew member of pilot Glenn Johnson and co-pilot Ralph Patton with the 331st Bomb Squadron and 94th Bomb Group stationed at Bury St. Edmunds.

The Shelburne Escape Line

Their B-17 was one of 112 bombers that hit the German airfield at Merignac near Bordeaux, France. After dropping their bombs on the target, they were returning to England when attacked by Focke-Wulf 190s over the Brest Peninsula and shot down. The ship broke in half when 20mm shells exploded between the ball turret and the radio room. Blye and waist gunner Isadore Viola were both blown out of the opening. Tail gunner Carlton Coleman was unable to get out and went down with the tail section that had been blown away.

The rest of the crew was able to bail out, but ball turret gunner James Stubblefield and waist gunner William Munson were killed when one's parachute did not open and the other's parachute wrapped around a wing of the plane. On the raid, 11 B-17s were lost, 49 damaged, and two were damaged beyond repair. Casualties were 11 killed, 21 wounded, and 110 missing.

Kenneth Blye landed in a field and was hidden by a French farmer for 11 days. The farmer then connected him with the French Underground where Blye met up with the other surviving members of his crew, including co-pilot Ralph Patton, and also with several other downed U.S. airmen who had evaded capture. The airmen were provided with forged papers, safe houses, food and clothing. In March, all the men were eventually able to return to England as part of Operation Bonaparte, the code name given to the "Escape by the Sea" mission of the French resistance network named the Shelburne Escape Line, operated by two French Canadians, Lucian Dumais, aka "Leon," and Raymond Labrosse.

Members of the Shelburne Escape Line had selected a small, isolated beach close to the village of Plouha on the Britanny coast as the best location for British gunboats to pick up small groups of downed airmen and take them approximately 90 miles across the English Channel to safety. Whenever a rendezvous had been arranged to pick up airmen, they would be gathered at a small stone farmhouse at Saint-Samson which became known as the Maison d'Alphonse (House of Alphonse). It belonged to resistance members Jean and Marie Gicquel and was located close to the beach.

For the evaders, the moments of silently waiting on the dark beach were exceedingly nerve-racking, but in time, small rubber rafts would appear out of the blackness. Once arms, money, and supplies had been quietly unloaded and brought up a cliff to the house, the airmen jumped in and the rafts slipped silently out to a waiting British gunboat, MBP (Motor Gun Boat) of the 15th Flotilla of the British Royal Navy which operated out of Dartmouth.

It is noteworthy that the Shelburne network never lost one airman. In fact, the only casualty was the Maison d'Alphonse which was eventually set on fire and blown up on July 24 by the Germans who suspected it was a resistance hideout. Altogether the Shelburne Line was only active for a short time, from January until August 1944; eight pickups took place which returned 136 evaders back to England.

Twenty years later, co-pilot Ralph Patton would contact two other men on the list of Americans who had escaped by way of Operation Bonaparte, and the three of them organized a reunion in Buffalo, New York, to honor their wartime helpers. The 1964 reunion was attended by 56 people: 32 evaders, 7 helpers, with the balance being family members. Thus began the U.S. Air Forces Escape & Evasion Society (AFEES) whose purpose "is to encourage airmen who were aided by resistance organizations or patriotic nationals of foreign countries to continue friendships with those who helped them." Ralph Patton would serve as its president for 27 years.

On January 7, three of Snyder's crew, Robert Benninger, Richard Daniels, and Ross Kahler flew a mission to Ludwigshaven, Germany, and the chemical works of I.G. Farbenindustrie. Benninger and Daniels flew with pilot Lt. Charles Kinsey, and Kahler flew with pilot Lt. Donald Tattershall. Fighter support was excellent although flak was extremely accurate with more than half the ships of the 306th suffering damage. During the raid, 461 tons of incendiary bombs and 548 tons of general purpose bombs were dropped on the target. Eike now had four raids in six days after it took him three months to get his first three. The other three officers of the *Susan Ruth* (Snyder, Benninger, and Daniels) still only had three each.

Scotland and Sick Leave

On January 9, Howard was given 10 days sick leave. With his leg in a cast, he went to Scotland with pilot Lt. Bob Fallow. Howard wrote,

> *We were supposed to fly up, but the weather was bad and had to take a train. The buildings in Scotland are all stone compared to brick as they are in England. The country is rough and hilly while England is a rolling peaceful scene. I like the Scots much better than the English—more friendly and polite. Edinburgh is a beautiful city, and its castle is most picturesque. All the buildings look so ancient and substantial, as if they will still be here unchanged for hundreds of years from now.*
>
> *We got a cab and drove all over town. I saw the royal palace where Mary Queen of Scots lived and saw the used beheading "block."*

Edinburgh is the capital of Scotland with prehistoric roots as a hilltop fort. Mary Queen of Scots, Mary Stuart, was beheaded in

1587, although not with a single strike. The first blow missed her neck and struck the back of her head. The second blow severed her neck, but not entirely, and the executioner had to cut through it using the axe. Afterward, he held her head aloft and declared, "God save the Queen." At that moment, the auburn tresses in his hand turned out to be only a wig, and the head fell to the ground, revealing that Mary had very short grey hair.

Snyder and Fallow then visited Glasgow, the largest city in Scotland and one of the largest seaports in the world, but Howard thought it was "a dirty town with lots of smoke." They also visited Loch Lomond which is a popular tourist destination and the largest inland stretch of water in Great Britain, containing many islands. From there, they went to Cambridge which Howard described as "a lovely place," and finally finished up in London where they saw several movies, including *Johnny Come Lately* with James Cagney and *The Girl from Monterrey.*

More Losses

On January 11, Ross Kahler flying with Lt. Bill Hilton's crew and Richard Daniels with Lt. Bill Quaintance's went on one of those missions when "IT" happens. The raid was to Halberstadt, Germany, an industrial center and railroad junction only 30 miles from Berlin. The huge Junker's aircraft manufacturing factory was located there which built one of the *Luftwaffe's* most effective weapons, the Stuka dive bomber.

It was the 100th mission for the 306th Bomb Group which put up 34 planes. The Group was led by its Commanding Officer, Colonel George Robinson, who was also leading the entire 40th Combat Wing. About one hour and ten minutes after leaving the target, the 306th was viciously attacked head on by about 40 Focke-Wulf 190s which came in three or four at a time in successive waves over and through the formation. Nineteen B-17s were in the formation when the attack started, and seven and one half minutes later just eleven ships remained. Five of the planes that went down were from the 306th with 43 men killed. The same day, Focke-Wulf pilot Hans Berger claimed a B-17 as his third "kill."

The B-17 of the 369th's Lt. Donald Tattershall had its tail shot off and disappeared near the Zuider Zee. Only Technical Sergeant James Hobbs, who was Howard's radio operator on his very first mission on November 3, survived and was taken prisoner. Among those who died was co-pilot Lt. Bill Grisham who had flown as co-pilot on Howard's second and third missions of November 26 and December 1.

Experienced 368th pilot, Willard Reed's *Rationed Passion* was hit hard on the right wing causing the ship to go into an uncontrollable spin and break apart. Waist gunner Albert Schaeffler died in the plane. The nine other crew members bailed out although co-pilot Tom Brady was killed when he hit the ground either because his parachute malfunctioned or he wasn't able to open it. Among the survivors were navigator Lt. Ivan Glaze, flight engineer T/Sgt. Orian Owens, radio operator T/Sgt. Charles Nichols, waist gunner S/Sgt. John Gemborski, and tail gunner S/Sgt. Warren Cole. More will be told about them later as the story unfolds.

Three planes from the 367th were lost. Veteran Lt. George Campert's *Arch Bishop* was knocked out of formation and the entire crew was killed. Lt. Perry Cavos and all his crew were lost, six in the plane and four from their wounds after reaching the ground. Lt. Ross McCollum's plane was damaged by a midair collision with another B-17, and on the return flight home was hit head on by three enemy fighters. The only survivor was bombardier Lloyd Crabtree who landed on the rooftop of a farmhouse near Appeldoorn, Netherlands, and was immediately captured.

All the ships got shot up, including Colonel Robinson's. The 369th's pilot Lt. Kinsey was badly wounded in the leg ending his combat career, but his co-pilot Theodore Czechowski took over and did a splendid job returning a badly shot up aircraft. Lt. Bill Casseday and his 369th crew had to crash-land at Horsham. Co-pilot Robert Crowley was severely injured, and their plane declared a total loss.

Lt. Kenneth Dowell and his co-pilot Charles Young of the 369th probably had the most difficult time of all. Their plane *Pretty Baby* suffered extensive damage, including the loss of their electrical system, and their #3 engine falling off the plane. Leaving the formation and flying alone, they were chased by enemy fighters but finally succeeded in making a crash-landing at the RAF base at Great Staling. Many of the crew were injured, radio operator Hugo Honkonen so badly he was sent back to the U.S. The plane was declared a total loss. Lt. Dowell received a Silver Star, the third highest military decoration awarded for valor and gallantry in action against an enemy of the United States. Co-pilot Young received the Distinguished Flying Cross for heroism and extraordinary achievement while participating in an aerial fight.

At least the gunner crews from the 306th were able to shoot down a significant number of enemy planes, led by Staff Sergeant Daniel Antonelli, tail gunner on Lt. Loren Page's 368th crew. Antonelli was credited with destroying four enemy aircraft. It was a record unequalled by any 306th gunner during the war and earned him the Distinguished Flying Cross.

After weathering the storm of enemy fighter attacks over the European continent, the returning ships learned that England was "socked-in," and according to the 369th Squadron Diary, they had to scatter like birds trying to find alternative airfields at which to land. Not a single plane landed back at its home base in Thurleigh, but instead at RAF bases scattered around the country. The intelligence officers practically lost their minds running around the countryside to perform mission debriefing interrogations. However, the combat crews were very grateful that the RAF bases, especially Hethel, welcomed them and went all out to make them comfortable, fed, and well inebriated. Halberstadt was a terrorizing mission, and one of the toughest of the war for the 306th. Most of the difficulty was due to lack of fighter escort support which was caused by unexpectedly bad weather.

23

ROCKETS AND A D-DAY DECEPTION

After the war, von Braun and 6,000 other German scientists and their families were taken to America along with 100 intact V-2 rockets.

The V-1 and V-2 Rockets

On January 14, Ross Kahler and Louis Colwart flew with Lt. Richard Wong and Richard Daniels with Lt. Bill Quaintance on a mission to Pas De Calais, France, where emplacements for Nazi V-1 and later V-2 rockets were located. The V was short for ***V**ergeltungswaffes* (meaning retaliation weapons) so named by Nazi propaganda as retaliation for the Allied bombers that were attacking German cities. The V-1s, known as flying bombs or buzz bombs, were liquid propellant rockets specifically designed for terror bombing London. At its peak, more than one hundred V-1s a day were fired on southeastern England.

The V-2 rocket was first launched in September 1944. It was the world's first long-range combat ballistic missile and predecessor of today's cruise missile. It flew into outer space and reached London in three minutes.

Hitler's goal was the complete destruction of London, and in six months, more than 3,000 rockets were fired on London and southeastern England. Hitler believed that the V-2 would devastate England and cause enough terror to make Churchill and the English people seek peace. He thought that the V-2 rocket was the wonder weapon that would save Germany and win the war, however, it came too late. Had it been available earlier, D-Day may never have happened. At a cost of $500 billion in today's money, the V-2 rockets only killed about 6,000 people. In hindsight, it was money that could have been spent to produce a vast number of airplanes—airplanes that Germany so desperately could have used.

V-1 Rocket

V-2 Rocket

Being the first human invention to enter outer space, the V-2 was the predecessor of all modern rockets, including those used by the United States and Soviet Union space programs. Wernher von Braun was the central figure in Germany's rocket development program and was responsible for the design and realization of the V-2. After the war, von Braun and 6,000 other German scientists and their families were taken to America along with 100 intact V-2 rockets. Eventually, von Braun and his group were assimilated into NASA (National Aeronautical & Space Administration) where he was the chief architect of the Saturn V launch vehicle that propelled the Apollo spacecraft and helped land the first men on the Moon in July 1969. According to many, he was the greatest rocket scientist in history.

Pas de Calais was a target the crews liked because the route was short and enemy resistance surprisingly weak. They described the mission as "a piece of cake" or "milk run." Twenty-seven B-17s from the 306th took part. Howard said,

> *The boys are getting a good many raids in. Eike has eight, Daniels, seven, Benninger, five, and several of the fellows who came a month after we did have 10 and 12. There will be plenty of bombing left when I start flying again. The earliest the Germans will be beaten, in my opinion, is next winter. A year yet. Then two or three years for Japan.*

Invasion Deception

After the raid to Pas de Calais, the weather prohibited any raids for several days. However, Snyder was able to start making practice flights again even though he couldn't manage too well with his cast on. Being grounded for so long, flying seemed strange to him, and he needed to get his coordination and sense of timing back, especially before flying combat missions again.

Pas de Calais was also the target of code name "Operation Bodyguard" employed by the Allied nations as a plan to deceive the

Germans that the invasion of Europe on D-Day was to occur there, rather than in Normandy. It was the most logical location for an invasion as it was the shortest crossing of the English Channel and offered the quickest route into Germany.

The key element of deception entailed the creation of a huge fictitious landing force, First U.S. Army Group, under General George Patton. The aim was to mislead the Germans into thinking the actual Normandy landing was simply a diversionary tactic with Calais the real objective. The phantom force was stationed at Dover, directly across the English Channel from Pas de Calais, and as a result, the German command took steps to heavily fortify that area of coastline.

Even after the Allies landed at Normandy, the deception worked perfectly and forced the Germans to keep most of their reserves bottled up waiting for the attack on Calais that never came. It gave the Allies valuable time to establish a foothold on the beaches and build upon it for their push inland. Operation Bodyguard was one of the most successful military deceptions employed during the war and arguably the most important.

Robert Benninger turned 21 on January 26 and George Eike turned 25 on January 27. They along with Howard and Richard Daniels just happened to be going on a pass then so they all celebrated in London. No details of the celebration were reported by Howard in his letters written to Ruth.

George Eike flew with Lt. Billy Casseday and Richard Daniels with Lt. Bill Quaintance on January 29's raid to Frankfurt, Germany, the country's largest medieval city and major industrial center. Leading the 306th Group comprised of 38 aircraft was Commanding Officer of the 369th Squadron, Major Robert Riordan, who completed his 28th combat mission. On the bombing run, a gap in fighter support enabled about 25 enemy fighters to attack from the tail, but good gunnery accounted for many destroyed, and no B-17s were lost from the 306th.

On January 30, Richard Daniels flew with Lt. Quaintance, George Eike and Ross Kahler flew with Lt. Casseday, and Robert Benninger flew with Lt. Rudolph Horst to Brunswick, Germany, noted for its aircraft production. From the 369th, Lt. Edward Murphy flew his 25th mission. Enemy opposition was slight, and no 306th aircraft were lost. The 369th didn't even suffer any flak damage. However, it was a difficult day because of very poor visibility.

Haze and contrails strained the crews nerves and considerable "sweating out" took place. It resulted in two planes of the 92nd Bomb Group in the 40th Combat Wing colliding in the target area and exploding. The contrail problem occurred because the hot moist plume of the engine's exhaust mixed with cold air. It created liquid droplets that froze and formed straight, white lines which then spread out to become virtually indistinguishable from natural cloud cover.

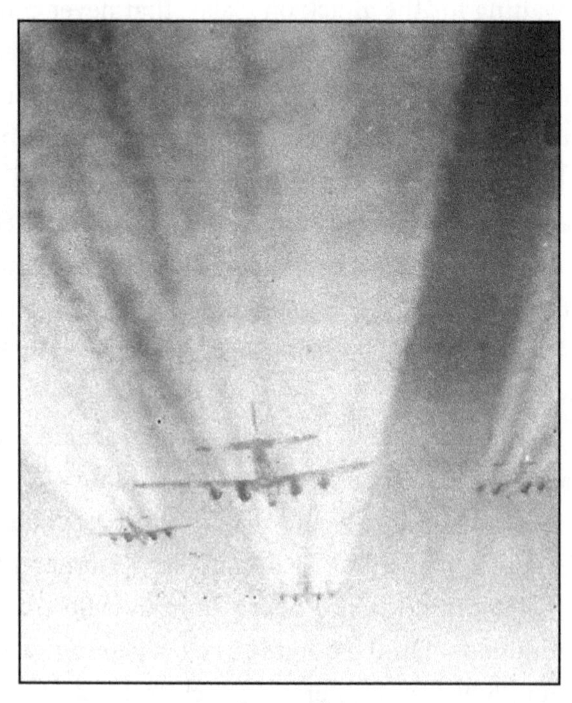

Contrails

Except for Halberstadt, January 1944 was a fairly successful month for the 306th. On the final two missions, the BG put up more than 40 aircraft on each mission, establishing a record. At one time, half that number was considered great. Everyone was glad and began to think that the end of the war was not as remote or intangible as it once seemed. Lt. Robert Fallow, whom Howard went to Scotland with and with whom George Eike flew as co-pilot on several missions, completed his 25th raid and returned to the States. Whenever a combat airman completed his required number of missions or "tour," he automatically became a member of what was informally called the "Lucky Bastards Club." He would also be "body painted" to celebrate the joyous event.

Lucky Bastards

24

FEBRUARY 1944 ... BACK IN COMBAT

After the bomb run, Dowell and Snyder's B-17 had their #1 engine knocked out by flak, and the plane started to lag behind the formation. Soon they were alone in the sky and a sitting duck for enemy fighters.

The Cast Is Off

The VIII Bomber Command began to see a much welcomed increase in long-range fighter escorts from the VIII Fighter Command in February. To further ensure the effectiveness of long-range escorts, General Jimmy Doolittle, now Commander of the Eighth Air Force, required "all qualified fighter pilots to fly escort missions and for escorting fighters to remain with the bombers at all times." Ironically, these orders were issued on February 8 which would turn out to be a fateful day for the *Susan Ruth* and its crew.

In February, the 1st Bombardment Division issued a citation to the 369th Squadron stating,

> *The 369th Bombardment Squadron, Army Air Forces, United States Army, for outstanding performance of duty in action against an armed enemy of the United States in the European Theater of Operations. In the aerial offensive against targets in Western and Central Germany, France, and other occupied territories, the 369th Bombardment Squadron has established an exceptional combat record . . . In these operations the 369th Bombardment Squadron, by extraordinary skill and great*

courage, has given evidence of unswerving loyalty and dedication to duty of the highest nature....

Although greeted with sour grapes by the other three squadrons, the commendation was the only one issued to the 306th BG during its three years of combat during the war.

Howard finally had his cast removed on the 1st and commented,

Finally have my cast off and does it feel good. My ankle is fine, and I will go on missions from now on. Will fly co-pilot on my first as I haven't had a chance to do any flying by myself as yet, and I don't feel that I should fly pilot until I get back in form. If I should misjudge my formation because of lack of practice, it would be my fault, and there are nine others who depend on the pilot.

The crew continued to worry about Richard Daniels' wife and her pregnancy. Virginia had still only gained four pounds, and her doctor thought the baby might be dead. Although she thought she could feel the baby moving, the doctor thought it might only be cramps.

Eike and I bicycled out in the country today and bought a dozen eggs. They will certainly taste good for a change. We will try to get some every week from now on. Eike and I went into town as I wanted to get my insignia sewn on my battle jacket. We had dinner and went to a show Wintertime *with Sonya Henie.*

The 306th returned to combat on February 3 with a raid to the shipbuilding yards of Wilhelmshaven, Germany. Although there were no enemy fighters and little flak, it was enough to bring down Lt. Richard "Calais" Wong of the 369th, the only Chinese-American pilot in the 306th, and three of his crew were killed. Wong had been the butt of many jokes and nicknamed "Calais" for the wrong turn he made on a practice mission when he ended up over Calais and was almost hit by German flak.

Howard finally flew another mission on February 4 to Frankfurt, Germany, to hit the railroad marshalling yards there. This time the 306th had 39 planes participating out of a total of 589 B-17s. Snyder flew as co-pilot on Lt. Kenneth Dowell's crew which included John Pindroch who was flying his first mission since suffering frostbite on the November 26 mission to Bremen. Dowell and his crew had had a very close call back on the January 11 raid to Halberstadt, Germany when their plane was nearly destroyed by *Luftwaffe* fighters, and several of the crew, including engineer and top turret gunner John Mellyn, were seriously injured. Dowell's B-17 barely limped back to England and crash landed at the RAF Great Saling airfield where his ship was declared a total loss.

The B-17G Howard Snyder flew in that day, aircraft #42-31143, was named *Satan's Lady*. It was considered a lucky aircraft and made it through 112 missions and returned to the U.S. in June 1945. Although it was shot up numerous times, none of the many crewmen who ever flew in it were wounded.

On the mission to Frankfurt, Richard Daniels flew with Lt. Rudolph Horst, and Ross Kahler flew with Lt. Alvin Schuering. No enemy aircraft were seen on the raid, but a great amount of anti-aircraft fire was encountered along the route. Bombing was by PFF again, and there was confusion in the Low Group during the bombing run because of the failure of the Lead Group to drop their bombs. Some aircraft returned to base with their loads and others bombed targets of opportunity that loomed up through occasional breaks in the overcast.

More Losses

The accurate flak in the target area accounted for the failure of two planes to return. On their way home, Lt. Henry Ware and his crew of the 367th B-17 *Round Trip Ticket* were shot down along the French coast near Calais. All the crew survived but were captured and became POWs. Lt. Charles Berry of the 369th took a direct hit over Cologne, Germany, in his right wing, and his plane burst into flames. With two engines out, the plane went into a spin and broke in two at the ball turret. The front section of the plane dropped out of the sky, and those in it were killed. The tail section stabilized long enough for the two waist gunners and tail gunner to bail out to safety. Lt. Berry was flying aircraft #42-31007, a B-17F model, which eerily was the plane Howard Snyder had flown during his missions on November 3, 16 and 26 the previous year.

After the bomb run, Dowell and Snyder's B-17 had their #1 engine knocked out by flak, and the plane started to lag behind the formation. Soon they were alone in the sky and a sitting duck for enemy fighters. They shot off flares signaling "help" to friendly fighters, and fortunately, four P-47s from the 78th Fighter Group came to escort them back to Thurleigh. Howard wrote, "Well, I'm at it again, number four today! The way we have been going on the raids they should mount up in a hurry from now on."

That same day, a B-17 from the 423rd crashed and burned on an attempted three engine takeoff from Drew Field, East Lothian, Scotland. All four officers, pilot Arthur Moseley, Woodrow Ellertson, Edward O'Malley and Michael Roskovitch, were killed. Originally a radio operator, Roskovitch was the first enlisted man in the Eighth Air Force to complete the 25 mission tour requirement. Being quite a character, he became known as "Rosky, the Mad Russian" because he had the nerve to cut the neckties off high ranking officers who flew on combat missions in his plane. He had been away for awhile to become a gunnery officer and had just recently come back to flying missions again.

For once, the weather was beautiful on February 5, when 21 planes from the 306th out of a total of 121 B-17s helped bomb the German airfield at Chateaudun, France, 60 miles southeast of Paris. It was a mission much more comfortable than those deep into Germany. Snyder flew again as co-pilot with Lt. Kenneth Dowell along with Daniels. Eike flew with Gerald Haywood, and Ross Kahler and Joe Musial flew with Alvin Schuering. It was ideal for visual bombing and pounding of targets in enemy occupied territory, particularly the bases from which the Nazis launched their nuisance raids on England. The 306th did an excellent job of pulverizing it as strike photographs showed. The flak was moderate and accurate. Fighter support was excellent, and no enemy aircraft were seen. All aircraft returned although a majority had flak damage. Lt. Robert Eckles from the 423rd came back with part of his B-17's wing shot away.

Snyder wrote to Ruth,

Hello Baby. Number five today. Two in two days, not bad. Hope I keep it up. The raid was easy today, and we were over France. It was a beautiful day, and I can almost say that I enjoyed it. It was clear over the target and we really knocked the h---- out of it. I flew as co-pilot again as I requested it. I can fly as good or even better now so will take my crew tomorrow. Daniels and Eike now have credit for 12 missions, Benny 7, Kahler 10, Musial 7, me, Colwart, and Holbert 6, and Slenker and Pindroch 5. It is natural, of course, to be disappointed that I haven't the raids in I would have had if it hadn't been for my ankle, but I shrug it off. Not only will it keep me away from you longer, but I would be a flight leader now and in line for my captaincy. I would *be leading the squadron on raids,* if.

Howard flew his third mission in a row the next day, February 6, to the German airfield at Nancy, France, and it was the very first mission that Howard's entire crew, including George Eike, flew together. It was hoped that the weather would be comparable to the day before, however 9/10ths clouds prevented the identification of the primary target, and various degrees of clouds prevented bomb runs on possible targets of opportunity. Anti-aircraft fire was negligible, and there was no fighter opposition.

The Group was proud that there was no indiscriminate bombing. It ended up being a "practice mission" for the 28 planes of the 306th and the other 300 some bombers of the Eighth Air Force that took off that morning. The plane Howard Snyder flew was aircraft #42-37953 and the B-17G that Alvin Schuering and waist gunner Harold Maron would be flying when they were shot the following month on March 29.

Howard wrote,

> *I am tired tonight as I flew another raid today. The third in as many days. Imagine, three in three months, and now three in three days. Eike flew with me today. The first time we have had the entire crew together since we arrived in England. Many of the fellows have flown seven raids in eight days and are pretty tired. I think we will rest tomorrow. I hope they keep pushing them to us, and I think they will. If we get a raid every fourth or fifth day, it will be all right. I would be home to my little family before you know it.*

Extreme Conditions

The conditions under which the air war was fought were extreme. Although the average flyer was only about 20 years of age, even for young men the missions were exhausting. The sheer anxiety of flying long combat missions for up to ten hours would subject the crews to continuous stress. Flying a lumbering bomber was no easy task either; brute strength often was needed to move the control column and rudder pedals, especially when an engine went out. Flying in close formation through low-visibility weather conditions was nerve-racking and made midair collision a constant hazard.

Besides the fear of being wounded or dying, they had to contend with loud noise, the constant hum and vibration of the plane, glare, bitter cold, heavy flight clothing and adherence to oxygen discipline. All this contributed to extreme fatigue even without the stress of flak and enemy fighters during combat. As a result of the constant battle with fatigue, most bomber crew members did little else but eat and sleep between missions. It was such stress that it sometimes resulted in a nervous breakdown. Mental stress ranged from simple flying fatigue to serious psychological disorders; formerly referred to as shell shock, it's now known as post-traumatic stress disorder. Crewmen who became jumpy and nervy were termed "flak happy."

However, the air war was much different than ground warfare. The air crews would experience bursts of fury and fear on combat missions often followed by several days of inactivity and boredom when the weather prohibited flying. Instead of lying in a fox hole, they returned to clean sheets, hot food, and adoring English girls. It had also been determined by the Eighth Air Force that regular and frequent leave or passes were essential in preventing flying fatigue. The passes gave the combat crews the knowledge and assurance that they would not be called on for duty within a set period of time and were thus able to completely relax. Passes and leaves gave servicemen the opportunity to travel outside of Thurleigh to experience places like London and Scotland. A nineteen- or twenty-year-old boy could be fighting over Germany during the day and back in London that night with the girl of his dreams.

Unlike the infantry, air crews also had a place that was their own, if not a room at least a bunk with a foot locker and some other space in which to keep personal items. Airmen had a respite between their encounters with the enemy, a night at the minimum or even several days, which gave them the opportunity to keep a diary or journal. Ground troops while in combat carried only what they needed to survive, and if pulled off the front line, their lodgings would still only consist of a tent without any amenities. As Howard wrote to Ruth, "I can't help but realize how fortunate I am in the Air Corps. I could just as easily be laying in some muddy, pest infested foxhole in the South Pacific instead of this comfortable room."

On February 7, Howard wrote to Ruth,

> *Not much doing today. We had a critique this morning on the last few raids. Everyone is resting, and they need it. I think the raids will go quickly from now on. We will probably fly every day we have good weather. I told Eike the story about George and Jane! We both were roaring so much Dan wanted to know what the trouble was. You and I probably have had more in one night than they have all the time they've been married. He never did appear to be very romantic, but I never thought he was that much of a flop! She should get a divorce. He is queer anyway, and I doubt if they would be happy even if their sexual relations were normal. I'm still laughing!*

25

FEBRUARY 8, 1944 ... TROUBLE

Then all of a sudden flak exploded and took three feet off their left wing, almost knocking the Susan Ruth upside down.

Frankfurt—Flying the Hole

Twenty B-17s from the 306th Bomb Group took off at 0809 hours from Thurleigh and flew Low Group to the 305th Lead Bomb Group in the 40th Combat Wing formation. A total of 236 B-17s took part in the Eighth Air Force mission to Frankfurt, Germany. It was only the second mission that the original 10 man crew of the *Susan Ruth* had all been on together. The *Susan Ruth* was one of the new B-17G models and had just recently been delivered to the 306th on January 21. It was carrying twelve 500-pound general purpose bombs.

For some reason, the High Group left the Combat Wing formation after crossing the English Coast. The 306th crossed the enemy Coast at 1013 hours and flew south of their briefed course to the vicinity of the I.P. The 306th then followed the 305th to bomb at 1127 hours. Bombing was by PFF due to 7/10ths cloud cover, most of which was concentrated over the target area. Crews saw Frankfurt between cloud breaks and strike photographs showed bomb bursts in fields north of the junction of the Rhine and Main Rivers, north of Biebrich and between Russelsheim and Wiesbaden.

As Howard recalls,

We were briefed to bomb Frankfurt. It was just another raid as far as I was concerned at the time. We had been there before

(February 4) and had an anxious and lonely time of it returning on three engines. But nothing happened to us, and the suspense and anxiety were unnecessary.

The *Susan Ruth* (aircraft #42-31499 J) was to fly the hole, number seven in the lead squadron of the Low Group. The hole position was the last plane in the bottom or Low Group of the formation. "When I saw my name on the formation board, I was a little apprehensive for a moment. I could not help but think of Berry who we lost flying that position a few days before, bombing the same target (February 4 to Frankfurt). However, I had long ago ceased to be nervous or afraid before a mission and the thought didn't remain with me long."

"The join-up was uneventful, and we joked over the interphone about our party the night before. Danny (bombardier Richard Daniels), Benny (navigator Robert Benninger), Eike (co-pilot George W.) and I had been on a little spree at The Falcon with some of the boys and were feeling surprisingly well for the condition we were in a few hours before. There is nothing like oxygen to clear up a fellow's blood." The Falcon was a 17th century English coach inn on the banks of the River Great Ouse. Now called The Falcon at Bletsoe, it is still in operation today and located on Rushden Road in the north Bedfordshire village of Bletsoe.

The Falcon Pub

We flew at 24,000 feet going in. The day was lovely way up there, with an almost solid layer of billowing, milky white clouds beneath us. The sky was a bright, almost pastel blue. We had a new ship (B-17G) which was performing beautifully, and we were in the lead squadron. It was easy to fly a good formation. No enemy fighters or flak were met on the way in. However, the usual intense flak was met over the target. It was barrage flak and accurate, rocking the ship. One burst pitted the windshield in front of me, and I was thankful we had bullet-proof glass in the ship. Several times the flak hitting the ship sounded like hail on a tin roof.

Daniels couldn't get the bomb bay doors open (because of being damaged by flak) so I gave the ship to Eike and proceeded to pull the emergency release when I saw the bombs begin to drop from the lead ship. They released without any trouble, and we made a sharp turn to the right and got the hell out of there (turning to the Rally Point). Flak continued to break all around us. Flak didn't scare me, but I could still feel my heart speed up as if it were thrown into high gear. My pulse throbbed as if the pressure would burst the veins. The sweat ran down my back and sides in small streams. I felt hot and flushed and all my actions sped up, making normal movements seem like slow motion. Whenever I left a heavy flak area, I cooled down as if after some sudden violent and heavy physical exertion. I don't think I can actually say I enjoyed the sensation, but I didn't dislike it. There is something invigorating and satisfying in knowing one can conquer fear.

Right in the midst of all the flak, ball turret gunner Louis Colwart yelled out over the interphone, "Wow! Look at those buildings fly apart!" He could see their bombs bursting right down through the center of the target. Then all of a sudden flak exploded and took three feet off their left wing, almost knocking the *Susan Ruth* upside-down. Colwart told waist gunner Joe Musial there was a hole in the belly of the plane big enough for him to crawl through. Upon the formation's return to Thurleigh, it was reported that seven of the 20 B-17s from the 306th were seriously damaged by flak.

Bomb Bay Trouble

Danny (bombardier Richard Daniels) couldn't get the bomb bay doors up, so I had him come up and try to wind them up mechanically, but he couldn't and finally had to give it up. Engineer Roy Holbert also tried but he too was unsuccessful. We were running low on gas as we had constantly pulled too much power, and now with the added drag of the open bomb bay doors, I was wondering if we would have enough gas to get us back. I had Eike constantly working on rpm to conserve as much fuel as possible.

Also that morning, fighter squadrons at various German air bases were alerted that U.S. bombers had taken off from England and were gathering over the English Channel. When the bomber formations reached the Continent's coastline, *Luftwaffe* pilots, including Hans Berger, received orders to take off. Squadrons then met up to form groups of 30 to 50 planes. Berger commented,

Through radio, we received azimuth and flight level data, had to gain altitude, and usually within half an hour or so we could far away in front of us perceive a lot of tiny black dots in the sky—the enemy bomber formations. A short while later, these black dots took the shape of 'laaaarge' four-engine airplanes.

Between 1235 and 1245 hours when the formation was crossing from Germany into France near Charleville, there was a gap in the fighter support. The American fighter escort that was visible was being engaged in a dog fight off to the right of the formation. Taking advantage of this gap, two German Focke-Wulf 190 fighters, one of them piloted by Siegfried Marek and the other by Lt. Hans Berger, popped out of the clouds from below, climbed in a sweeping curve to the front, and swept back through the formation firing their 20 mm cannons.

It must have been an hour before I heard one of the gunners (waist gunner, John Pindroch) call out, "Two 190s at five o'clock." We had seen no fighters up to this time and only scattered bursts of flak on the way out. It wasn't but a few seconds later until we had "had it." He (Pindroch) called out again, 'Watch 'em! They're coming around to the front!' Then Dan, ready at the chin turret guns, responded, 'I see them. Let 'em come!' Well, they came, and if he had known what was to happen, he wouldn't have been so anxious to receive them.

Singled Out

Suddenly the nose guns were thumping away. I could hear the dull crackling fire through my headset, as if the guns were a great distance away. The vibrations of the firing shook the ship, and as I looked from one ship to the other above me, I could see the empty cartridges fly out of the nose turrets into the slipstream and whiz past our cockpit.

The bursting of the Focke-Wulf's 20 mm cannons around our ship was the first indication that we had been singled out. Then the celestial dome (a radar installation on the bombers) blew up in front of me. After that I could hear 20 mm striking and exploding as they hit the ship. Pieces of equipment and parts of the ship were flying about, striking my feet and legs.

Daniels was badly wounded when an unexploded shell entered his right arm, tearing away most of his bicep and exiting through his back.

When the oxygen cylinders exploded, I didn't realize what had happened. The noise of the explosion was muffled by my helmet and headset, but the concussion stunned me for a few moments.

In addition to fragments from the exploding 20 mm shells, tracers were being fired as well which caused the escaping oxygen to catch fire. Someone lighting a match in a gas-filled room would cause much the same effect as the explosion. Only, instead of flames decreasing immediately after the explosion, they seemed to continue all around us with the same intensity.

Tracers are bullet or cannon caliber projectiles that are built with a small pyrotechnic charge in their base. When ignited, they burn very brightly, making the projectile visible to the naked eye. This enables the shooter to follow the projectile trajectory in order to make aiming corrections.

As I looked around in a half-dazed state, I became slowly conscious that the entire cockpit was filled with smoke and flames. I must have been knocked unconscious for a period of time. It was difficult to see through the smoke and flames, but I could see the terrified face of Eike, his eyes almost out of his head, looking crazily around him as he tore frantically at his flak suit and safety belt. I think Holbert (Roy, the flight engineer) had already jumped as I couldn't see him at all.

After trying to get the bomb bay door up, Holbert had returned to his gun turret. He recalled,

I looked down to my right and saw fighter planes through a break in the clouds. A few moments later two FW 190 fighters were attacking us. I could see one FW 190 making his attack from the front, but he was too low for me to fire my gun at him. When he opened fire on us, he knocked out our no. 2 and 3 engines setting them on fire. One 20 mm shell went between my legs tearing a hole in my flight suit and bursting on the bomb bay door behind me. The back of my legs were sprayed with fragments.

26

DISASTER

I had been a good while without oxygen and was feeling the effects as I fell. We were at 20,000 feet. I was determined to make a delayed jump and as I extended my arms to stop somersaulting, I caught a glimpse of what I thought were eight billowing chutes.

Abandon Ship

A full burst of 20 mm cannon shells came right through the ball turret, practically blowing it out of the plane, and killed Louis Colwart instantly. The cannon fire also knocked Joe Musial's gun position right out of the plane. Musial witnessed a 20 mm round hit radio operator Ross Kahler in the temple, killing him instantly. Attempting to drag Kahler's body toward the side escape hatch, Musial took a direct burst to his left leg that tore it off. Another shell deflected off the back of his flak jacket, knocking him forward like a rag doll.

Musial was momentarily knocked unconscious and when he came to, he was lying against the tail wheel and trying to determine how he had gotten there. Amazingly, it wasn't his leg that hurt but his back, and he said it felt like someone had hit him with a baseball bat. He was sitting in all this blood, his blood, with his leg a tangled mess and thought "just blow the hatch and stick it outside like the training manual said. I stuck my leg out into the air and the blood froze. Just like they taught us to do."

Musial continued:

There was nothing more I could do but crawl back to the escape hatch (the main hatch on the side of the plane) and bail out because the plane was a blazing inferno. And I had to get out before I lost consciousness from the lack of oxygen and loss of blood. The other waist gunner, John Pindroch from Cleveland, didn't even have his chute on. We all wore a harness but laid the chutes next to us. The damn plane was on fire and starting to go, and Johnny was so petrified he couldn't move. I threw shell casings at him to get him to react.

With the main hatch open, the thin cold air was no longer a friend, for in a few minutes it could rob them both of consciousness, causing them to lay down and pass out in the dying plane. The short stocky Musial grabbed Pindroch, clamped his chute on the harness and threw his fellow waist gunner out. Then Musial jumped himself. William Slenker, who had been hit in the knee and leg, got out through the escape hatch located in the tail.

Musial said,

I knew I was out of the plane because it was all so damn peaceful suddenly. I pulled the ripcord, and all I could think of was my back. Then my foot began to feel cold. I don't know how I ever made it out and to the ground alive! It was just one of those miracles of combat.

Snyder recalled,

As I looked back at Eike, after trying to see Holbert, he seemed *absolutely mad and out of his head. Then, as my mind seemed to clear a little more, I too became absolutely terrified. I had been frightened before but never completely lost my wits from terror. It was horrible. I tried to yell or scream, but the sound died in my throat and my open mouth emitted no sound. I tried to jump out of my seat, but my safety belt held me there.*

My only thought was to get out of that terrible fire. I couldn't think as I clawed wildly for my safety belt. The fact that I had buckled my safety belt under my flak suit on this raid, instead of over it in my usual way, was the only reason I was able to regain a semblance of sanity. For as I endeavored to unfasten my safety belt, I could not realize in my terrorized and stupefied mind why I could not find it. It was only with great mental effort that I figured out why and thus started my thought process again. As I looked down and realized what the trouble was, a little of the terror left me. But it wasn't until l I had thrown my flak suit from me and unfastened my safety belt that I regained control of myself.

The explosion that had dazed him and ignited the oxygen happened in but a few seconds and as the smoke cleared somewhat, Snyder saw his cockpit was a mass of fire with great tongues of flame shooting out between the seats and around his and Eike's head. Snyder, continuing,

Eike had just taken his chute pack from beneath his seat and made his way to the nose hatch to jump. I hesitated momentarily, not knowing what to do and switched on the auto pilot. Although not terrified as before, I was still greatly shaken and afraid. I acted more from instinct; I don't recall any thoughts. I grabbed a fire extinguisher, but it had no more effect on the blaze than an eyedropper. Deciding it would be impossible to save the ship, I threw the extinguisher down, climbed back from between the seats where I had been standing, held the emergency switch on and began calling through the interphone for the crew to jump. I don't know how long I continued to call, but not getting any response, I felt they had jumped.

Holbert continued,

Moments later, I heard the bail-out alarm. As I came out of the turret, I saw George Eike leaving his seat and he motioned for me to follow him. I grabbed my parachute and snapped one side

to my harness and followed him toward the nose of the plane. As he reached the nose, he turned back and motioned for me to jump. I pulled the handle to release the nose hatch, but nothing happened. I pulled again, and one pin came loose causing the wire to pull through my hand and cutting my fingers to the bone. Eike pushed the door open and held it while I proceeded to leave the plane. The door caught my feet and I was hanging outside the plane with my feet being held by the door. I lost everything out of my pockets, even my dog-tags. I kicked myself loose from the door.

Meanwhile, Snyder said,

The fire was getting so hot I could hardly stand it. My neck was burning and I pulled my scarf over the exposed skin. My nose, cheeks, eyebrows, eyelids and lower forehead must have been burned when I was using the extinguisher. I don't recall any pain from my face until I was on the ground. It was impossible to go back through the fire to see if they had jumped from the rear of the ship, and as I couldn't get any response from anyone, I left the cockpit. As I crawled down to the escape hatch, I was surprised to see Benny and Dan still in the nose. As I made my way toward them, Benny looked down and saw me. I motioned for him to come. He hit Dan on the arm and they both dived toward their chutes. We went out through the nose hatch.

It didn't occur to me at the time, but I believe the interphone and auto pilot were shot out. The crew in back must have jumped earlier because of the smoke and fire, and they possibly could have seen Holbert or Eike jump. Because the ship crashed one or two kilometers from where I landed (at the ferme de la Distillerie or Distillery Farm in Macquenoise, just north of the French border), the auto pilot could not have held level flight for very long. Of course, the ship could have exploded soon after we jumped. With the fire so fierce, it would not have been unlikely.

When I jumped, our bomb bay doors were still open. As I crawled through the escape hatch, I recalled the discussion we had about clearing them when jumping and I wondered if I would. I did! I had been a good while without oxygen and was feeling the effects as I fell. We were at 20,000 feet. I was determined to make a delayed jump and as I extended my arms to stop somersaulting, I caught a glimpse of what I thought were eight billowing chutes.

On his back, with his feet elevated, Snyder plunged toward earth. He could hear nothing but roaring wind.

Someone had told me that we would fall about 10,000 feet a minute so I started counting to sixty as I fell through the clouds, vapor and then clear air. But after reaching sixty, I still couldn't see the ground. I started counting again but gave it up and watched the ground. As I came out of a cloud, the earth appeared for a second and then disappeared again as I reached another cloud. I was falling in the country. There were little clusters of white farm buildings, green squares of pasture and dark brown, irregular and leafless woods. Then as the earth appeared again, I waited until I could distinguish objects very clearly and pulled the rip cord.

It seemed natural to wonder if the chute would open. I knew soon enough as the air caught, filled the chute, and the jerk nearly snapped off my head. The rushing air roaring in my ears stopped suddenly and a most wonderful and peaceful quiet settled over me. It seemed as if I had come out of that hell above into a heaven of peace and rest. Up above, I could now hear the heavy deep sound of the "Forts" mingled with angry rasps of the fighters. But with the peaceful country coming up to meet me, baked in sunshine, the war and all that had happened only a few seconds before seemed like a bad dream long ago. A light breeze seemed to carry me toward a wood, and I reached up to grab the shrouds in order to guide myself into a pasture. I found I was so weak I could hardly lift myself up in my harness. I was too close to the ground to pilot my course. I placed my feet together and resignedly watched the trees rush up at me.

The Caterpillar Club

Anyone who successfully used a parachute to bail out of a disabled aircraft and save his life became a member of an informal association called the "Caterpillar Club." The name makes reference to the silk threads of which the original parachutes were made and recognizes the debt owed to the silk worm. The Club's motto is "Life depends on a silken thread." On February 8, 1944, Howard Snyder, George Eike, Robert Benninger, Richard Daniels, Roy Holbert, John Pindroch, Joe Musial, and William Slenker became members awarded by the Switlik Parachute Co. located in Trenton, New Jersey. However, they weren't the only ones who bailed out that day.

Although the crew was unaware of it before having to abandon their plane, both German fighters had been hit and shot down during the attack. It was sometimes difficult and at other times impossible to determine what gunner from which bomber actually shot down an enemy fighter during combat because usually so many gunners from so many bombers, not to mention U.S. fighter planes, were often firing at the same time. In addition, with the German fighters attacking the bombers head on, and at a combined closing speed of 500 miles per hour, both sides had only seconds to make their fire count. It could not be confirmed which B-17 actually shot down the Focke-Wulf piloted by Siegfried Marek.

The 306th Mission Report of February 8 contains statements from returning crew members stating that Marek's plane "caught on fire and a lot of pieces flew off." "He rolled over on his side and then went into an uncontrollable dive straight down with his engine flaming." Marek went down with his plane, and it crashed near Rue des Usines in Bourlers, about two miles southeast of Chimay. Years later in the 1980s, the plane was dug up. Along with pieces of Marek's boots, parts of the plane that were found were the pilot seat, machine guns, rear wheel with a Michelin tire, and the tail.

It was the gunners of the *Susan Ruth* who had succeeded in knocking down the other Focke-Wulf which was confirmed by its pilot, none other than Lt. Hans Berger. With his plane severely damaged, Berger bailed out. He recounted, "Hanging myself on a parachute, I could see the American crew members on their parachutes not too far away and coming down some place in the middle of nowhere. Some were coming down a mile or more away and soon being taken prisoner by local police forces. All you can think in such a condition is that you thank God to be still alive and in fairly good shape, and then you have to see to it that you get back to your air base in some way or another." Lt. Hans Berger's Focke-Wulf crashed down nearby at Beauwelz, Belgium. Slightly wounded, he was able to make it back by train to his unit at Dortmund Air Base in Germany. His next sortie would be on February 21.

Berger survived the war and said years later,

> *It was hell! And I am still today wondering how and why I survived these fights (as a matter of fact, very, very many of us did not)... They (the U.S. flyers) were beloved sons of their mothers and fathers, as we were the beloved sons of ours. They thought they were fighting for the right cause and so did we. The question that we have now come to ask ourselves today when thinking back on those war days is: Why on earth did we have to shoot at each other???*

On the mission to Frankfurt, a total of 236 B-17s left England of which thirteen were lost, two were destroyed, and another 108 were damaged. Louis Colwart and Ross Kahler along with nine other airmen were killed in action (KIA) and 130 were missing in action (MIA), eight of those from the *Susan Ruth*.

27
BELGIUM

... set up a government in-exile in London and announced its resolve to continue the war and fight at the side of the Allies. Thus began four years of German occupation for the Belgium people under which conditions were severe.

Some History

The country of Belgium is about the size of the state of Maryland and came into its present form as a result of the Belgian Revolution in 1830. It has two main linguistic groups. Dutch speakers (about 60 percent) are located in the northern region of Flanders bordering the Netherlands; and French speakers (about 40 percent) are located in the southern region of Wallonia bordering France. The capital region of Brussels is officially bilingual. Also bordering Belgium is the North Sea to the west and Luxembourg and Germany to the east. Belgium is famous for waffles, chocolate, French fries with mayonnaise, and beer.

Belgium is known for its high quality chocolate and its more than 2,000 small and large chocolatiers. In fact, the world's biggest chocolate selling location is the Brussels National Airport. Contrary to their name, French fries (*pommes frites*) are claimed to have originated in Belgium. Traditionally, they are served in a *cornet de frites*, a cone-shaped white piece of cardboard then wrapped in a piece of paper with one of a variety of different flavored mayonnaise sauces on the top. Some Belgians believe that the term "French" was introduced when American soldiers arrived in Belgium during World War I. They

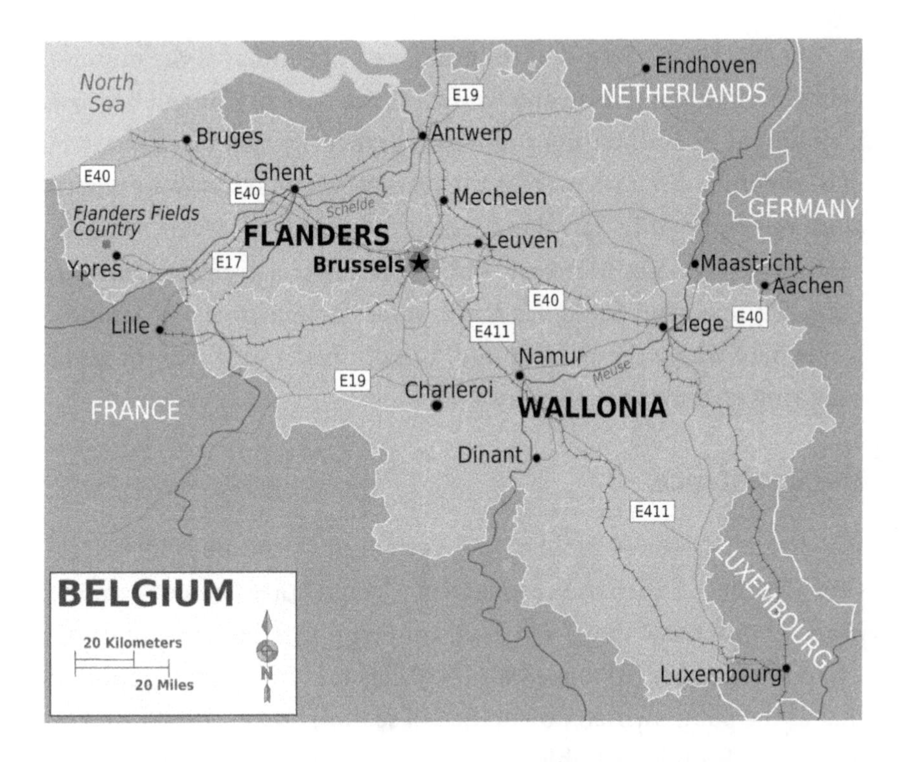

supposedly called them "French," because it was the official language of the Belgian Army at the time.

Today, Belgium produces over 1,100 varieties of beer and has more distinct types of beer per capita than anywhere else in the world. The biggest brewer in the world, ABInBev (Anheuser-Bush InBev which brews Stella-Artois) is headquartered in Leuven. Belgium is also home to the unique Trappist beers brewed by six monasteries. There are only two other monasteries in the world that brew and sell Authentic Trappist Product—one in the Netherlands and one in Austria. One of the more well known Trappist beers is the Chimay Brewery founded inside Scourmont Abbey in 1862 in the Belgian municipality of Chimay located in the Belgian province of Hainaut in French speaking Wallonia.

Chimay is about 35 miles south of Charleroi, the biggest city in the province and the second largest in Belgium after the capital city of Brussels. Located about eight miles west of Chimay is the municipality of Momignies in an area known as the Boot of Hainaut because it's a tongue of land jutting south into France. In fact, three quarters of Momignies' circumference is the French border. It has some woodland but is mainly farmland and composed of seven villages: Momignies, Macon, Monceau-Imbrechies, Macquenoise, Beauwelz, Forge-Phillipe, and Seloignes and several hamlets such as Cendron. It was here where the B-17 *Susan Ruth* crashed and where the eight surviving crewmen's destiny awaited them.

The Resistance

A Belgian lad, Albert Brouns, who lived at the ferme de la Distillerie (The Distillery Farm) in the village of Macquenoise just north of the French border saw the *Susan Ruth* coming down. He said, "It didn't explode but rather fell to pieces." The villagers on the ground reported that as the plane swirled down, the tail section broke off, followed by an engine. Both Ross Kahler and Louis Colwart were thrown free of the plane as it was coming down, and their bodies fell onto the snow covered ground.

Albert Brouns recalled, "It was a little after noon and I was going to fertilize the fields. The machine guns crackled. The clouds were so low that one could distinguish nothing. One only waited. And then a strong wind let loose from the sky, and I saw pieces of an airplane falling. I thought that we were lucky that the wind carried the debris beyond the farm. And then I saw a man falling, and I ran toward the spot. I touched the soldier (Ross Kahler) and he was dead."

While Brouns threw lumps of dirt on the parachute to prevent the wind from carrying away the body, other neighbors also came running. One of them searched Kahler's pockets and found a rosary, a photograph, and an identification bracelet. "That evening," Brouns said, "I regretted not getting a souvenir myself so I went to the house of the neighbor who had taken the objects and told him so. He opened a drawer and handed me a bracelet." After the crash, Mr. Brouns was inspired to join the Belgium resistance, White Brigade, but decided he had too much work on the farm to get involved.

Distillery Farm

Susan Ruth crashed at Macquenoise

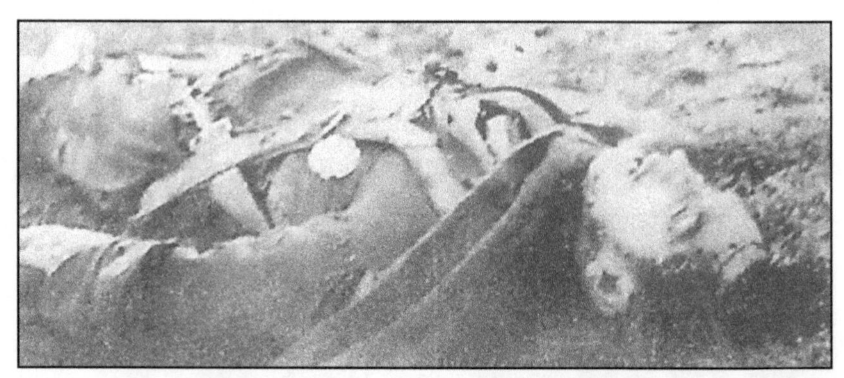

Bodies of Louis Colwart and Ross Kahler

Although Belgium was a neutral country, its strategic location as a pathway to France made it an invasion target for Germany in 1940. France and Britain sent soldiers to aid in the fight against the Germans, but despite their efforts, Belgian King Leopold III capitulated and asked the Germans for a suspension of arms to spare his people further bloodshed. The King was made a prisoner of war and the Belgian Cabinet (which had disassociated itself from his actions) set up a government in-exile in London and announced its resolve to continue the war and fight at the side of the Allies.

Albert Brouns

Thus began four years of German occupation for the Belgium people under which conditions were severe.

On December 12, 1941, the day after Hitler declared war on the U.S., he had issued the notorious *Nacht und Nebel* (night and fog) decree whereby enemies of the *Reich* in occupied countries would not be put to death but put to an endless night of silence, to make them vanish, never to be seen again. The procedure was to arrest people in the middle of the night and take them to prison or concentration camps hundreds of miles away as quickly as possible where they would be interrogated and tortured. There was no trail, no explanations, and nothing said. Relatives would never know where the person went, if they were alive or dead, and if they died where they were buried. As Hitler intended, the *Nacht und Nebel* decree intensified the terror throughout Europe, particularly in France, Holland, and Belgium.

After a period of depression and confusion, many Belgians began to rise up against the Nazis. During the occupation, their resistance spirit slowly developed and materialized into underground actions in conjunction with various military-related groups. Two main underground organizations emerged, the Secret Army in the north and the White Brigade in the south, both doing what they could to help their country. The White Brigade got their name because of the white butchers' coats they wore while "above ground." They hid people who refused to work in labor camps, hid downed Allied airmen trapped behind enemy lines and/or helped them to escape, and aided young men who wanted to join the Allied forces in England. Many escape networks were created to hide individuals who wanted to escape the hated Gestapo.

Collaborators and the SS

The Gestapo, an abbreviation of ***Ge****heime* ***Sta****ats****po****lizei* (meaning Secret State Police), was the official secret police of Nazi Germany and Nazi occupied Europe. Anyone living in Nazi controlled territory lived in fear of a visit from them. It was under the jurisdiction of Heinrich Himmler who headed up the *SS*, an abbreviation for

Schutzstaffel (meaning Protection Squadron). The *SS* originally began as a small guard unit known as the ***S**aal-**S**chutz* (Hall-Protection) to provide security for the Nazi political party. Later on it was renamed the ***S**chutz-**S**taffel* and eventually grew to more than one million men. It was responsible for the vast majority of Nazi war crimes.

In particular, the *SS* was the primary organization which carried out The Holocaust—from the Greek word *holókauston*, which referred to an animal sacrifice offered to a god in which the whole (*olos*) animal was completely burnt (*kaustos*). The term "Final Solution" was used by the Nazis to refer to their plan to eradicate the entire Jewish population. The Holocaust is used to define the Nazi's genocide of six million Jews, two-thirds of the total who resided in Europe before the war. However, the definition could be expanded to include the mass murders of Romanians, Soviet Union prisoners of war, Polish and Soviet civilians, handicapped, homosexuals, and other "undesirables" which would put the death toll up to around 20 million.

There were Belgians who collaborated with the Nazis and were a dangerous threat to anyone who did not cooperate with the Germans. Before the outbreak of World War II, Fascism was quite popular in Belgium, and there were pro-Nazi political organizations such as the *Vlaamsch Nationaal Verbond* (VNV) in Flanders and the *Rex* in Wallonia. Each of these movements had subtly different ideologies, their own paramilitary forces and printed their own newspapers. These organizations were also instrumental in encouraging Belgians to enlist into the German army.

A Catholic-fascist political party, the Rexists, was founded in 1930 by Léon Degrelle. It not only welcomed German occupation but assisted the Germans with their repression and anti-Semitic policies. Soon the Catholic Church denounced Rexism as a menace to society and branded Degrelle an extremist and Nazi sympathizer. Degrelle would later join the *Légion Wallonie* which was a German army unit manned by French speaking Walloons and later became the

"Wallonien" Division of the *Waffen SS*, meaning armed or weapons, which was the armed wing or military force of the *SS*. Degrelle became a full-fledged Nazi and poster child for Nazi collaboration and would later serve as the Division's commander.

The Rexist party ran across the country, but was most popular in the southern French-speaking area of Wallonia where the *Susan Ruth* crashed. Any downed flyer was to be turned over immediately. If anyone was discovered helping flyers, all the men were lined up and shot on the spot and the women sent to concentration camps. It is estimated that approximately five percent of the Belgian population was involved in resistance activity, putting the number of resistance members killed during the war to more than 19,000, roughly 25 percent of its "active" members.

The day after the *Susan Ruth* was shot down (February 9), a local priest was planning to perform last rites and a Requiem Mass before burying Kahler and Colwart, but when the villagers arrived at dawn for the funeral service, they found that the Germans had set up guards and sealed off the area. The Germans did this whenever an Allied bomber crashed so they could search the wreckage for any useful information. The Germans also went through the area rounding up civilians and interrogating them on the whereabouts of the other American airmen from the downed B-17.

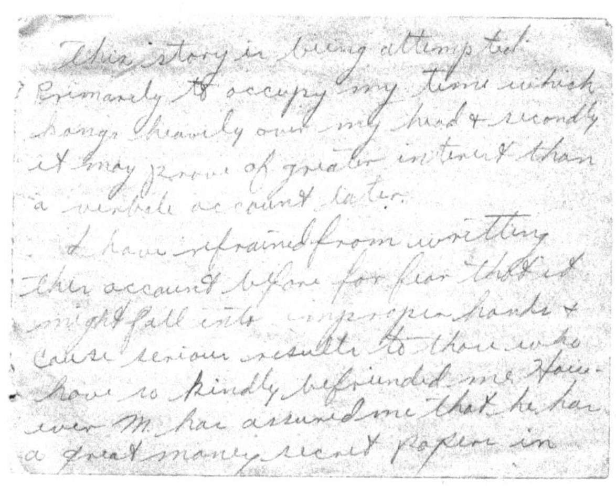

This story is being attempted
primarily to occupy my time which
hangs heavily over my head & secondly
it may prove of greater interest than
a verbal account later.
I have refrained from writing
this account before for fear that it
might fall into improper hands &
cause serious results to those who
have so kindly befriended me. However M. has assured me that he has
a great many secret papers in

Excerpt from Howard Snyder's diary

28

FATE OF THE CREW

At the German controlled clinic, they secretly sneaked Slenker through the back door where his leg was fluoroscoped and 20 mm shell fragments were found and removed from his leg, knee, and foot.

Bill Slenker

Staff Sergeant Bill Slenker had not actually bailed out of the plane but was thrown clear sometime after the tail broke off. He pulled the rip cord and landed safely, coming down south of Signy la Petite, France, near the village of Auge where he was rescued by members of the resistance. Slenker was taken to a home where he received first aid for the shrapnel wounds on his right leg and foot. However, his injuries were too severe, and he needed medical attention so a local doctor was called. The doctor said it appeared there was a shell imbedded in Slenker's foot, but even after probing, could not locate it and said Slenker needed to go to Dr. Tragaux's medical clinic in Chimay.

So that night, heavily armed members of the French resistance fighters known as the Maquis arrived in a truck to take Slenker across the border into Belgium to Dr. Trigaux's medical clinic which was controlled by the Germans.

Aided by British intelligence and encouraged and equipped by General Charles de Gaulle's Free French Army in London, the Maquis was a ragtag group of rough individuals that developed into a ruthless guerrilla army. They engaged in aggressively fighting the Germans by sabotaging railway lines, ambushing German troops and assassinating German officers.

While Slenker rode in the cab of the truck, ten Maquis members rode in the truck bed with pistols and rifles at the ready in case they ran into any Germans. One of the men had on a German soldier jacket that had a large bullet hole in the chest. At the German controlled clinic, they secretly sneaked Slenker through the back door where his leg was fluoroscoped and 20 mm shell fragments were found and removed from his leg, knee, and foot.

Slenker was then sneaked back out and driven to the home of Mrs. Josephine Collet who lived on Rue Van Humbeck #12 in Chimay by 37 year old Fernand Delporte who was the local chief of the *Front de l'Indépendance* (Independence Front) for the districts of Beaumont and Chimay. Delporte went by the codename of "Albert," and in his civilian life, he was a civil engineer and road superintendent. The Liberation Front was one of the many Belgian resistance movements which conducted sabotage operations, assisted escape routes, provided false documents, and distributed underground publications. It was highly active in preventing large numbers of Belgian men being made to leave the country to work as forced laborers in Germany.

Collet's Home at Rue Van Humbeck #12 in Chimay;
Fernand Delporte aka "Albert"

Joe Musial and Richard Daniels

Once Musial was out of the plane, he lost consciousness when his chute opened. When he recovered, he began to examine his painfully sore back with his hand, but he could find no evidence of blood. Suddenly, he became aware that a foot felt terribly cold and glanced down to see that it had been severed. Musial landed in a snowy field at La Neuville, Belgium, just north of the French border and his parachute dragged him up against a barbwire fence. Soon a farmer ran up and told him to follow him, but Musial knew if he tried to hide, he would bleed to death. With gestures, Musial had the farmer cut one of the parachute lines and together the two men fashioned a tourniquet.

Shortly after that, a German car drove up with two soldiers in it. They were there to take him prisoner, but realized the seriousness of Musial's condition so took him to the first house they came to in the village to seek medical assistance. Musial said, "They put me in the back of the car. It has no backseat, just straw on the floor. A young German soldier sat next to me. I was having one helluva time with what was left of my leg, trying to hold it out of the dirt and the soldier just reached over and took this 'piece of meat' and laid it across his lap. We had been told how horrible the Germans were, but human nature is pretty much the same."

Fanny Melament

Once at the house, a Russian woman doctor and member of the underground, Fanny Melament, was called and after a morphine injection, a tetanus shot, and new tourniquet was applied, Dr. Melament amputated more of his lower leg to make it a clean cut. The next morning when Musial awoke, an old man was standing in front of him dancing. He lifted the leg of his trousers to show Musial his artificial leg as a gesture of encouragement.

The Germans then took Musial to the medical clinic in Chimay, and on the way, they found a wounded Richard Daniels aimlessly walking alone. So both airmen were driven to the clinic for treatment where, at that very moment, Slenker was secretly receiving medical care. Daniels' arm was so severely damaged that Dr. Tragaux came close to amputating it. After Musial and Daniels were stabilized, they were then transferred to the *Luftwaffe* Hospital at Saint-Gilles Prison outside of Brussels and questioned.

Saint-Gilles Prison, Brussels, Belgium

"It was like a third rate movie," Musial said.

We were told in England what it would be like if we were interrogated, that the Germans would tell us they were going to shoot us if we didn't cooperate because no one knew we were prisoners anyway. You just didn't tell them anything and hoped the training people knew what they were talking about.

Roy Holbert

After Holbert finally broke free and escaped from the plane, he said,

> *When my parachute opened, I realized I had forgotten to fasten the other side to my harness. I did not have the strength to pull myself up to fasten it. It caused me to be pulled sideways, and I hit the ground on one leg injuring my knee and back and knocking me out. When I came to, a man with an axe over his shoulder tried to talk to me, but I did not understand him. I could not understand, or speak French. After he left, I crawled to a brush pile and hid my chute, then crawled away from it. The back of my flight suit was burned half way up the legs. About thirty minutes had passed before the Germans found me. They took me to a clinic or small hospital in Hirson, France.*

It was located about 10 miles west from where Holbert landed in France south of the Belgium border.

In the evening, a *Luftwaffe* pilot came to the clinic and said he was flying one of the FW-190s that had attacked 306th formation. Holbert said, "He shook hands with me and said he was sorry it had to be me but that was the game of war. He was only 19-years-old and spoke good English as he had been educated in New York." Holbert was told that the pilot who shot down the *Susan Ruth* was an "ace" which meant he had been credited with shooting down several enemy aircraft. After the war, the surviving members of the *Susan Ruth* joked they were glad at least they were shot down by a *Luftwaffe* "ace" and not some mediocre pilot. The ace of all fighter aces of all nations was German fighter pilot Erich Hartmann ("the Blond Knight") with 352 "kills!"

> *After several days and when my knee and back would allow me to hobble around, I was taken by closed truck for about a 30 minute ride and was shown the tail section of my plane. When*

the guard opened the curtain and asked me if that was my plane, I asked him what it was. My response made him mad and he slapped me across the ear with a cupped hand. I was returned to the clinic. After several more days of recovering at the clinic, I was moved by night to the Saint-Gilles Prison in Brussels. I spent two weeks in a room with nine other men sleeping on the concrete floor. Every morning we could hear gunshots coming from the direction of the courtyard. We assumed it was the executions of the day.

John Pindroch

After being thrown out of the plane by Joe Musial, John Pindroch pulled the ripcord on his chute, but it didn't open and so he frantically started tearing at it. He was greatly relieved when it finally did open, but the shroud lines and chute bag struck him in the face when the parachute unfurled. Evidently when Musial fastened the parachute to Pindroch's harness, he only fastened one of the two clips which allowed it to flip up. However, Pindroch was lucky his parachute even stayed on, and he didn't free fall to the ground. He landed in France at a place called "Croix Colas" northwest of the village of Signy-le-Petit, and was picked up by two members of the French underground.

Pindroch had suffered serious burns and shrapnel wounds to his leg so he was also smuggled into the medical clinic in Chimay where he received treatment. On February 10, the two underground members took him to the dairy farm of Georges and Nelly Collet Deshorme at Rue Trieu Godin #38 located halfway between Chimay and the village of St. Remy. Like other municipalities in Belgium, Chimay was comprised of several villages and hamlets which included St. Remy, Rièzes, Lompret, Vaulx, Bourlers, and Forges.

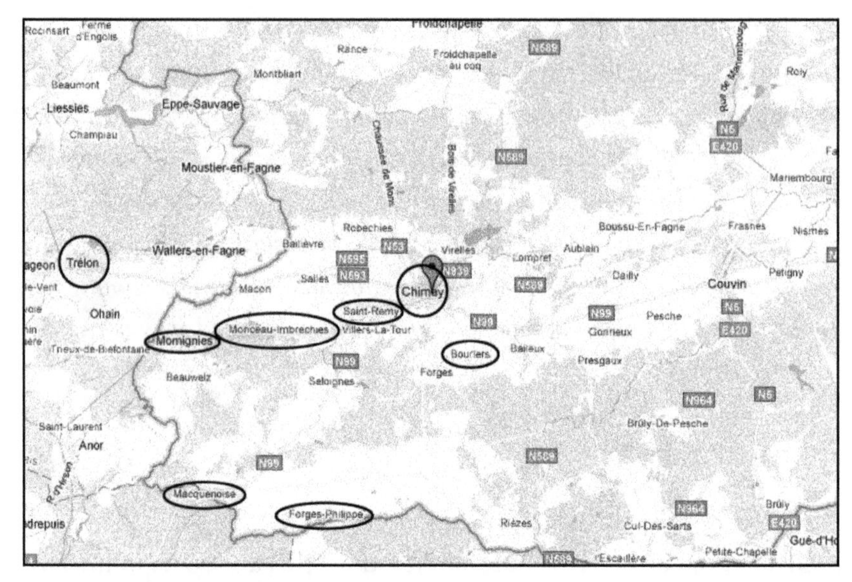

Map of Southern Belgium

Nelly Deshorme recalled,

On one day I saw three men coming up to our farm. The man in the middle seemed to be limping and was being helped by the other men. When they started talking, I understood that they were French. They asked me if we would agree to house this American airman whose leg had been badly injured. I got a bit upset at the time because they could have been German collaborators and were trying to set a trap. I asked them many questions to check if they were telling the truth, and they seemed to be all right.

Nelly continued,

I let them in and I saw something unbelievable; the men had tied a French flag around John's waist. What a terrible blunder! Had the Germans discovered this, it would have been the end of the war for all of them. We prepared a room upstairs for him and made a hole in the wall between his room and the hayloft in case he needed to escape in an emergency.

Georges Deshorme;
Deshorme Dairy Farm at Rue Trieu Godin #38 in Chimay

George Eike and Robert Benninger

George Eike and Robert Benninger also landed in the area south of Signy-le-Petit. Members of the resistance initially brought them across the border to Mrs. Collet's house in Chimay right after Slenker had been taken to the medical clinic. They were quickly moved from there to the Belgium village of Rièzes for a couple days where Eike stayed with Mr. Robert Bertrand and his aunt Martha Bertrand-Bultot, and Benninger stayed with sisters Valerie and Esther Fosset.

Eike and Benninger were then led to a camp set up by the resistance at Gros Fau, called "Camp de Rièzes," in the nearby woods south of the village. Gros Fau is a beech tree that grows in the French forest, about halfway between the villages of Rièzes and Beaulieu. The camp had been set up by two men from Chimay, Fabien Pierra, code name "Commandant Yvon," and Fernand Delporte, the so-called "Albert."

The camp had been established to house people who had escaped from German POW or labor camps; people who had received orders to work for the Germans; people wanted by the Gestapo; wounded resistance fighters; and downed Allied flyers. When Eike and Benninger arrived, the group consisted of about sixty men and was comprised of

Belgians, French, Algerian and Tunisian soldiers, and a mixture of Russians, Poles, and Yugoslavians.

Howard Snyder

Because Howard Snyder was the last man to bail out of the plane, he came down about 10 miles further west than the rest of the crew. When he landed in Macquenoise, Belgium, at around 1:30 in the afternoon, his parachute snagged in some trees, leaving him hanging some twenty feet above the ground. Two young Belgian farmers, Raymond Durvin and Henri Fraikin, saw Snyder coming down and ran to the area.

Seeing him dangling from the trees, they went to get a ladder and rope to rescue him. When they came back, they threw him the rope so he could tie it around his waist, and then Durvin pulled him over to one of the tree trunks from where Snyder was able to climb down the ladder to the ground. They told him to remain hidden where he was for the time being to avoid the German patrols and their dogs that were prowling the area hunting for him and the other members of his crew who had bailed out. It helped that there was snow on the ground; the German dogs had trouble tracking.

Trees where Howard Snyder's parachute was caught

Woods where Howard Snyder landed

Henri Fraikin;
Henri Fraikin next to tree from which Howard Snyder was freed

Under cover of darkness, Raymond Durvin came back that night. Snyder could not speak any French at that time, but communicated using gestures and the little French/English dictionary that was included in his escape kit (it also contained folding money of different European countries, first-aid kit, waterproof silk map, small compass, and a few rations).

After Durvin hid Snyder's parachute, he took him to his parents' farmhouse in Macquenoise just north of the French border. There,

Durvin's mother bandaged Sndyer's leg wounds caused by shrapnel from the fighter attack. He had also suffered burns from the fire in the plane, but they were not very serious.

House where Howard Snyder spent his first night

Battles between U.S. bombers and German fighters often took place above the French/Belgium border and attracted the attention of people on the ground from Couvin to Macquenoise. People would come out on their door steps to watch and sometimes machine gun bullets crashed to earth or a string of shell casings splattered on the tiles of their roofs.

Hector Marlair who was 22-years-old at the time, relates,

On the ground, the German machine gunners sprayed the men who were falling. I saw a flyer (Snyder) in a parachute not opening up. The wind made it deviate one or two kilometers, and he thus escaped the bullets. Then, miraculously the parachute was entangled in a tree! Raymond Durvin hurried forward and was able to pull the American from his uncomfortable position. He came out with his ankle a little injured and also had wounds on his leg.

At nightfall, I was called to serve as interpreter for the American. Not very sure of my English, I went there. Howard Snyder was stretched out on the bed in a basement room. I asked him if his ankle was causing him pain. He said no and very quickly unfolded a letter to show me that he was to go to Spain. While talking, I went to the window and saw Germans on bicycles circling around the house. 'You are a funny one!' I told him. 'The Germans are out looking for survivors and you expose yourself with all the lamps lit up!' We shut the drapes.

Because there were so many German patrols in the vicinity looking for the downed flyers and the Durvins were being watched closely by the German Gestapo, it was too dangerous for Snyder to stay there any longer than one night. Paul Tilquin, a customs officer and member of the underground, was called to move Snyder to a safer location in Chimay.

That night, Paul Tilquin came and took Snyder to his home nearby so Snyder could put on one of Paul's uniforms to wear as a disguise. Paul's wife, Nelly Bastien-Tilquin, later said she giggled when she saw Howard in it because he was so much taller than her husband and the trousers were way too short. "It was the uniform of a border patrolman, including a long khaki cape and the peculiar square pill box cap they wore," Howard remembered.

Paul and Howard then ventured out. Howard recalled,

It was a miserable night, cold, black as the ace of spades, and raining cats and dogs. We left riding a tandem bicycle which I could only pedal with my right leg as my left leg had been injured during the attack by the FW-190s. So I could only wait until the right pedal came around for me to step on it. We came to a hill, and since I could not pedal and Paul was unable to pedal both of us, we got off and started pushing. I used it as a crutch.

There was a tavern or café at the crest of the hill, and when we reached it, two German Luftwaffe officers, came out with their girlfriends who were laughing and giggling. When the tavern door opened, you could hear music and see people dancing inside. They were pretty looped and feeling no pain.

One of the officers came up to my side, put an arm around me and proceeded to jabber some drunken German asking for a light for their cigarettes. I was scared because I spoke no German or French and did not know what to do. Fortunately, Paul did. He gave them a light, the German let loose of me to light his cigarette. The German was real friendly and wanted to talk, being very gregarious because he was tight. Paul made up some excuse to get away, and we hurried on as quickly as we could. I thought it was kind of exciting. Perhaps these German pilots were even the ones who shot my plane down.

Eventually, they made their way to the home of Mr. Sohie, the bailiff of Chimay. The next day Germans came to the Durvin house to interrogate Raymond, but just before they arrived he received warning from a young 16-year-old girl named Mary Lou. Barefoot, he ran into the woods barely escaping being captured. In 1949, Raymond and Mary Lou would be married.

Paul Tilquin (both photos)

Paul Tilquin with his son and friend with tandem bicycle and road
Howard Snyder and Paul Tilquin rode on to Chimay

Mr. Sohie's House in Chimay where Howard Snyder
spent his second night

29

MISSING IN ACTION

"We women have to stick together in these trying hours.
I feel if we trust in God and pray earnestly enough,
our men will be brought back to us.

Bravery on the Home Front

It wasn't until February 23, 1944, when the wives and/or mothers of the crew received a Western Union telegram from the War Department that they found out about the *Susan Ruth* being shot down. Ruth Snyder's telegram read, "The Secretary of War desires me to express his deep regret that your husband First Lieutenant Howard J. Snyder has been reported missing in action since 8 February over France. If further details or other information are received you will be promptly notified. Major General J.A. Ulio Adjutant General." On February 25, a follow-up letter was received from Major General Ulio confirming the telegram. He went on to state that, "The term 'missing in action' is used only to indicate that the whereabouts or status of an individual is not immediately known. Experience has shown that many persons reported missing in action are subsequently reported as being prisoners of war."

Immediately, the families of the crew started writing letters to each other. In shock, they never thought this would/could happen to their "boys." Initially, they weren't even sure what crew members were flying together that day as it had seemed to vary a lot. However, they quickly found out that it was indeed Howard Snyder's entire crew.

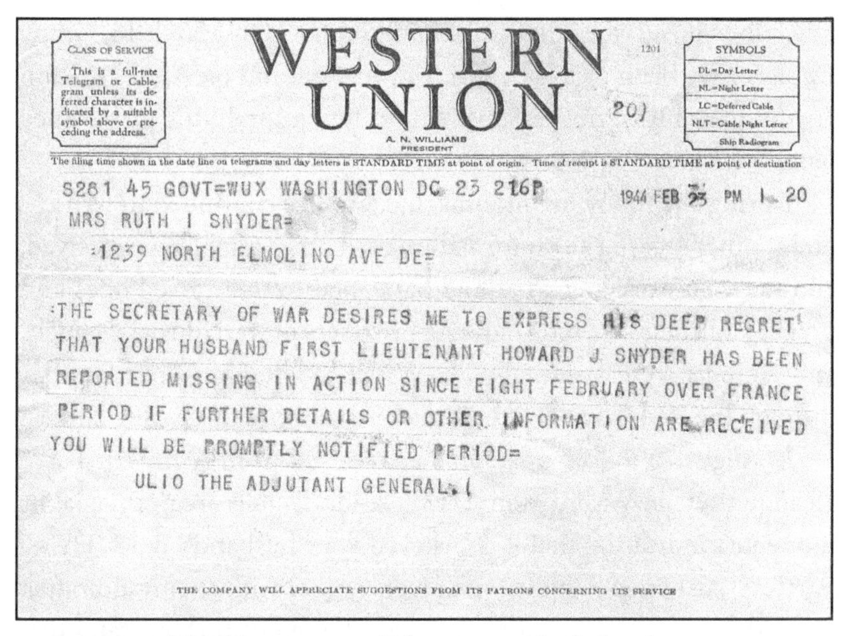
WESTERN UNION

CLASS OF SERVICE
This is a full-rate Telegram or Cablegram unless its deferred character is indicated by a suitable symbol above or preceding the address.

A. N. WILLIAMS
PRESIDENT

SYMBOLS
DL=Day Letter
NL=Night Letter
LC=Deferred Cable
NLT=Cable Night Letter
Ship Radiogram

The filing time shown in the date line on telegrams and day letters is STANDARD TIME at point of origin. Time of receipt is STANDARD TIME at point of destination

S281 45 GOVT=WUX WASHINGTON DC 23 216P 1944 FEB 23 PM 1 20
MRS RUTH I SNYDER=
1239 NORTH ELMOLINO AVE DE=

THE SECRETARY OF WAR DESIRES ME TO EXPRESS HIS DEEP REGRET THAT YOUR HUSBAND FIRST LIEUTENANT HOWARD J SNYDER HAS BEEN REPORTED MISSING IN ACTION SINCE EIGHT FEBRUARY OVER FRANCE PERIOD IF FURTHER DETAILS OR OTHER INFORMATION ARE RECEIVED YOU WILL BE PROMPTLY NOTIFIED PERIOD=
ULIO THE ADJUTANT GENERAL.

THE COMPANY WILL APPRECIATE SUGGESTIONS FROM ITS PATRONS CONCERNING ITS SERVICE

War Department Telegram to Ruth Snyder

On February 25, Richard Daniel's wife Ginny wrote to Ruth Snyder, "Although it's a dreadful shock, I have high hopes and trust in God I will receive good news." George Eike's wife, Helen, wrote on the 28th, "I don't have to tell you what a shock all this has been. I felt that it would never happen to us. It's going to be hard to sit here and wait for news, but we've got to be as brave as our husbands are and have faith and trust in them and God. Oh Ruth, I feel so terrible when I think of the long days ahead. They'll come back to us."

On March 4, Louis Colwart's mother wrote, "I can't sleep or eat thinking of those poor boys. I called them my boys and I'd always told Louis to tell my boys hello, and that I'd pray for them, especially the pilot because he had a big job to do." On March 12, Roy Holbert's mother wrote, "We women have to stick together in these trying hours. I feel if we trust in God and pray earnestly enough our men will be brought back to us. I say men for although they may have been boys when they left, they will be men when they return. I have three other sons in service. That's all I have to give." On March 14, Ginny Daniels gave birth to a baby girl, Donna Rae, and on April 28, Ruth Snyder gave birth, not to Steve, but to her second little girl, Nancy Jane.

During the following months, the families continued to write to one another seeking any information each other might have received, all the while worrying what had happened to their loved ones and praying for their safe return. Being prisoners of war, Musial, Daniels, and Holbert were eventually able to write letters to their families through the Red Cross so it became known those three were alive.

In August, a follow-up letter was received from Army Air Force Headquarters in Washington, D.C. It read, "Details are not available, the report indicating that it is believed your husband's B-17 (Flying Fortress) sustained damage with an encounter with enemy aircraft at approximately 12:35 p.m. over France. The report further states that parachutes were used, but the exact numbers are unknown." Attached was a list of those who were in the plane and the names and addresses of their next of kin.

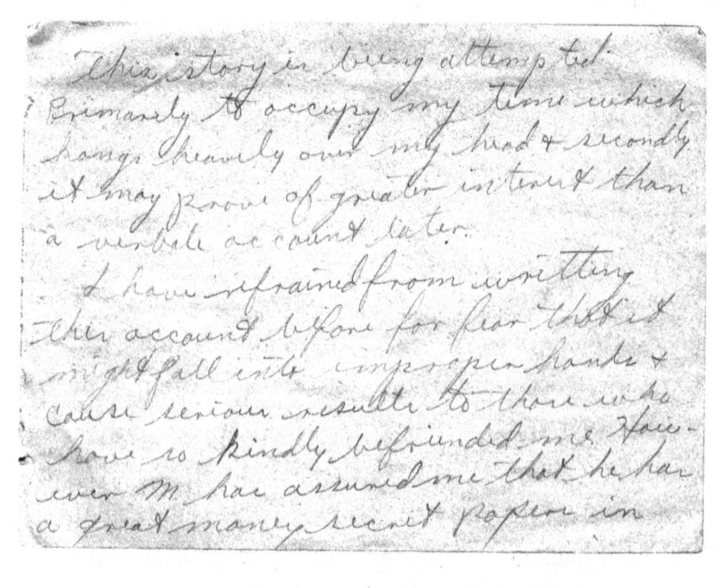
This story is being attempted
Primarily to occupy my time which
hangs heavily over my head & secondly
it may prove of greater interest than
a verbal account later.
I have refrained from writing
this account before for fear that it
might fall into improper hands &
cause serious results to those who
have so kindly befriended me. However M. has assured me that he has
a great many secret papers in

Excerpt from Howard Snyder's diary

30

CHIMAY ... THE RESISTANCE

Many members of the escape routes were betrayed and hundreds were arrested or shot. If arrested, they were interrogated and tortured, then either executed or deported to German prisons or concentration camps which usually meant death.

The Freedom Trail

Shortly after Eike and Benninger arrived at "Camp de Rièzes," they were joined by five other airmen from the 306th Bomb Group. From 368th Squadron's Rationed Passion were navigator Ivan Gaze, radio operator Charles Nichols, waist gunner John Gemborski, tail gunner Warren Cole, and flight engineer Orian Owens who had been shot down a month earlier over the Netherlands on the infamous January 11 raid to Halberstadt. Their plane had crashed at the village of Nijverdalseberg, near Nijverdal. Pilot Bill Reed, bombardier Myron Dmochowski, and ball turret gunner Joe O'Connell had also bailed out safely but were captured and taken prisoner.

The five who showed up at Camp de Rièzes were able to evade capture with the help of the Dutch resistance who helped the flyers make their way to Belgium. There, all the airmen waited for arrangements to be made by the underground to get them out of occupied Europe through Spain and back to England.

The five U.S. airmen were hoping that their time in Belgium would be temporary, and that they would soon be able to return to England through several secret escape routes over the central Pyrenees known as *Le Chemin de la Liberté* (The Freedom Trail). Resistance groups in the Netherlands, Belgium, and France helped downed American flyers return to Britain. Airmen who evaded capture by the Germans were hidden in attics and cellars, fed, clothed and given false identity papers. A network of people, mostly ordinary citizens, then guided them south through Nazi occupied France over the Pyrenees into fascist, but officially neutral Spain at San Sebastián, and then home via British-controlled Gibraltar. Many members of the escape routes were betrayed and hundreds were arrested or shot. If arrested, they were interrogated and tortured, then either executed or deported to German prisons or concentration camps which usually meant death.

The "Comet Line" (*Le Réseau Comète*), founded by Andrée de Jongh (nickname Dédée), was the most famous, but not the only line of escape, stretching for 1,200 miles. The work of running such a line needed a vast number of operatives (around 2,000) who had to take care of shelter, food, clothing, false papers and guides. Even though it was known as a safe escape line, transporting more than 700 Allied military personnel during the war, the "Comet Line" was fraught with danger and still very susceptible to infiltration or German counterespionage. No less than 800 of the operatives of Comet Line were arrested and at least 155 of them were executed or perished in German camps.

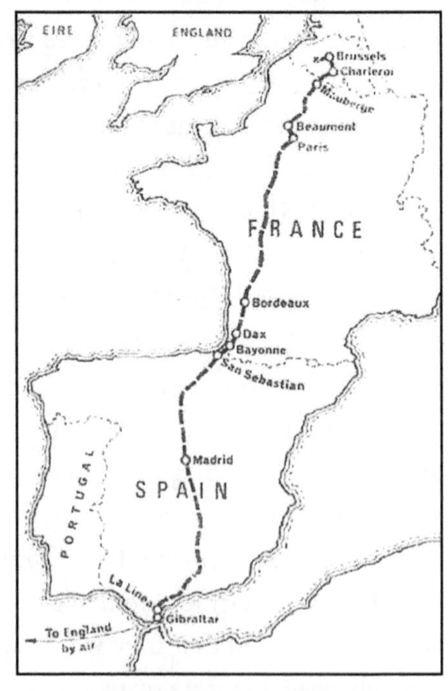

Pyrenees Escape Route

Andrée personally escorted 118 airmen over the Pyrenees herself, and was arrested in 1943 during her 33rd journey to Spain. Only 26-years-old, she was interrogated and tortured by the *Gestapo* and admitted that she was the organizer of the escape network. However, the *Gestapo* didn't believe she was capable of such an undertaking and let her live.

Getting captured or shot going over the Pyrenees was not the only danger involved. The journey, usually under cover of darkness, was grueling and exhausting as they had to cross forests and rivers, scale massive granite boulders, and climb higher and higher into the cold and snow of the mountains. Most of the men fleeing from the Germans were exhausted and weak from lack of food. Some were injured and had received little or no medical help. They were without any climbing clothes, boots, or gear; they only had the clothes and shoes they wore.

Camp de Rièzes

Camp de Rièzes was camouflaged and well hidden in the forest. It had three log barracks covered with grass and ferns and was relatively comfortable and well equipped. They had a kitchen, electricity, telephone connections, a radio, and transmitter/receiver. Security outposts connected by field telephones provided protection.

Camp de Rièzes

Supplies for the camp were first gathered at the small village of Vaulx-lez Chimay where they were hidden in a small barn on the farm of Julien Jacquart. From there, the supplies would be brought to the Chimay railroad station and secretly loaded onto a narrow gauge train which would take them to the village of Rièzes, about 10 miles away. A young farmer, André Mairiaux, code name Constant, would then bring the supplies by wagon to the camp. Even though the camp received these supplies, food was still scarce—mainly, bread filled with sawdust as flour was hard to come by. The rough men at the camp would eat their food in the barracks and not clean up which resulted in their living quarters being infested with rats. Initially this was deplorable to the Americans, but they eventually learned to get used to it.

At daybreak on February 25, the entire area around Rièzes was surrounded by three thousand Germans; very likely it was a result of information supplied by Belgian collaborators. Referred to as the "Rafle de Rièzes" or "The Rièzes Raid," the Germans thoroughly searched every house in the villages, and twenty-nine people were imprisoned. Even though being in the resistance had a high price, the people of Rièzes were just one example of how ordinary citizens fought against the atrocities the Nazis committed against them. The Fosset sisters were arrested by the *Gestapo* and sent to Ravensbrück, the notorious women's concentration camp in northern Germany. They would not to return home until May 8, 1945.

Loading supplies at the Chimay railway station for Camp de Rièzes

Located about 45 miles north of Berlin, Ravensbrück was Germany's largest women's concentration camp, and from 1939 to 1945, approximately 132,000 women from 47 countries were imprisoned there. More than half were executed or died from malnutrition, sickness, exhaustion from heavy labor, or from the after effects of medical experiments. One of the most famous survivors of Ravensbrück was Christian author and speaker Corrie ten Boom who was arrested along with her family for harboring Jews in their home in Haarlem, The Netherlands. The ordeal of Corrie and her sister Betsie is documented in her book *The Hiding Place* which was eventually made into a motion picture.

One of the German patrols searching the area was spotted by André Mairiaux who ran to warn the men at the camp, but he was shot at and wounded by the Germans before he could do so. However, the camp was alerted by the sound of the gunfire, and the men all fled in different directions. The American flyers were taken to a small wooden cabin in the Bois de Pleumont (Pleumont woods) where they stayed hidden in freezing conditions without food or water for two days.

Cabin in the Bois de Pleumont (Pleumont Woods)

Life with the Resistance

They were startled late at night when they heard someone call out to them in English. When the men came out to see who was there, they were greatly surprised to be greeted by another U.S. airman, Billy Huish, who was accompanied by a farmer, Florent Simon, who lived in the area at Rue du Fourneau #96 in St. Remy, Chimay. Huish was the navigator on the B-17 Skunkface of the 91st Bomb Group that had been shot down just a few days earlier on February 20. They were on a raid to Leipzig, Germany, when their ship was shot down and crashed near the Belgian villages of Vaudignies and Chièvres. Huish had bailed out and been taken prisoner by the Germans, but he managed to escape and be taken in by the underground.

Fearing that the Americans would be found by the Germans, 54-year-old Florent Simon walked them through the snow to an abandoned and broken down old shed (called Baraque Bébert or Bebert's Shack) in the woods a little east of the Terne des Vaches (Hill of the Cows), south of the village of St. Remy. It was just an old, one room building 15' by 18' that had no windows, no cooking facilities, and just two beds. Their food was prepared by Simon's wife, Jeanne Humblet Simon, and brought to them. With a stream nearby, they had plenty of water, but they didn't know that it ran through another farm upstream and was polluted from the animals. They all became ill with dysentery which along with the cramped living quarters and ice-cold temperatures made life there pretty miserable.

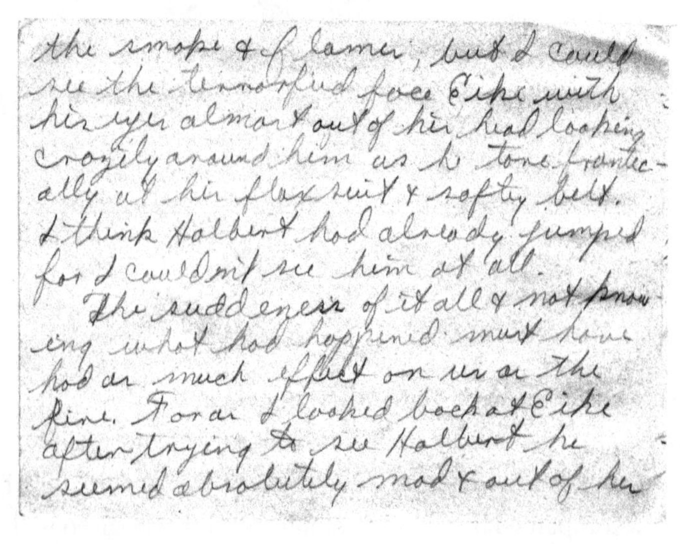
the smoke & flames, but I could
see the terrorfied face Eike with
his eyes almost out of his head looking
crazily around him as he tore frantically at his flax suit & safety belt.
I think Halbert had already jumped
for I couldn't see him at all.
The suddeness of it all & not knowing what had happened must have
had as much effect on us as the
fire. For as I looked back at Eike
after trying to see Halbert he
seemed absolutely mad & out of his

Excerpt from Howard Snyder's diary

31

SHELTER

It was on March 25 that John Pindroch and another downed American flyer, Vincent Reese, who was also being hidden in Chimay, decided to join up with the Americans hiding in Le Bois de la Champagne (The Champagne Woods).

The Hut at Champagne Woods

After a week or two, Florent Simon decided to build a new hut for them in the Bois de la Champagne (Champagne Woods) just east of the St. Remy woods. With the help of Fernand Fontaine, and the aid of the American flyers, a larger structure was finished around March 10. It was made of logs and branches and half buried in the ground so that its roof touched the ground on two sides. The inside dimensions were 10 feet in width and about 25-30 feet in length with one door facing south. Along the east wall was a long bed made of straw and in the middle was a large wooden table. Both were big enough to easily accommodate all the men.

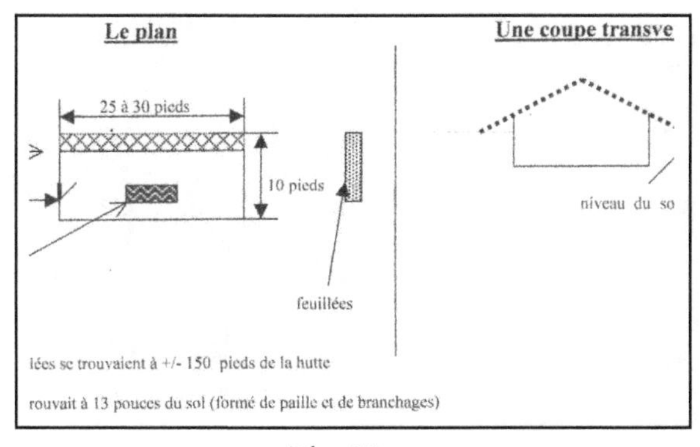

The Hut

Fernand Fontaine was 56 and had fought in World War I and suffered from respiratory problems caused by exposure to Mustard Gas. His disability made it necessary for him to work outdoors in fresh air so he worked jobs as both a forestry worker and a gamekeeper. He and his family lived in a modest house on Rue les Haies at the edge of the forest in Haies de St. Remy about a 30 minute walk to the hut. His wife, Maria Prince Fontaine, prepared food for the Americans and washed their clothes.

Fernand's 24-year-old son, Henri, was the courier for these items and spent a lot of time with the airmen. Henri had received a compulsory notice to work in a German labor camp so he had to stay out of sight and carried a pistol in case of trouble. Occasionally, Henri would take one of the men to his parent's home to spend the night. There a good meal, a hot bath, and a comfortable bed were very much appreciated. Maria was an exceptional cook with her specialty being a delicious *Pot-eu-fau* (French beef stew).

Back at the Deshorme's farmhouse, Georges and Nelly did their best to make Pindroch feel at home. They ate meals together, and

The Simon Family

Jeanne (Humblet) and Florent Simon (inset photo); the Simon Farm

Fernand Fontaine; Henri Fontaine

Nelly often played chess or cards with him to "kill time." Unfortunately, Pindroch's leg continued to bother him and he became quite depressed; he longed to escape and return to England. Feeling cooped up and isolated, he became nervous and angry. Poor Nelly was at a loss to please him.

Once or twice a week, Fanny Melament, the Russian doctor, would ride a bicycle to the farm and care for Pindroch's injured leg.

The first time she did so, the doctor leaned her bike up against the house facing the road when she arrived. While the doctor was treating Pindroch's leg, Nelly glanced outside and nearly fainted at what she saw. Tied to the bike was a French rifle! Anyone passing by could have seen it. Nelly couldn't believe how careless the doctor had been, and didn't even want to think about what the Germans would have done! From then on, she had the doctor always put the bike inside the stable.

Nelly would wash Pindroch's clothes with theirs. She was hanging the laundry on the clothes line one day when her neighbor commented about Nelly having so many clothes for only two people. Wittily she answered, "You know on a farm, clothes get dirty very fast."

Although the Deshormes were quiet people, they were brave members of the underground and the Belgian resistance effort. During the night, Nelly and Georges would nail anti-Nazi posters and fliers on utility poles. Although the German occupation was a time of deprivation, generous farmers in the resistance network would donate food that Georges would collect and take to the Americans hiding in the hut. Like many other Belgian patriots, the Deshormes took great risks and had to be extremely careful. In their particular case, there was a collaborator that lived just west of their dairy farm who would surely have turned them in to the *Gestapo* if he "saw anything" or obtained any evidence of their "crimes."

While Pindroch was being hidden by the Deshormes on the west side of Chimay; Slenker was being hidden by the Collets on the east side. After awhile, the two *Susan Ruth* crew members began writing messages to each other which were carried back and forth by the Deshormes and other members of the underground. Once again, it was a risky undertaking. If stopped and frisked by the *Gestapo*, a messenger carrying letters written in English would have been immediately arrested and tortured for information.

After exchanging letters for awhile, Pindroch wanted to go see Slenker, but the Deshormes said it was impossible. It was way too dangerous. Slenker was on the other side of Chimay, and the town was swarming with German soldiers, *Gestapo* agents, and collaborators. Pindroch didn't speak French, and if asked for his papers, that would be it! With his injured leg, he was still limping so not only would it be difficult to walk, but he would be easily spotted.

For awhile Pindroch listened to them, but he became more and more nervous and anxious. Eventually, he insisted on seeing his friend, and the Deshormes gave in. Although the Deshormes were scared to death, they started out at night holding up Pindroch between them. On their way, they ran into a German convoy and weren't sure what to do. They were afraid that if they turned around that the Germans would become suspicious so they tried their best to act normal and to their great relief made it safely past. After reaching the Collets, Pindroch and Slenker were ecstatic to see each other and be reunited. Not only were they fellow crew members, but they were also best of friends. Pindroch and Deshormes made it back to their farm without any incident.

The three of them made one more trip together to the Collet's house. During that visit, Pindroch and Slenker discussed some escape options but couldn't come to any decisions on what to do. Thereafter, the Deshormes thought these sojourns were just too dangerous and refused to make anymore, much to Pindroch's chagrin.

It was on March 25 that John Pindroch and another downed American flyer, Vincent Reese, who was also being hidden in Chimay, decided to join up with the now eight Americans hiding in *Le Bois de la Champagne* (The Champagne Woods). Reese had been a waist gunner on the B-17 *Women's Home Companion* of the 303rd Bomb Group which was shot down on the December 30, 1943, raid to Ludwigshaven and the I.G. Farbenindustrie chemical works. His plane crash landed in a field at Cerfontaine, Belgium, near the Luxembourg-French-Belgian border.

Vincent Reese evaded capture and was helped by the underground, in particular Julien Lehouck, the major of the village of Senzeilles, who connected him with members of the resistance. A short time later,

Julien Lehouck was arrested by the Nazis so his wife had Reese come stay at her chateau at Senzeilles in the municipality of Cerfontaine. After that, Reese went to the home of Maurice Van Cantfort

at Vellers-Deaux-Eglies in Cerfontaine for awhile and eventually was taken to Chimay, about 12 miles south, where he was hidden. Julien Lehouck would eventually be executed by hanging at Breendonck prison located near Antwerp, Belgium. Mrs. Lehouck and her son were deported to the German concentration camp at Bautzen. It is believed that Mrs. Lehouck survived the war, but that her son died in the camp.

Although Pindroch and Reese were being safely hidden by members of the Belgian underground, they wanted to join up with their fellow airmen so they would all be together when it came time to escape for Spain. By this time, Nelly Deshorme had grown very fond of John Pindroch, calling him "her John," and came to view him as her younger brother. She was very sad about him leaving, and she and her husband, Georges, tried to dissuade him but to no avail. William Slenker though continued to stay in Chimay with Josephine Collet and her two daughters, Gisèle (27) and Paula (20), although he kept in contact with the other men through messages passed by the underground.

Josephine Collet; Gisèle Collet, William Slenker, and Paula Collet

Now there were ten Americans hiding in the woods biding their time. They mostly talked about home and their loved ones who didn't know if they were alive or dead; only that they were "missing in action." Living in such close quarters combined with boredom, inactivity, constant danger, uncomfortable conditions, and inadequate food created definite tension between the men.

Compounding all this was the fact that they were different ages, came from different backgrounds, and had different religious views. At 36, Vincent Reese from Philadelphia, Pennsylvania, was by far the oldest of the group, with John Pindroch the youngest at age 19. Both were devout Catholics, and they had heated discussions with Billy Huish, a 25-year-old Mormon from Douglas, Arizona. Ivan Glaze was 26, from Indianapolis, Indiana; John Gemborski 24, from Chicago, Illinois; Orian Owens 29, from Lisbon, Iowa; Charles Nichols 28, from Stockton, California; and Warren Cole 22, from Illinois. Eike, Glaze, and Gemborski were married and the rest were single.

The Americans were getting very antsy about trying to return to England. Warren Cole and Ivan Gaze felt there was little chance of moving such a large group of men through an escape route so they decided not to wait any longer for the underground's help and headed out on their own in early April. After they left, Henri Fontaine moved into the hut which was actually safer than staying at his parents' house.

From then on, Florent Simon would most often bring them meals prepared by his wife, Jeanne Humblet Simon, who also cleaned their clothes. The overall distance from Simon's farm to the hut was about a mile and a half. Florent Simon would travel up a steep grade on the *Chemin du Terne des Vaches* (Hill of the Cows Road), turn off on a path for about 300 yards, and then make his way through the forest another 60 yards or so to the hut. Due to the risks involved traveling to and from the hut, Florent would often spend one or two nights there to break up the repetitiveness of the trips.

He would hang two jugs on the back of his bike and pretend he was going to milk his cows in the meadow located about halfway up the hill. He had to take a lot of precautions in case he was being watched and faced a big problem. When he left his farmhouse, the jugs were heavy with food when they should have been empty and light. Then on his way back from the hut when the jugs should have been heavy with milk, they were very light with only clothes to be washed. His solution was to act like it was easy pedaling up the hill, and on the way back down he did the opposite. He pretended he was trying to hold on to the supposedly heavy jugs, and he skidded his boots along the ground to look like he was trying to keep the bike from going too fast.

Hill of the Cows Road (*Chemin du Terne des Vaches*) on way to the Hut

Pathway to the Hut off the Hill of Cows Road

Although the U.S. airmen wanted to get back to England, the underground was having difficulties arranging their escape out of Belgium. Life at the hideout had become tedious and routine, and the men started feeling pretty safe. They began accompanying Florent to and from the Fontaine's house, and people living in the area could see them coming and going. Gradually, more and more people in the villages of St. Remy and Chimay became aware of the Americans' presence.

Fontaine Home

As the days passed, the men had grown more and more impatient about staying any longer in the cramped and cold confines of the hut. Even though Maria Fontaine, Nelly Deshorme, and Jeanne Simon cooked for them, having adequate food was a constant problem. Trying to feed ten young men would have been a chore in the best of times. Coupled with the scarcity of food during the German occupation and the logistics of getting food to the hut, it was a major ordeal. The men wanted to get back to England and began discussing the possibility of leaving on their own in pairs like Ivan Glaze and Warren Cole did.

To prepare for their escape, all of the airmen dressed in civilian clothing except for Eike and Benninger who still wore their khaki shirts and pants. Eike also wore his leather flyer's jacket. They also had been provided with false identity papers, but still wore their dog tags which identified them as military personnel. Actually, Vincent Reese had left his dog tags with Maurice Van Cantfort and was wearing ones he had carved out of wood. None of the men were armed, but two rifles and a pistol were in the hut that had been brought by the Simons. The time for their escape was getting closer, and on April 20 Fernand "Albert" Delporte came by to give each man 1,000 francs for their journey.

John Pindroch sent a note to Bill Slenker asking him to be his partner when they left for Spain. In turn, Josephine Collet and her daughters did their best to dissuade Slenker. They knew it was too dangerous for the Americans to try and escape on their own without the help of the underground. However, Slenker was getting more and more nervous about staying because so many of the local people knew about him; so much so, that he was actually becoming something of a celebrity.

With the chances of him being betrayed increasing, Slenker not only feared for his safety but for the safety of the Collets as well. However, a major obstacle that stood in the way was that he was still recovering from the shrapnel wounds to his knee and ankle and wasn't fit enough to make such an arduous trip of 1,200 plus miles over the Pyrenees. Because of this fact, and the Collets' insistence that it was far too perilous, Slenker decided to stay. He made his decision on the evening of April 21, and it was a decision that would save his life.

out of a cloud, the earth appeared for
a second & then disappeared again
as I reached another cloud.
I was falling in the country, there
were little clusters of white farm
buildings, green squares of pasture
& dark brown irregular & leafless
woods.
Then as the earth appeared again
I waited until I could distinguish
objects very clearly & pulled the
rip cord.
It was only natural to wonder if
the chute would open. I knew soon

Excerpt from Howard Snyder's diary

32

A TRAITOR AND CAPTURE

While standing there, Minet glanced over at the trucks and saw Joseph Simon in one, his face bloodied, and realized the worst had happened; the Americans had been discovered.

Betrayal

Unbeknownst to everyone was a meeting that took place on April 19 at police headquarters in Charleroi led by a Belgian traitor, Charles Lambinon from Brussels, who was chief of the Belgian *Service de Securite et d'information* (SI), a Rexist organization similar to the *Gestapo*. Also in attendance were Jacques Derby, chief of the SI unit in Charleroi known as the Police Merlot, and three German officers. Based on information from an informant, they made plans to surround and capture the group of American flyers and the people who were helping them; all of whom the Germans considered "terrorists."

The morning of Saturday, April 22, at 5:00 a.m., Fernand "Albert" Delporte was woken from a peaceful sleep by the rumbling of trucks. As he looked out the window and saw trucks full of soldiers coming down the road from Charleroi, he knew immediately what it meant and rushed to the telephone to warn members of the Resistance. The lines were dead; the Germans had cut them. He said, "Ordinarily if the Germans or Belgium *SS* were to make a raid in the area, I would know about it, but this raid was very secret and I believe it was a result of a denunciation by somebody in St. Remy who knew that the American flyers were in the woods at St. Remy." For his own safety, Delporte hid the rest of the day.

Chimay Intersection

The entire area around the town of Chimay (including its villages such as Bourlers, Rièzes, and St. Remy) was completely surrounded by Lambinon's combined forces of about 1,500 men. There were SI units from Brussels, Charleroi, and Mons, the 3rd Company of the *Garde Wallonne* (Walloon Guards) which was the Rexist Party security/police force based in Mons commanded by Captain Marcel Jaye, a Rexist Brigade Z which was a unit of collaborationist thugs, the German *Gestapo*, the German *feldgendarmerie* (military police) lead by Leon Bertand, and two companies of Russian soldiers fighting for the Nazis. The Russian troops were part of Soviet General Andrey Vlasov's Russian Liberation Army which had defected to the Nazi's in July 1942, after being defeated and captured at Leningrad.

Although the convoy of trucks passed by the homes of Fernand Delporte and the Collets, many other resistance members were not so fortunate and were arrested. At around 7:00 a.m., some of the trucks stopped at the Simon farm while others continued to destinations up the Hill of the Cows Road. While Florent's wife Jeanne and 22-year-old son Joseph were eating breakfast, hundreds of heavily armed German soldiers and Belgian *SS* jumped out and surrounded the farm. Jeanne Simon testified, "My son Joseph opened the door and the Germans rushed in, put my son in the kitchen with his face against the wall and hands over his head and searched the entire house and cellar. They found quite a bit of food and civilian clothing and they took everything."

Joseph Simon

The Germans interrogated the pair about the supplies and about a pistol clip and a note with English writing on it that was in Joseph's coat. Joseph was shoved in the back of a truck with other civilians who had been arrested to be taken to the *Ecole Communale de Chimay* (school house) where the Germans had set up their headquarters.

The entire scene was witnessed by 19-year-old Roger Motquin who was studying to be a doctor and had come home from medical school because he was ill. His father operated the pumping station across the road from the Simon farm that supplied the city of Chimay with drinking water from the White Water (Eau Blanche) River. He was in bed in the upstairs living quarters of the station and was looking out the window when some of the Vlasov Russian troops rushed into the station to search it. To their surprise, Roger Motquin's father started speaking to them in Russian which he had learned during World War I when he was in a German prisoner of war camp with some Russian soldiers.

Hearing their native tongue, they stopped their search and sat down with the father who then made them breakfast. Talking and laughing, the Russians forgot all about their mission and left wishing senior Motquin a pleasant afternoon. This was very fortunate for if the Russians had continued their search, they would have found a stash of weapons that Motquin, being a skilled mechanic, regularly repaired for the resistance.

German Convoy arrived from bottom of picture.
Pumping station, with Simon farm behind it, is on left.
Bridge over White Water River is on right.

At the hut, the airmen along with Florent Simon and Henri Fontaine had risen around 6:00 a.m. Billy Huish and Henri Fontaine then walked to the Fontaine's house to get some soup for breakfast and returned between 7:00 and 7:30. After eating around 8:00, Florent walked to the latrine which was about 100 yards from the cabin. Just as he was starting to head back, he heard Germans yelling followed by automatic gunfire. He testified, "I started to go back to the camp when someone shot at me. I hid behind a tree and then escaped into the woods. While in the woods I heard explosions of grenades." He knew that someone had betrayed them and feared that all the Americans were being shot.

Knowing it would be suicidal to go to his farm and scared for his life, Florent Simon fled deeper into the woods. Running frantically, he ran out of his clogs and continued barefoot until he came to a road where he saw Joseph Bernard riding a bicycle. Seeing Simon was barefoot, Bernard let him ride the bike and ran alongside him to the home of Bernard's brother-in-law, Fernand Malacord.

Simon stayed there the rest of the day and that evening his daughter, Fernande Simon Buet, came and told him that his wife and son had been arrested. His daughter also brought him some money. Although Simon did not know it at the time, the eight Americans and Henri Fontaine had not been killed, but captured. After two days, Florent fled to Fourmies, France, where he found refuge with a Maquis unit until France and Belgium were liberated by U.S. troops at the end of August and beginning of September.

Road taken by Florent Simon and Joseph Bernard

Fernande (Simon) Buet; Fernand Malacord home

Fernande's husband, Jules Buet, had narrowly escaped being captured on the morning the 22nd. As usual, he was riding his bike to the Simon farmhouse before going to work. He didn't see the German troops until he rounded a corner and rode right into the swarm of heavily armed soldiers. Realizing what was happening and that there was nothing he could do about it, Buet just kept on riding as if nothing was the matter and continued on to the center of town where his brother lived. The Germans did not know he was Florent Simon's son-in-law so they paid no attention to him.

Naturally, Buet was worried sick about what would happen to his wife. Fortunately, Fernande had not been arrested by the Germans and she was allowed to stay at the Simon farm where she was later joined by her brother Joseph's fiancée, Claire Fontaine (no relation to the Fontaine family). Jules Buet, suspecting that the Germans only did this to set a trap to capture more partisans, decided it was too risky to join them and went to stay with a friend, Mr. Casselin, until September 3 after the area was liberated.

Claire and Joseph Simon; Jules Buet

While all this was happening, other trucks in the convoy had gone to the farm of another resistance member, Albert Minet, which was located off the Hill of the Cows Road. Albert lived there with his wife, Léopoldine Clercx, and his two daughters, the oldest being 14-year-old Henriette. As German and SS troops started to surround the farm, the Minets became panic stricken and quickly tried to hide guns and ammunition in the hayloft. Once the troops reached the farm, the Minets were herded outside and watched in terror while all the farm buildings were systemically and brutally searched. While standing there, Minet glanced over at the trucks and saw Joseph Simon in one, his face bloodied, and realized the worst had happened; the Americans had been discovered. Minet was arrested and put in a truck with other prisoners and taken to the school house.

Albert Minet; Minet Farm

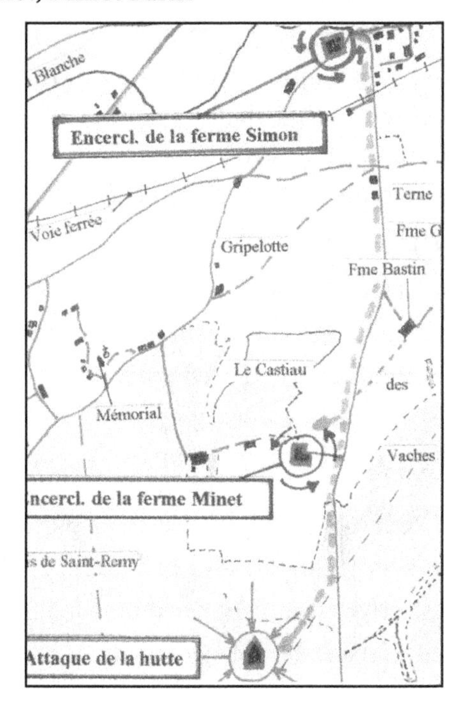

German convoy route down The Hill of the Cows Road - Simon Farm at top, Minet Farm below and the Hut at bottom

About an hour after Huish and Henri had left the Fontaine's house, Fernand Fontaine came out of his house and saw about 300 to 400 Germans starting to surround the woods. He said, "I thought that they were on maneuvers but I left to go to the hut to warn my son and the flyers that the Germans were coming. The woods are about 500 hectares (over 1,200 acres). I got to within 50 meters of the hut when I saw some Belgium SS men throw hand grenades into it."

However, the flyers were no longer there as they had already been taken prisoner. He continued saying, "Just then somebody fired two shots at me; I started to run away but was taken prisoner by a German officer. I was asked for my papers which I showed them but was held by the Germans until 12:30 in the afternoon."

After Fernand was released, he went home and stayed there the rest of the day. The next day, he and his brother Alphones went back to the hut to see what had happened, but they could not get close because it was being guarded by Wallones guards and SS men. All they could see was that it was burning. It wasn't until three or four more days that they were able to reach the hut. They examined the area for blood or graves to indicate if any of the men had been wounded or killed, but didn't find any. All they found were some bullet holes in the roof of the hut and nearby trees.

At the school house, Jeanne Simon was kept in a small room from 9:30 to 2:30. While she was there, Henri Fontaine was brought in and his face was bleeding. He told Jeanne that her husband, Florent, had escaped but said nothing about the flyers. At 2:30, the thirty-three civilians who had been arrested were taken by truck to the jail in Mons.

Captured and Executed

Taken totally by surprise, the American airmen had no time to escape and were quickly and easily captured. Like the Belgian civilians, the U.S. flyers were arrested and taken by truck to the *Gestapo* Headquarters under Commandant Markus at the school house in Chimay for interrogation. On the second floor, the Germans confiscated the Americans false papers and dog tags, and stripped them of all their clothing except their underwear. The Germans also took their watches but not their rings.

Chimay School House (*Les Ecoles Communales de Chimay*)

The interrogations lasted for two to three hours, and afterwards the airmen were loaded into a truck and driven back along the Hill of the Cows Road into the Champagne Woods. The truck stopped at the pathway entrance to the hut where Captain Karl Benner, commander of the German *Feldgendarmerie*, ordered a perimeter to be set up around the area. The Americans were ordered out of the truck, lined up in a row, and led into the woods on the path.

With two Feldgendarmerie guards behind each airman, they were then taken in different directions off the path, and Captain Benner yelled out, "*Sie wissen bescheidt!*" (You know what to do!) After walking further into the woods, each American was shot in the back three or four times and left there. The next day the Germans came back, loaded the bodies into a truck, and took them to an area near the Charleroi airport where they were buried in a common grave.

Executing prisoners without a trial was a complete violation of the laws of war as outlined at the 1907 Hague Convention, but in this instance, the Nazis were not deterred by it. Normally, the Germans sent captured U.S. airmen to *Luftwaffe* prisoner of war camps. Perhaps finding the three guns in the hut and the one that Henri Fontaine carried, the Nazis determined them to be guerilla fighters. No one will ever know. Evidently, the Germans did not know about the Fontaine's involvement with the American flyers as Henri's parents were not arrested. Henri just had the misfortune of being in the wrong place at the wrong time. Otherwise, the Germans had been well informed by local collaborators and knew where to go. Ignoring other farms in the area, the trucks in the convoy went directly to three locations: the Simon farm, the Minet farm, and the hut.

After the war, the U.S. Army War Crimes Department investigated the tragedy and interrogated a number of individuals. Twenty-one year old Henri Bastien was a member of the resistance and along with his father ran a bakery business in St. Remy. At 6:00 that morning, ten armed German soldiers came to his father's house while Henri was still sleeping. He testified,

> *The Germans came into my room, searched it and then arrested me. Then I got dressed and they took me to the school house in Chimay. When I got there, I was taken upstairs and as I went by the door on the right which was a big room, I saw the eight American flyers. There was a big table in the room. The flyers had their civilian clothes on the table and had their hands over their heads, and the Germans were searching them. One flyer, the tallest one, turned his face around to look at me and the Germans hit the flyer with a club. I then continued on to another room and never saw the flyers again.*

Eloi Patat, a 32-year-old Belgian farmer and resistance member, testified,

I knew that eight Americans flyers were in the woods in Chimay and was asked to get some civilian clothes for them and did get them, but it was too late. The morning of April 22, between 8:00 and 10:00, I got a telephone call that there was a raid in Chimay by the Germans. Shortly thereafter, the telephone wires were cut and I stayed home. Later I heard that the eight American flyers had been captured.

Patat had known Marcel Jaye since 1939 before the German occupation, and on the following day the two had breakfast together. Patat testified that Jaye told him, "I had orders not to take any prisoners and I killed them. They are in the woods."

Fernand Joly was a member of the Merot Police from Charleroi and following the war was interned at Camp de Fourcaul in Dampremy, Belgium. The 42-year-old Joly testified,

I was doing Gestapo *work checking the black market. The* Gestapo *and Merlot police were the same. The raid took place in the early morning on 22 April 1944. I was not there. The day after the raid I spoke with Jacques Derby and asked him what happened. He told me that they had captured eight American flyers in a cabin in the woods in Chimay and that they had been shot without a trial, near the woods of St. Remy. Derby did not tell me that he had killed any of the Americans.*

Twenty-four-year-old Jacques Lefèvre, a non-commissioned officer of the 3rd Company *Garde Wallonne* said that Marcel Jaye ordered him to join one of the German *feldgendarmerie* who was behind the second American flyer in line, and they started walking into the woods. Lefèvre testified,

While going through the woods for about 200 to 300 meters, I heard a shot and suddenly the flyer in front of me started to run away. I pulled my pistol and shot at him and hit him in

the shoulder. In the meantime, the German NCO had taken out his pistol, ran after the flyer, shot three or four times and the flyer fell to the ground dead. The NCO went to the body of the flyer, looked at it, came back to me and said, "Finished; we can go back." Just then there were more shots from various parts of the woods. We went back to our truck and left the body of the flyer in the woods.

POWs and Political Prisoners ... Their Fate

Captain Marcel Jaye of the 3rd Company of the *Garde Wallonne*

On August 15, Jeanne Simon, Joseph Simon, and Henri Fontaine were taken from Mons to Saint-Gilles Prison in Brussels and tried before the German Military Tribunal where they were convicted of resistance activities and aiding U.S. airmen. Joseph and Henri were transferred to Buchenwald concentration camp on September 1, and eventually to Dachau concentration camp. In March 1945, Joseph Simon was working as part of labor detail repairing railroad tracks near Koblenz, Germany, when he was killed during an American bombardment. A French newspaper, *Libres*, dated September 27, 1945, reported Henri Fontaine was alive in the Russian zone of Germany, having been liberated from Budapest, but was never heard from again.

On September 2, Jeanne Simon was among 1,370 political prisoners and 41 Allied airmen POWs loaded on a train to be transported to the Neuengamme concentration camp near Hamburg. This was devastating news to them as it seemed it ended their dreams of being liberated by Allied troops who were rapidly approaching Brussels. In Claude Lokker's 1985 book *'Des bâtons dans les roues* (*Stick in the Wheels*), it reports that the women being driven in trucks from Saint-Gilles Prison sang the Belgian national anthem and threw out scraps of paper containing messages to their families and friends asking them not to lose hope and to keep the faith.

The train was referred to as the "Nazi Ghost Train" although the name was really a misnomer because all the Belgian railway workers knew about it. It was intended to leave the Brussels Mid-Way train station in the morning, but it was delayed several hours by the railway workers. Further delays and problems caused by sabotage resulted in the train returning to the Brussels La Petite-Ile station the next morning. Following more confusion caused by the railway workers and through negotiations by the Red Cross, the political prisoners were reluctantly released. By this time, the German SS troops in charge of the train were starting to panic, and they and other Germans in the area jumped on board and left with the POWs. Because of resistance efforts, the train only made it about two miles to Schaerbeek where the POWs escaped. Jeanne Simon would return to the family farm in St. Remy on September 6 to be reunited with her husband, Florent, who had come back from France after U.S. troops liberated the area. Albert Minet was also freed during this time and went back to his farm.

After the capture of the eight Americans, the Germans stepped up the frequency of their searches in Chimay trying to find more flyers being hidden by the Belgian underground. One day a bunch of motorcycles and cars roared up the street stopping at the Delporte home at Rue Van Humbeck #7 while Slenker watched in terror from the Collet's house. While Fernand Delporte bolted out the back door, Mrs. Delporte opened the front door to see an *SS* commander standing there. To her uncontrollable relief, all he wanted was to ask her if he could have a few of her prize roses that were blooming in the front yard.

Delporte Home at Rue Van Humbeck #7 in Chimay

33
BELGIAN HELPERS

Danger was everywhere. Every knock on the door could be the Gestapo resulting in possible arrest, interrogation, torture, prison camp, or death.

Uncertain Survival Even with the Resistance

During World War II, there were 4,000 airmen of the Eighth Air Force who were shot down and evaded capture. It was a nerve-racking experience to say the least. Most downed flyers had medical needs, either being injured or ill. They were under a great deal of psychological stress of being alone in an unknown land and of constantly living with the risk of being caught hanging over their heads. Additionally, it was frustrating not being able to speak a foreign language and be able to communicate with the people who were trying to help them. They had to put their complete trust in strangers, some of whom could be Nazi collaborators or spies. Those who were not able to get to an escape route back to England could only sit around day after day, waiting and waiting, under the continual pressure. This was the fate of William Slenker and Howard Snyder.

During his stay in Chimay, William Slenker didn't know French, and Mrs. Collet and her daughters did not speak English so they communicated with each other through the use of gestures. Slenker stayed in a room upstairs and celebrated his birthday while he was there on April 29. Paula Collet would often play the piano and sing songs. The local butcher brought them rations of meat each day. On one occasion the area was bombarded and some of the bombs came down so close to the Collet's house that Slenker said the explosions were "breaking all the windows and knocking all the doors off the hinges of our house." The concussions from the exploding bombs were so great that the Collet's heavy piano was shoved across the room.

Collet's Home at Rue Van Humbeck #12 in Chimay

The Colet home was a grand house with three stories. Mrs. Collet and her husband had been wealthy merchants and when war was imminent, used their money to buy large quantities of food, chocolates, tobacco, wine, etc., knowing that money itself would have little value when war came. However, the Germans discovered all these goods and stole everything leaving the Collets with nothing. Mr. Collet was so despondent that he committed suicide by hanging himself in the family's warehouse behind their home.

Slenker was provided with false identity papers under the name of Emile Louis Gaston Dupont from Namur, Belgium, with his occupation being listed as a cow laborer. The Collets thought Slenker being a "cowboy" was quite amusing since after all he was an American. Just down the street at rue Van Humbeck #7 lived the 38-year-old district resistance leader, Fernand Delporte, ("Albert") and his wife.

Because Delporte had an important job, the Germans let him keep his car that he used to move downed flyers from one location to another. "Albert" regularly checked in on Slenker to make sure everything was OK. Also stopping by from time to time to clean his wounds was the female Russian doctor, Fanny Melament, who had treated members of the crew after they were first shot down.

Danger was everywhere. Every knock on the door could be the *Gestapo* resulting in possible arrest, interrogation, torture, prison camp, or death. Local people knew that Slenker was being hidden, but fortunately, they were sympathetic and never said anything to betray him or the Collets. He said, "I felt that it was only a matter of time until I would be captured. I also knew that these people that were hiding me would be shot first and then me."

Whenever word came that a house-to-house search was imminent, he was forced to leave the Collets and go to outlying areas for periods of time. He said, "The *Gestapo* knew that Allied airmen were hiding in the area, but the resistance seemed to know when their searches would occur." After the danger of capture subsided, he would return. Once it was suggested that since he could be killed at any time and was never far from death, he should see the local Catholic priest and take confession to make sure he went to heaven. When he said he was Protestant (actually a Lutheran like Howard Snyder), he was told that made no difference in such times as this.

One time when word came that the Germans were going to be conducting a house-to-house search, Fernand Delporte drove him out into the country to hide. Slenker said, "We drove in broad daylight with both German soldiers and local Belgians walking all around. The local people were all looking at the car to get a glimpse of the U.S. airman they had heard about. Some were even waving! I was terrified!"

For about a week, Slenker stayed with some people, but he never knew who they were because there was no communication. He couldn't speak French and they couldn't speak English. The people had a big Flemish dog called a Bouvier des Flandres which is a French name meaning "Cow Herder of Flanders." They had trained it to bark whenever it heard the boots of German soldiers clicking on the cobblestone street as they walked by the house. Whenever the dog barked, Slenker said he would jump with fright.

Also hidden at the same house was a Russian submarine officer whose ship had been sunk in the North Sea. He had been captured and taken prisoner but managed to escape from the German prison camp. The Russian and Slenker would play cards and discuss politics. The Russian liked Americans and thought no one else in the world was any good except Americans and Russians. He would tell Slenker what a vicious guy he was and what he would do to any Germans he came across.

One day a mailman came by and knocked on the door. The uniform he wore looked very similar to those worn by German soldiers, and the Russian thought he was one. He pulled out a gun to shoot, but fortunately for the mailman, Slenker knocked the Russian's arm and the bullet barely missed or the innocent mailman would have been murdered. Slenker believed that eventually the Russian "would needlessly kill a German one day and everyone in the region would suffer in retaliation. I had to get away from this crazy man and I did."

Up the street, no more than a block away from the Collet's home was the Chateau de Chimay, an ancient castle that the Germans used as a garrison. Every day, an attachment of German troops would march in formation down the street past the Collet's house, sometimes singing. Fearing that they would break into the house one day and search for him, Slenker desperately wanted to escape from his situation but realized it was impossible to do it on his own.

"A particular problem," said Paula Collet, "was that in the building next to our house a livestock office had been set up where cattle were requisitioned for the Germans. There was a woman there who came in every day and was always going to the bottom of the garden to look closely at our windows. What if she had ever seen the cellar curtains moving or noticed the silhouette of a man in this house where there were only women?! We were very afraid because she could have turned us in."

After a few months, Slenker's wounds had healed sufficiently that Paula and Gisèle thought walks would do him good so at dusk they started taking him out on short strolls. Although he was wearing civilian clothes, he was very nervous about it. Since most all the young local men had been taken away to labor camps, he felt he stood out like a sore thumb. The Collet sisters loved these outings and would point out all the local sights such as the bordellos and bars saying, "Bad girls in there!" All Slenker could think about, however, were all the Germans walking all around carrying guns.

His worst fear finally came true when one evening a drunken German soldier walked over to him and the sisters, and Slenker thought he was doomed for sure. However, Paula and Gisèle were both fearless and Paula whispered, "I'll take care of this," but before anything happened the German's buddies grabbed him and told him to leave the Belgians alone. Well, that was quite enough for Slenker, and he never ventured out again.

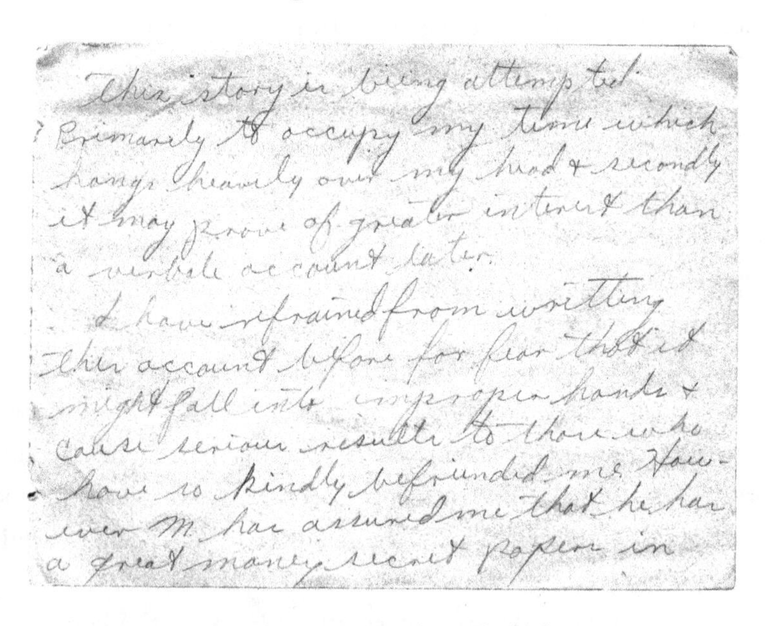
This story is being attempted
primarily to occupy my time which
hangs heavily over my head & secondly
it may prove of greater interest than
a verbal account later.
I have refrained from writing
this account before for fear that it
might fall into improper hands &
cause serious results to those who
have so kindly befriended me. However M. has assured me that he has
a great many secret papers in

Excerpt from Howard Snyder's diary

34

HOWARD ... ON THE MOVE

Maurice took him upstairs to a trap door in the ceiling and told him to climb up on the roof and to stay there until he came back. On the roof, Howard could hear the Germans talking and yelling as they searched the house.

Musical Chairs with the Resistance

Over the next four months, Howard Snyder was moved back and forth to various places such as farms, homes, and different buildings with the mode of transportation also varying from bicycle, street car, or railroad. The length of his stays depended on the people he stayed with. Some were "scared to death", and if so, he was moved quickly. Others were extremely brave with whom he might stay with for up to six weeks. He went back to Macquenoise where he stayed with the Fraikins at their farmhouse for 10 days and then was taken up to Charleroi, 30 miles north of Chimay.

Fraikin Farm House in Macquenois;
Fraikin Farm House (arrow indicates room where Howard Snyder stayed for 10 days)

In Charleroi, Snyder stayed off and on with Ginette Gadenne at Rue de Gozée 156, and they developed a deep friendship. Her husband, André, was a captain in the French Army and in a German prison camp. Harboring a downed airman put her in extreme danger, and she dyed her hair in an attempt to avoid being recognized. Regardless, she was still picked up by the *Gestapo* who interrogated and beat her.

Ginette Gadenne and Howard Snyder

Ghislaine Bailleux, Howard Snyder, and Ginette Gadenne

Maurice Bailleux

Charles Schuyteener

Mimi Gabriel, Howard Snyder, Ghislaine Bailleaux, and friend

For a few weeks, Howard stayed at the home of Maurice and Ghislaine Bailleux on Rue Volta 12 in the Marcinelle section of Charleroi. Their next door neighbor, 16-year-old Mimie Gabriel at Rue Volta 13, would play cards and monopoly with Howard and teach him French. Howard also passed the time reading and doing crossword puzzles. For six weeks, Howard stayed with Charles Schuyteneer who lived at Rue de la Révolution 32 in the Jumet section of Charleroi.

Also in Marcinelle, Howard stayed with Eva Laurent-Martin and her two daughters, Maggy 22 and Jacqueline 18, on Avenue Eugène Mascaux 702, and it was Eva who gave him a civilian suit to wear. Eva's husband was John "Jack" Martin (51-years-old) who although born in Philadelphia, Pennsylvania, was a British citizen. He had served as a captain in the British Army as a member of the Duke of Wellington Regiment and the Royal Gurkha Rifles, a unique infantry unit recruited from Nepal with a reputation of being amongst the finest and most feared soldiers in the world. The British referred to them as "The Bravest of the Brave" and their motto was "Better to die than to be a coward." In 1940, Jack and his family were planning on leaving Belgium for Arras, France, but he was arrested by the *Gestapo* for being British and taken prisoner. In addition, the Germans dispossessed the family of all their goods.

At various times, Mrs. Eva Laurent-Martin had hidden other downed airmen before taking in Howard, and the Germans had become suspicious of her so she placed Howard for awhile with Victor and Aimee Kuyls who lived nearby at Avenue Eugène Mascaux 672, Charleroi. It was a good thing because the *Gestapo* searched the Martin's house twice and once arrested Maggy. After aggressive interrogation she was released, but as a result of that horrible experience, she said she could not stand to hear a single word of German anymore.

Aimee and Victor Kuyls

Ginette Gadenne, Howard Snyder, and Victor and Aimee Kuyls

After this happened, Eva thought the probability that the Germans would come back to search her house again was very low, so Howard moved back in. Eva reasoned that the Germans would never imagine that the wife of a British war prisoner and mother of two young daughters would take such a risk as hiding an American pilot.

However, the Germans did come back to search her home. They told Eva to line up her two daughters beside her and asked her if she was hiding any British or American soldiers. She answered no. Two more times they asked her the same question, and each time she said no. The Germans then started to search the house, but only went into the living room and the kitchen. They didn't search the entire house because—logically—they thought she would not take such a risk, being the wife of a German POW and the mother of two daughters.

Jack Martin spent the rest of the war in various prison camps and prisons where the Nazis performed medical experiments on him. Towards the end of the war, he was repatriated to Bradford Royal Infirmary in Bradford, England, where the doctors tried to restore his health. After a couple years of treatment and recovery, he returned to his family in Belgium where he died in 1952 of cancer, believed to have been caused by the tests and injections the Nazis performed on him.

Jack Martin and Eva (Laurent) Martin circa 1950

Although no one ever asked him for it, Howard had been given a forged identity card stating he was deaf and dumb, and wherever he traveled another underground member was always with him. Under constant protection of the Belgian underground while he was missing in action, Howard often found himself in the immediate vicinity of German occupation forces. On one occasion, Eva and her daughters went by train with Howard to take him to another town, and some German soldiers came into the car and sat down next to them. They started to talk to Howard in French, but he pretended to have a coughing fit so Eva answered them while Jacqueline and Maggy pretended to take care of Howard. Fortunately, a moment later the train stopped at the next station, and the Germans got off.

The Germans were always trying to catch men involved in underground activity and/or hiding downed airmen. They would throw up a blockade at an intersection and surround the whole block. Then they would interview all the males, mostly older men because the young ones were at labor camps. If the Germans determined men were guilty, their entire families would be arrested. The women might eventually be let go, but the men were either shot or taken to concentration camps.

One night after dinner at the home of Maurice and Ghislaine Bailleux, there was loud knocking and banging on the front door. Maurice went to see what it was and after talking for awhile came running back telling Howard to follow him. Maurice took him upstairs to a trap door in the ceiling and told him to climb up on the roof and to stay there until he came back. On the roof, Howard could hear the Germans talking and yelling as they searched the house. Maurice didn't come back to get Howard until the next morning so Howard had to stay up on the roof all night in the cold. After this happened, he was moved because it was too dangerous to stay there any longer.

Another incident happened when he was staying in a house near a railroad marshalling yard, always an excellent target for American bombers, when the area was hit. Smoke from bombs of the first wave of planes obscured the marshalling yard which resulted in the next wave dropping their bombs very near the house he was. Snyder couldn't go down into the cellar to seek cover because neighbors and friends were seeking protection there who didn't know he was being hidden in the house. He couldn't risk them seeing him in case any of them were collaborators or had "loose lips" so he had to stay upstairs and stand under a doorway, praying he wasn't killed by his own Eighth Air Force. Fortunately, the house was not hit.

As in all occupied countries in Europe, food and clothing were strictly rationed by the German authorities. Regardless, a significant black market existed, supplying food illegally at very high prices to those that could afford it.

As Howard explained,

> *If people were fairly well-off and had a little money, they bought food on the black market and you ate pretty well. If not, you ate potatoes five days a week. Food of any kind (livestock, eggs, produce, crops, etc.) was supposed to be turned over to the Germans for rationing, but the stuff they sold using coupons was lousy. For example, flour had sawdust in it and when it was baked, you had to burn the outside to get the inside done. Many farmers sold their goods on the black market, and word would get out on who had what to sell. However, poor people couldn't afford black market prices.*

Howard with Belgian helpers

35

PRISON CAMP

Joe Musial stayed at Saint-Gilles Prison for four more months, 21 days in solitary confinement, and finally left in June 1944. Sent to Stalag Luft VI like Holbert, Musial, along with other prisoners, was shipped in boxcars with no food, no water, and no place to sit.

POW

Kriegsgefangenenlager was the German word for prisoner of war (POW) camp and prisoners of war were referred to as "*kriegies.*" Stalags (short for ***S****tamml****ag****er*) were operated and used for non-commissioned personnel (enlisted ranks of the Army). Officers were held in separate camps called *Oflags* (short for ***Of****fiziersl****ag****er*). The German Air Force operated *Stalag Lufts* (*Stalag der Luftwaffe*) in which flying personnel, both officers and non-commissioned officers, were held and received better treatment than infantry soldiers in the Stalags.

Roy Holbert was moved from Saint-Gilles by night to the Dulag (***Du****rchgangs****lag****er*) Luft at Oberursel near Frankfurt. The main purpose of this camp was to act as collection and interrogation center for newly captured air crews before they were transferred to the permanent camps. Holbert said, "I spent 22 days in solitary confinement, and was threatened every day that I would be shot as a spy, because I did not have any identification (which he had lost while trying to bail out of the *Susan Ruth*). They finally gave up on me and sent me and others by '40 and 8' boxcars to a prison camp, Stalag Luft VI at Heyderkrug, East Prussia (now Lithuania)." The box cars were called "40 and 8" because they held either 40 men or 8 horses. The cars were stubby, only 20.5 feet long and 8.5 feet wide.

Joe Musial stayed at Saint-Gilles Prison for four more months, 21 days in solitary confinement, and finally left in June 1944. Sent to Stalag Luft VI like Holbert, Musial, along with other prisoners, was shipped in boxcars with no food, no water, and no place to sit. Making conditions worse, the boxcars had previously been used to transport livestock so the foul smell was overwhelming.

The compound at Heydekrug was an isolated and remote place a few miles from the Baltic Sea, and the ground there was either knee deep in snow or a sea of mud. The Stalag Luft VI Commandant was Oberst Hermann von Hoerback, an old-line Prussian army officer. He was very strict but basically fair and did not commit any acts of cruelty. As spring came, conditions improved. More Red Cross food parcels came and many social activities were organized to pass the time. Barracks even formed up teams for various sports (softball, rugby, boxing, basketball, and football) and theater groups. With books sent by relatives back in the States, the prisoners were even able to set up a library. Relatives could send parcels to the POW camps although this became problematic if prisoners were moved frequently from camp to camp. Although both Holbert and Musial were at this same camp, they were unaware of each other's presence there.

By cablegrams sent through the Red Cross, Musial and Daniels were able to write back home and let their families know they were alive and "relatively" safe. They also confirmed that besides Louis Colwart and Ross Kahler, the other eight crew members all bailed out and were thought to be safe on the ground. From Saint-Gilles Prison, Joe Musial had written to his older sister Sophie on May 22, 1944:

> Dear Mom (as he called her because she was so much older),
>
> *Well, I've finally finished the war. I have been severely wounded in the left leg. Don't worry. I am getting good medical attention.*

Also, write to my squadron and tell them Lt. Daniels and myself are both wounded and in the same hospital. The Red Cross authorities will let you know what to send to me. Tell everyone to write. I can only write one letter a week here. Please don't worry about me. Just go on as if nothing happened and someday I'll be back with you all again. God bless you and thanks to all of you for just being my family.

After Helen Eike heard the very welcome news that her husband George and Howard Snyder had bailed out, she wrote to Ruth Snyder saying that the news "is such a ray of hope." Daniels learned that his wife, Ginny, had given birth to their first child, Donna Rae, born on March 14, 1944. He and Ginny would give birth to ten more children.

Roy Holbert's parents back in North Carolina didn't know what had happened to him. The first word they heard wasn't until May when they received more than 35 letters and postcards from people who heard his name broadcast on the radio that he was a German prisoner.

Virginia Daniels with 4-month-old Donna Rae

From the *Luftwaffe* Hospital at Saint-Gilles Prison outside of Brussels, Richard Daniels was first taken to Oflag IX A/H located in the beautiful 12th century Spangenberg Castle in the small town of Spangenberg in north-eastern Hesse, Germany.

After a short stay at Oflag IX A/H, Daniels was sent to a large hospital, Reserve Lazaret, under the administration of Stalag IX-C, in the town of Obermassfeld, southwest of Erfurt, Germany. It was a three-story stone building and prior to the war it was a resort run by the Nazi-controlled *Kraft durch Freude* which stood for "Strength through Joy." It was a large, leisure organization which became the world's largest tourism operator of the 1930s.

Most of the patients sent to Obermassfeld had been seriously wounded, suffering amputations and infected wounds, and the facilities there were designed to take care of orthopedic cases, predominately arm and leg injuries. Daniels had developed osteomyelitis or chronic bone infection in his injured arm which was a common and major problem during the war when treating compound fractures. Both the care and the conditions were very good. The hospital operations were actually run by British medical personnel who had been captured in the 1940 Battle of Dunkirk on the coast of France and had been prisoners ever since. From the Germans, the prisoners learned about the Allied landing at Normandy, France on June 6, 1944, better known as D-Day.

During the Battle of France, the British Expeditionary Force, the Belgian Army, and the French 1st Army became trapped at Dunkirk, but the German command inexplicably decided to stop its Army's advance. Helped by a flotilla of more than 800 English ships of all sorts (minesweepers, destroyers, torpedo boats, ferries, fishing boats, plus private yachts and motorboats) approximately 340,000 Allied soldiers were evacuated to England during the week of May 27 to June 4, without any interference from the German Army. It was called "The Miracle of Dunkirk" and in the eyes of the British, it was seen as a victory. However, the British Army left behind the majority of their equipment (ammunition, guns, tanks, vehicles, etc.) which took months to re-supply. Nevertheless, Dunkirk was one of the great turning points of the war.

The "Protecting Power" and the Red Cross

On July 19, Richard Daniels, along with other injured prisoners, was transferred by truck to a prisoner of war hospital at Meiningen, Germany. Here the men began their convalescence. It was also at Meiningen that Daniels went before a medical board set up by the

Protecting Power (Switzerland) and representatives from the International Red Cross. After his medical condition was reviewed, he was approved for the next exchange of wounded prisoners scheduled for January or February of 1945.

During the war, Germany and the United States had cut off diplomatic relations so Switzerland, being a neutral country, acted as a third-party Protecting Power. The prisoners referred to the medical board as the "D.U. Board" for "Desirably Unfit," and those approved received a D.U. chit signed by both the German chief physician and by the Swiss which became the prisoners' exit paper from Germany. This process of returning severely wounded prisoners back to their home countries was called repatriation.

Because of the Russian pressure against the Germans along the eastern front, Stalag Luft VI in Hedyekrug was closed in July 1944. Evacuation of the camp was in several phases. On July 14, Roy Holbert was among 1,000 American prisoners moved by train from Heydekrug to Memel, East Prussia (now known as Klaipėda, Lithuania), a seaport on the Baltic Sea. From there, they were put in the hold of a captured Russian coal boat, *SS Masuren*, and shipped to Swinemünde, Poland. In the dark hot hold, the POWs were stuffed in like sardines. There was little food available, sleeping was out of the question, and there was no means for the men to relieve themselves. The Germans would lower a bucket with drinking water, and when it went back up, it was full of filth and slop. They were aboard the freighter for 56 hours.

After arriving, the prisoners were put on a train to Stalag Luft IV at Gross Tychow, Poland, arriving on July 18. Gross Tychow was located in a thick pine forest between Stargard and Belgard. After being unloaded from boxcars at the railroad station at Kiefeheide, they started marching in pairs, shackled ankle to ankle and wrist to wrist, for four miles toward the camp; but soon the march turned into a fast walk, and then a run.

Chaos and Cruelty

The prisoners had to start shedding their overcoats and dropping all the belongings they were carrying. Regular soldiers and young 18 or 19-year-old naval cadets, called *Kriegsmarines*, were shouting and yelling and vicious guard dogs were snarling, barking, and snapping. Any prisoners who lagged behind were slashed with bayonets, beaten by rifle butts, and/or bitten by the dogs. As the guards jabbed with their bayonets, they'd yell out the name of a German city that had been bombed: "Eine fur Hamburg!" "Eine fur Koln!"

A wild and crazed red-headed Nazi captain, *Hauptman* (Captain) Walther Pickhardt, shouted and cursed (*Schweinhunde* meaning pig-dog and other choice words) at the prisoners and urged his troops to be even more brutal, ranting over the destruction of German cities. It was absolute chaos and several hundred prisoners were badly injured.

Hauptman Walther Pickhardt

Holbert was handcuffed to a buddy who had been a prizefighter back in Pennsylvania, and he held Holbert up so he wouldn't fall down. When Holbert's mouth got dry, his buddy gave him a pebble to put in his mouth to suck on to keep his mouth moist. Holbert gave his buddy a lot of credit for not letting him give up and said he might not have made it if it were not for the friendship and encouragement of his friend. The incident became known as "The Heydekrug Run."

Afterwards, the POWS learned that the run up the road was really an attempt to have them escape. All along the woods on each side, soldiers with machine guns were ready to open fire. The Germans wanted the prisoners to panic, so they could cut the *krieges* down. Pickhardt's officers and guards would become known for their individual cruelty and savage nighttime intrusions into the barracks.

The conditions at Gross Tychow were worse than at Heydekrug. The barracks were overcrowded, food was scarcer, and morale suffered. The prisoners were fed very little, and as long as they were in a POW camp, their main source of food was Red Cross parcels. Each Red Cross package weighed 11 pounds, and the selection of items in it would vary. However, with prison camp diets consisting largely of starchy foods, the selection would attempt to supply the minimum requirements of proteins, fats, vitamins and minerals. In addition, foods were selected that could last up to twelve months, require little or no cooking, and included cigarettes, soap, and chewing gum. If a horse died that pulled the "honey wagons" emptying the septic tanks, the prisoners would get horse meat the next day.

Joe Musial had also been sent to Stalag Luft IV, and it wasn't until there that he and Roy Holbert were finally reconnected after being shot down six months earlier. Musial was shocked to discover that Holbert's once jet black hair had turned white. Holbert's fiancée had given him a New Testament which he carried with him at all times, and he said it really helped him a lot; that he had to rely on a higher power to pull him through the ordeal. Thankfully, little by little things started to improve. By September 1944, Red Cross parcels started arriving more regularly (usually once a week), a theater was built, and a library started.

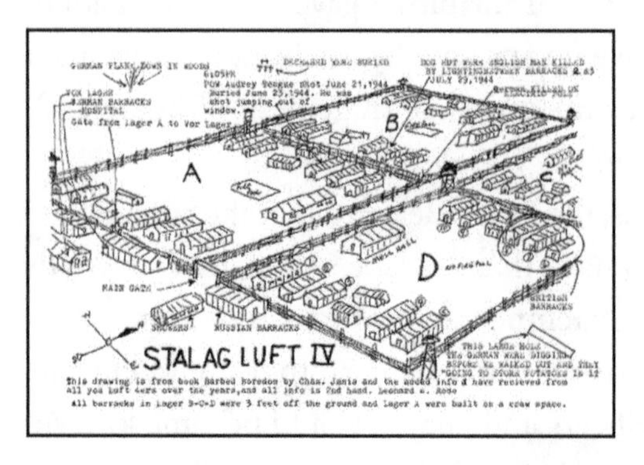

Stalag Luft IV at Gross Tychow, Poland

Back on the March 29 mission to Helmstadt, waist gunner Harold Maron who flew with Howard Snyder on his first and third missions had been shot down flying with pilot Gerald Haywood's crew. Six crew members were killed, including Haywood and co-pilot, William Daniels. Maron and four others were captured and first processed at Dulag Luft, near Frankfurt for interrogation. Afterwards, Maron was taken to one of the most notorious German prisoner-of-war camps—Stalag 17b at Braunau Gneikendorf in Austria, near Krem. It was labeled 17b because it was the second prison camp in the German 17th military district.

As the United States and Great Britain intensified their strategic bombing campaigns forcing the Germans to consolidate camps, the American population at Stalag 17b eventually swelled to more than 4,200. However, the American prisoners shared their misery with more than 25,000 other POWs who were prisoners there. The U.S. section of the camp was flanked by international compounds stuffed with French, Italian, British, and other Allied nationalities. Especially ghastly was a "village of the damned" saved for the Russians. Detested, feared, and treated worse than animals by the Germans, Russian prisoners suffered beyond comprehension and died in droves.

Russia was not a signatory to the 1929 Geneva Convention agreement, which on paper guaranteed humane treatment for prisoners of war. As a result, the Germans took no responsibility for Russian prisoners, letting Russian prisoners starve and freeze to death, die of diseases, or simply shoot them to avoid the troublesome problem of having to feed and care for them. Desperately hungry during the winter months, Russian prisoners would prop up dead comrades in their lines for roll call each morning to be counted by unknowing Germans, who issued rations based on shoe count. When German soldiers were captured by the Russians, they acted likewise and treated prisoners just as bad or even worse. At least Western captives had the Geneva agreement working in their favor, and the American flyers received a semblance of respect from the Germans.

36
THE MAQUIS

It was extremely dangerous for Snyder to join, for if captured, Maquis members faced torture, death or concentration camps where few survived. Still, Snyder felt like he was doing something to help the war effort.

Joining the Resistance

Several times Snyder was set to start out on the journey over the Pyrenees via one of the escape routes to Spain, but one thing or another would go wrong and the plan would be aborted. He said later, "I thought I was having a great deal of bad luck getting back for arrangements were made at least four times for my return and each time something happened to prevent it." Obviously this was very disheartening to him, and finally Snyder became tired of continually waiting, being moved from house to house, and living with the constant threat of being captured by the Nazis. He thought he might as well do some good and be proactive against the Germans so he decided to join up with the Maquis, the rural guerilla band of French resistance fighters. Maquis, or *maquisards*, was a Corsican name for a local scrub brush that resistance fighters on the island of Corsica used for cover during their eighteenth century revolution. By July, it had also become too dangerous for Howard to stay in Belgium any longer so he was moved to the La Fagne region in northern France where he was connected with the French Maquis.

Howard asked one of his Belgian helpers, Aimee Kuyls, to take him across the border into France, and at first she said no; it was too dangerous. When he said he would just go alone, she knew that was not a good idea so she relented and got two bicycles for them to ride. As they traveled westward along one side of the road, they came across thousands of German soldiers retreating along the other side heading east. Howard recalled,

> *They were in bad shape and all banged up. It amused me that here I was, an American pilot, in the midst of them, within spitting distance. When we got into France, I was turned over to George Pirau, the French equivalent of a forest ranger. He took me to a farmhouse, Ferme de L'Ermitage (The Hermitage Farm) in Wallers on the lands of the Princess of Merode where the Maquis unit stayed.*

There, Howard was incorporated into Commandant Marais' resistant unit of the French Maquis comprised of about 20 men. Commandant Marais had been a lieutenant in the French Army and was captured by the Germans but managed to escape. By this time, Howard could speak conversational French fairly well.

Aimee Kuyls and Howard Snyder;
The Hermitage Farm (Ferme de L'Ermitage)

Howard Snyder at Hermitage Farm in 1994;
Paul Delahaye at Hermitage Farm in 1994

In general, the French Maquis were very diverse in their makeup and nationality. They were soldiers from defeated armies, escaped prisoners, students, right-wing nationalists, socialists, communists, and anarchists. In the unit Snyder joined, there were a few Frenchmen, a few Belgians, and several black Algerians who were particularly fierce fighters. It was extremely dangerous for Snyder to join, for if captured, Maquis members faced torture, death or concentration camps where few survived. Still, Snyder felt like he was doing something to help the war effort and was once again fighting the "Krauts" or "Boches" as the French called them. Little did Snyder know how valuable his previous army infantry training would become.

Even though Snyder had been seen descending in a parachute and required assistance to the ground after dangling in the trees, he was not immediately accepted as an American airman by the Maquis. He said,

> *The German military often dressed their own men in various Allied uniforms and bailed them out over territory they held. The purpose was so these men who spoke whatever language was necessary for the ruse might be picked up by the underground members and thus later be able to give away the identities and locations of underground participants and residences to the* Gestapo.

Although the Maquis used whatever arms they could get their hands on, they relied heavily on airdrops of weapons and explosives from the British. They also used German weapons captured throughout the occupation such as the Mauser 98K rifle and the MP 40 submachine gun. In fact, the MP 40 became so common that a resistance fighter was quoted saying, "They are as common as hookers on the streets of Paris, and they get about as much action." Snyder was given a back-pack, dynamite and blasting caps, a submachine gun that he carried over his shoulder, a Spanish-made Llama .45 pistol that he wore on his hip and an ammunition belt.

Aided by British Intelligence

Snyder later confirmed, "We received our orders by radio from England to harass and destroy German military targets. Somehow they knew every German convoy that came through our area. British planes dropped arms, ammunition and explosives to us. Our job was to do as much damage as possible. Hiding by day and hitting at night, we blew up portions of motorized military columns and troops. On the narrow country roads, we'd place explosives in a zigzag pattern in the road so the tanks or trucks would be sure to hit them. The operation was run like a business."

The major reason the British knew so much was that they were able to decipher Germany's secret messages. Prior to Germany's invasion of Poland, the Polish had broken German military texts enciphered on its Enigma machine, and before being actually invaded, Poland informed the British about it. Decryption of Enigma messages was so effective, it was joked that "the British knew orders before the German generals in the field did." Some estimated that it shortened the war by two to four years. Winston Churchill went as far as to say, "It was thanks to Ultra (code name for the British signals intelligence) that we won the war."

The band of guerillas Snyder was with was involved in a lot of action. Once, they were waiting to attack a German convoy when to their surprise a squadron of American fighters came swooping down on the convoy. Howard said, "They strafed them just like in the movies and blew up every truck. We had ringside seats and just watched in amazement."

Another time, they had been notified that a German Field Marshall and his staff would be coming down a road and sure enough, three cars came along "going like hell" around 3:00 in the morning. Howard was manning a BAR (Browning automatic rifle) which was a .30-06 caliber light machine gun fired from a bipod. He said, "We shot the daylights out of them. We disabled one car, and some of the soldiers in that car hopped in another and took off. I don't know how many we got, but we hit some of them. They were scared to death, and I bet the Field Marshall must have wet his pants."

On the Hermitage Farm, Howard stayed in an upstairs room in the farmhouse while the Algerians stayed in the barn. He was shaving one day and heard Germans driving up to the house and thought they were coming after him. With shaving cream on his face and wearing just his undershorts, he frantically jumped out a second story window and ran into the nearby woods where he hid until they left.

One time after they had set up explosives on a road, a German convoy came by and the lead tank hit one. The explosion knocked the track off on one side and caused the tank to tip at an angle so its 88 mm gun was pointing up. Even though the German tank crew couldn't lower it, they still opened fired. With the trajectory being too high, the shells were crashing into the forest, and trees were splintering apart and crashing down all around the Maquis unit. The noise was deafening and Howard said, "Scared the hell out of us!"

The next morning, the group came back and found a German sergeant who had a broken leg still inside the broken down tank. The group took everything of use, including some cigars and a bottle of cognac. They even took the sergeant's belt off him as a souvenir which Howard ended up with. "We decided to just leave him there because we didn't know what else to do with him."

Meanwhile back in Chimay on August 12, Paul and Nelly Tilquin lived through a frightful experience due to a common occurrence of people talking too much and not considering the consequences. Because of the foolish and careless talk of

Howard jumping out of a jeep with other members of the Maquis unit

Henri Fraikin, both he and Paul Tilquin were arrested. The *Gestapo* came to the Tilquin house at 5:00 in the morning. Nelly and Paul were still in their night clothes, and their two children were terrified.

The Germans were angry because of the assistance Nelly and Paul had given to Allied aviators and brutally searched their house, ripping it apart and destroying their possessions in the search for clothing that Howard might have left behind. The Tilquins' protests and denials only served to intensify the Germans' anger which became worse when they found a Belgian Army Browning HP 9 mm handgun that Paul had hidden. Under Nazi occupation, a German ordinance prohibited the possession of firearms. After the search, Paul and Henri Fraikin were beaten over the head and taken to a jail in Charleroi where they were told that their fate was sealed for having helped in the escape of an Allied aviator. With her house being pillaged, Nelly had to abandon her home to go live with her parents.

Nelly and Paul Tilquin with daughter and a friend

37

LIBERATION

Patton's men had only one general order: "Seek out the enemy, trap him, and destroy him." General Patton didn't believe in defensive tactics but in attacking, telling his soldiers, "When in doubt, attack."

Operation Overlord

D-Day had taken place on June 6, 1944, launching the Allied invasion of German occupied Western Europe. Troops from Canada, United Kingdom, and the United States landed on the beaches of Normandy, France. It was the first step of Operation Overlord, the code name for the Battle of Normandy. A 12,000-plane airborne assault preceded the amphibious landing assault that involved almost 7,000 vessels. The effect of the American P-51 Mustang fighters on the German fighter force had been decisive as the *Luftwaffe* simply could not sustain the losses the American fighters and bombers inflicted on it. The result was that the *Luftwaffe* was notably absent over the skies of Europe by D-Day. Not a single German plane was seen over the Normandy beaches.

The reasons for the Mustang's successes were due to America's industrial might, the Mustang's tactical use in combat, and its offensive capabilities which truly separated it from its contemporaries. Looking at combat aircraft production numbers demonstrates the differences in German versus American industrial might. During 1943, Nazi Germany produced 18,953 combat aircraft compared to 101,639 produced by the U.S. During 1944 the numbers were 33,804 to 125,718. During 1945 the numerical difference was even greater, at 6,987 to 60,494.

The Allies' strategy of using large formations of bombers to attack targets deep within German-occupied territory forced the *Luftwaffe* to fight a war of attrition. However, the war of attrition was just as much, if not more, one of human attrition because of the *Luftwaffe*'s "fly till you die" policy. Pilots were pushed to their limits with no rotation home for time off and no limit on the number of missions or combat hours. This severely hampered the *Luftwaffe*'s ability to turn out large numbers of well-trained pilots later in the war. By mid 1944, most of the *Luftwaffe*'s most experienced fighter pilots had been killed.

The various factions of the French Resistance had been included in the plan for D-Day and Operation Overlord. Through a London-based headquarters that embraced all resistance groups, a massive campaign of sabotage was initiated. The Allies developed four strategies for the French Resistance to execute: sabotaging the rail system, destroying electrical facilities, delaying operations of enemy forces, and cutting telephone lines and teleprinter cables. On June 24, 1944, a U.S. Army Intelligence Annex stated,

> *The French Maquis (Partisans) in southern France has been rendering far more assistance to the Allied invasion than was ever thought possible. Not only did their activities delay for several days the movement of the 2nd SS Panzer Division from Toulouse to Normandy, but it now appears likely that both the 9th and 11th Panzer Divisions will be pinned down in southern France in an attempt to restore the situation for the Germans. In addition to the enemy armor, the Maquis are also tying up substantial numbers of German Infantry Troops.*

Nearly 160,000 Allied troops crossed the English Channel and landed on the beaches of Normandy making it the largest amphibious invasion in world history. By the end of August, more than three million troops were in France. Following two months of slow fighting in the hedgerow country of France, the Americans finally broke through the German defenses and were soon racing across France.

Patton's Third Army

The U.S. Third Army, led by their commander General George Patton, did not take part in the initial stages of Operation Overlord but arrived in France in early August 1944. Once they got started, there was no stopping them. The speed of the Third Army's advance at 40 miles a day forced the Germans to break into a haphazard, hasty retreat. Patton's men had only one general order: "Seek out the enemy, trap him, and destroy him." General Patton didn't believe in defensive tactics but in attacking, telling his soldiers, "When in doubt, attack." He knew that to defeat the Germans, they had to be on the offensive at all times. Like a boxer, he understood that once you got your opponent on the ropes, you had to keep at him until he went down. You couldn't let up and give him a chance to rest. He was nicknamed "Old Blood and Guts" and his men would say "His Guts and Our Blood."

In an ironic twist, Patton grew up in San Marino, California, a small town in Southern California just south of Pasadena, where Howard Snyder and his family would move to in 1949 and live there until 1974.

By 22 August, the Falaise Pocket which the Germans had been fighting desperately to keep open to allow their trapped forces to escape was finally sealed. The ten day battle of the Falaise Pocket (or Gap) was the decisive engagement of the Battle of Normandy. It resulted in the destruction of the bulk of Germany's forces west of the River Seine and opened the way to Paris (liberated on August 25) and subsequently the German border. General Eisenhower recorded that:

The battlefield at Falaise was unquestionably one of the greatest 'killing fields' of any of the war areas. Forty-eight hours after the closing of the gap, I was conducted through it on foot, to encounter scenes that could be described only by Dante. It was literally possible to walk for hundreds of yards at a time, stepping on nothing but dead and decaying flesh.

Retreat

The Germans were now in full retreat eastward, trying to reach the Siegfried Line which was a defense system just inside the western German border. The Line was built between 1938 and 1940 and was comprised of more than 18,000 bunkers, tunnels and tank traps; it stretched more than 390 miles running from the Netherlands to Switzerland. However, it was actually far more valuable as a propaganda tool than as a military defense. Although the Line was portrayed as an unbreachable bulwark, the bunkers could not withstand the more recently developed armor-piercing weapons.

Day after day disheveled German divisions marched through Chimay heading east. During their retreat, soldiers would come to the Collet's home wanting to purchase food, but there was none to sell. In an attempt to catch up to the main column, stragglers would come to the house looking for horses and other means of transportation. One day Slenker was upstairs taking a bath when he heard loud knocking at the front door. After getting dressed, he came downstairs and almost walked into a room full of Germans, but said, "I had wisely peeked through the keyhole before entering." The soldiers had just come to the house to trade some of their sugar for coffee.

William Slenker could hear the low rumble of artillery fire in the distance and hoped it wouldn't be long until the U.S. Army advanced into the area, and he was finally liberated. Then at 9:30 on the morning of September 2, 1944, the 39th regiment of the 9th Infantry Division, First U.S. Army crossed the French border into Belgium over the

Wartoise Bridge at the border hamlet of Cendron, near the village of Forge-Philippe.

First U.S. troops entering Belgium on September 2, 1944

The Fighting Falcons of the 39th regiment had been the first unit of American combat troops to set foot on foreign soil when they stormed the beaches of Algiers in November 1942. The following year while fighting in Sicily, the regiment was given its triple A-Bar Nothing (AAA-O) slogan: Anything, Anywhere, Anytime—Bar Nothing. Their commander, the legendary Colonel Harry "Paddy" Flint declared, "The enemy who sees our regiment in combat, if they live through the battle, will know to run the next time they see us coming."

As U.S. jeeps, trucks, and tanks started pouring into the country, the local citizens could hardly believe their eyes. People start coming out from all the nearby villages to celebrate. For over four years, the people of Belgium had experienced the horrors of war and the oppression of the Nazis. They endured starvation, arrests, curfews, torture and death. So many tears, so much pain and so much terror were now over. The Allies' "V" victory sign replaced the Nazis' "Heil Hitler" salute. It was a day filled with so much happiness!

U.S. troops

Belgians greeting the American troops

There were still skirmishes however. The first fighting for the liberation of Belgium took place later that morning at 11:30. On the ridge of Monceau Imbrechies, the U.S. 60th regiment of the 9th Division was engaged by remnants of the German 2nd SS Panzer Division Das Reich, an elite Tiger tank division of the *Waffen-SS*. The *Waffen-SS* (weapons or armed) was the military combat branch of the *SS* and was separate from the German Wehrmacht or regular armed forces. The German tanks were firing from the village of Macon about a mile below the ridge in an attempt to delay the American advance. The fighting didn't last too long, about three hours, and wasn't much of a battle, but twelve G.I.s (a major, lieutenant, and ten enlisted men) were killed in the fighting. They were the first Allied fatalities in the liberation of Belgium.

At the post-war Nuremburg Trials, the *Waffen-SS* was condemned as a criminal organization due to its close connection with the Nazi Party and its involvement in numerous war crimes. *Waffen-SS* veterans were denied many of the rights afforded to German veterans who had served in the regular German Armed Forces. The exception was *Waffen-SS* conscripts (captured soldiers from defeated countries) sworn in after 1943, who were exempted because of their involuntary servitude.

Howard Snyder and Bill Slenker ... Liberated

The Maquis unit Snyder was with was setting up a barricade to detain retreating Germans, when they received news that American troops were in the village of Trélon, France. "The Germans never showed, so we hurried back to Trélon. I saw an American major from the Third Army of General George Patton standing on a corner and identified myself to him. He sent me to the local headquarters where I was interviewed by G2, Army Intelligence, and my identification was verified."

Howard Snyder at Trelon, France, in 1983

At 4:40 p.m., the U.S. First Army advanced into Chimay, Belgium, and Slenker came out to meet them, though still fearful that the Germans might counter-attack. But it wasn't to be. Bells ran out. Children and teenagers climbed on the vehicles. Mothers kissed the young G.I.s who rained cigarettes, chocolate, and chewing gum on the adoring crowds.

A couple days later, Bill Slenker hitchhiked a ride with some troops to Paris and went to Army headquarters where he was interrogated to make sure he wasn't a Nazi spy. Now that it was safe, downed airmen who had been in hiding started popping up all over the Netherlands, France, and Belgium. With Supreme Headquarters, Allied Expeditionary Forces (SHAEF) now located in Versailles outside of Paris, they all headed there.

A few days later Slenker was flown back to England and returned to Thurleigh where he immediately contacted his family and the relatives of his crew. There he learned that his pilot, Howard Snyder, had successfully evaded capture too and was on his way back. To Slenker's knowledge, Eike, Benninger, and Pindroch had been captured and were being held as prisoners of war. It was rumored by local villagers that Paula Collet had "sweet eyes" for the American airman and that she was extremely disappointed when Slenker went back to the States and got married.

Snyder also went to Paris, hitching a ride with an Army convoy that was taking German prisoners there. Snyder was interviewed further and then flew on a C-47 military transport aircraft to London. On the following day, he wired his wife Ruth that he was alive and well saying, "Is that sweet little chin still up? Fit as a fiddle. Will write. Love, Howard." It was the first news of him since she received the telegram from the War Department on February 23, informing her that he was missing in action. Seven months of silence ended in unsurpassed happiness.

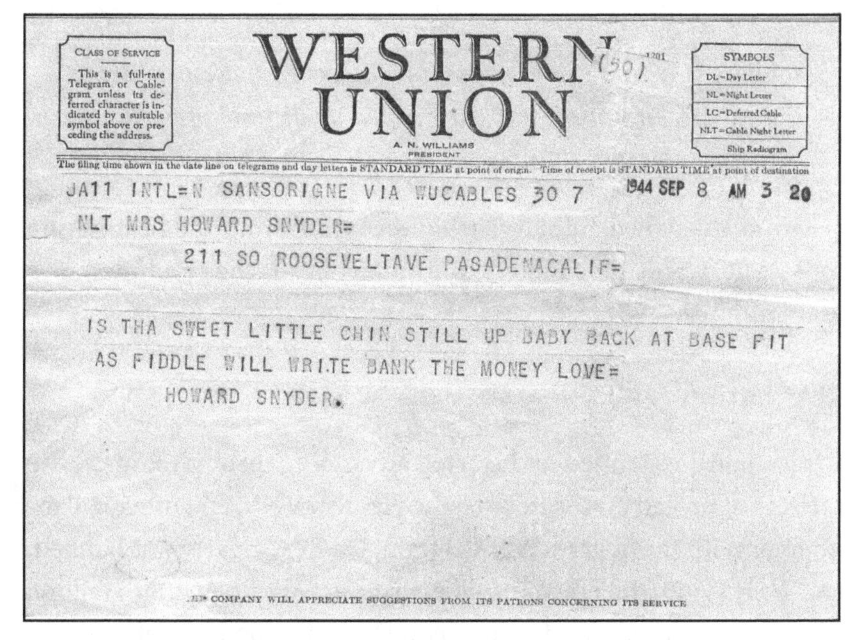

WESTERN UNION

A. N. WILLIAMS
PRESIDENT

CLASS OF SERVICE
This is a full-rate Telegram or Cablegram unless its deferred character is indicated by a suitable symbol above or preceding the address.

SYMBOLS
DL=Day Letter
NL=Night Letter
LC=Deferred Cable
NLT=Cable Night Letter
Ship Radiogram

The filing time shown in the date line on telegrams and day letters is STANDARD TIME at point of origin. Time of receipt is STANDARD TIME at point of destination

JA11 INTL=N SANSORIGNE VIA WUCABLES 30 7 1944 SEP 8 AM 3 20

NLT MRS HOWARD SNYDER=

211 SO ROOSEVELTAVE PASADENACALIF=

IS THA SWEET LITTLE CHIN STILL UP BABY BACK AT BASE FIT AS FIDDLE WILL WRITE BANK THE MONEY LOVE=

HOWARD SNYDER.

THE COMPANY WILL APPRECIATE SUGGESTIONS FROM ITS PATRONS CONCERNING ITS SERVICE

Howard Snyder's Telegram to Ruth

Happiness also came to Paul and Nelly Tilquin for, with the Germans in retreat, there wasn't time for them to execute her husband Paul and Henri Fraikin. Instead, they were put in trucks bound for

Germany. Fortunately, the truck Paul and Henri were in broke down, and the Germans were forced to leave them at Saint-Leonard prison in Liège, just 25 miles from the German border. Then because the speed of the Germans retreat increased even more, the prisoners were completely abandoned at Liège and freed by Belgian patriots on September 9. Paul was reunited with his wife on September 11.

Nelly said,

> *We had prayed hard, and God had heard our prayers. He didn't allow my husband to be executed as a result of his doing a good deed in saving a soldier momentarily overcome by the enemy. Today, however, we are proud. We have reached the hour of victory over a fierce and brutal enemy, and we have recovered our liberty. Our admiration for the valiant Allied soldiers is without limits, and our thanks go out especially to the American nation who has helped us in time of peril and preserved us from slavery.*

Unfortunately, Paul never truly recovered from the beatings he took. Afterwards he suffered continuous headaches and died of a brain tumor in 1951.

Retribution

After the Allies landed and started advancing through France, the resistance turned on the Rexists, the Flemish VNV, and other collaborators. With the liberation of Belgium, the Rexist party was banned, and Nazi sympathizers and soldiers suspected of being SS Wallone Legionnaires were rounded up. Léon Degrelle who had betrayed his countrymen fled to Spain which was still a fascist country.

Bill Slenker said that the heads of female collaborators were shaved to mark and shame them. He was asked if he wanted to shave some of them himself but declined. However, he said the Russian submarine officer gladly "went right at it." Like the Russian boasted, he really was a "holy terror." For a while, a civil-war-like situation took place and all sense of justice was lost as collaborators were killed in targeted assassinations.

The families of Eike, Benninger and Pindroch still didn't know the fate of their boys but hearing that Slenker and Snyder were back safe raised their hopes. George Eike's wife Helen wrote on September 6,

> *Ruth, I'm so scared now, I can hardly control myself. Howard will surely know something about my George. Maybe they are together and his cable got through first. Anyway, I'll soon know the answer but these few hours or days of waiting shall be unbearable. I'm so thankful to God that your Howard is safe. We've all been praying for him you know. I feel now that I shall hear from George soon now, perhaps even today. Oh how wonderful that would be. I feel like a criminal who is waiting for the jury to pronounce life or death for me.*

On February 8 in a letter to Ruth, Howard wrote,

> *Seven months ago today I was shot down! Now that I am back it seems very anti-climatic. It is impossible to tell you by letter of all the heartbreak, disappointments and experiences I have had in that time. How I worried about you carrying the baby and learning that I was missing. I don't know what they are going to do with me. I have been at Headquarters for several days and in two or three more will go back to my field for some time as least.*
>
> *We were shot down by fighters. Kahler, my radio man, and Colwart, ball turret, were killed. The rest of us jumped and were all hidden. I never saw anyone after we left the ship. The ship was on fire, and it was impossible to put it out. Several times arrangements were made for me to return, but each time something happened to prevent my return. It was terribly disheartening the first three or four months, but finally I resigned myself to the*

fact that I would have to wait for the liberation by our armies. After hiding in many places, I finally got someone to take me out of Belgium into France where I fought with the Maquis for several weeks before our armies reached me.

On September 9, Robert Benninger's mother Jane wrote to Ruth,

You don't know how happy I am for you, Mrs. Snyder, for it has been a terrible strain on you and them two small children. When I got the word I went upstairs and went to bed and I cried for I was so happy to hear your husband is safe. I do wish I get news like that. I don't think it will be long till he (Robert) gets home and I don't think it will be long till this war is over and then all our boys will be home.

Robert Benninger with parents (Curtis and Jane) and older brother Roy

On September 11, Howard wrote again,

Back at Headquarters after a visit to my old Squadron (369th). It seemed strange to go back. Nearly everyone I knew has either gone back to the States or gone down. Eleven of the fourteen or so crews in my squadron at the time I was shot down have gone down too. I learned that Daniels and Benninger are prisoners.

It made my heart ache, Sweetheart, to find out that you did not know I was all right. I sent three messages to you by the Underground and was certain one would get through. The first few months I was miserable knowing how you and mother (Minn) would worry, but I gradually felt better thinking you knew for I had sent those messages. I got your letter saying we had another girl (Nancy Jane, born on April 28). I was very glad to know! I had wondered a great deal. I don't know how long I will be here. All my clothes and personal belongs have been sent back to the States. In fact, you may have them by now.

Colonel Riordan, my Squadron C.O., Capt. McKim, the Squadron doctor, and Capt. Williams, the Squadron Executive Officer were all very glad to see me.

Captain Williams, (nicknamed "Wee Willie") had replaced John Stanko who had suffered a mysterious gunshot wound and was sent back to the U.S. Rumor was he either shot himself after getting a "Dear John Letter" from his wife or his Bedford sweetheart shot him.

There was a big party Saturday night. It was the second anniversary (of the 306th Bomb Group's arrival in England in September 1942). I am very fortunate compared to some, and of course, unlucky compared to others, but we cannot have everything. So many things have happened it is hard to know what to say. In your prayers darling, thank God that you are an American and not a European. Keep smiling, Precious, you will never know how much I missed you.

On September 17, Ruth wrote to Ginny Daniels, "My anxiously awaited letter from Howard has arrived, filled both with happiness and sorrow. I am the happiest girl in the world and yet my heart is filled with sorrow for Mrs. Colwart and Mrs. Kahler."

And on October 8, one of Benninger's older brothers, Oliver, wrote to Howard,

> *Welcome home Skipper. We learned from Sgt. Bill Slenker that Bob was taken prisoner by the Germans on April 22, at which time he was well and in one piece. He said Bob, Eike, and Pindroch were living on potatoes for those 2 ½ months of playing hide and seek. After all these months of chasing rainbows and ending up empty handed, we have finally hit pay dirt with word from the front. All the families of your crew have corresponded with each other, and in that way, a large family was born, bound together in a common cause.*

On September 23, John Pindroch's girlfriend Charlotte wrote to Ruth, "We (she and John's mother) were so happy to hear your good news. I cried and laughed all at once. I can just imagine how you felt. I wonder what I'll do when I hear from Johnny and how I pray it will be soon."

On September 28, Howard sailed into New York Harbor and then reported in at Mitchell Field on September 29, 1944, ending his assignment to the European Theater of Operations. Howard was actually the first member of the crew to return to the U.S. as Slenker got back four days after him.

That same day Howard returned, George Eike's younger brother Richard, who was a B-17 co-pilot in the 34th Bomb Group, was shot down over Aix-la Chapelle (Aachen, Germany) on a mission to Merseburg, Germany, and killed when his plane sustained a direct flak hit and exploded. Listed as Missing in Action (MIA), it wasn't until June that the Eike family was notified that their son had been killed.

In October, Ruth received another Western Union telegram from Adjutant General J.A. Julio at the War Department which read, "Am pleased to inform you your husband First Lieutenant Howard J. Snyder has returned to duty." What an understatement!

38

THE WAR COMES TO AN END

POW EXCHANGE

Back in Meiningen, Germany, Daniels and the other wounded prisoners scheduled to be repatriated back to the U.S. were taken by train to Stalag IV-D/Z in Annaburg, Germany, arriving on December 1, 1944. It was designated as a *Heilag* (short for ***H**eimkehrer**la**ger*), a repatriation camp for POWs waiting to be either exchanged or returned home on medical grounds. By that time, the Allied forces had driven deep into Germany so the prisoners felt the war was coming to an end and their days as POWs were drawing to a close.

Compared to what the prisoners had been used to, the conditions at Annaburg were unbelievably good. There were pillows, sheets, and blankets on the beds, and the rooms had working fireplaces. Through the Red Cross, there was ample food, medical supplies, and clothing. The Germans even took group pictures of them to take home. Thinking all this was too good to be true, the prisoners became very leery and thought it might all be a propaganda stunt.

Annaburg, Germany, POW Repatriation Processing Center

However, on January 14, 1945, they were taken by train to the Germany-Switzerland border. In the custody of German authorities, a total of 497 American prisoners from various German camps and

American prisoners: Richard Daniels, back row, third from right

hospitals were brought by rail to Konstantz, a small town on the German side of the border. It was a very slow journey because so many of the German towns they passed through had been destroyed by Allied bombings and rubble was everywhere. Even in the countryside, the going was slow due to train wrecks caused by bombings from American fighter planes. In fact, American planes caused two frightening incidents. Once when the train came to an abrupt stop and backed up into a mountain tunnel to avoid being strafed by U.S. fighters, and another when the train was strafed. The cars were hit by bullets, but no one was injured and the engine escaped damage.

The exchange of the seriously sick and seriously wounded prisoners of war took place in the Swiss border town of Kreuzlingen on Lake Constance. Approximately 5,000 persons, comprising military and civilian personnel and merchant seamen, were included in this exchange of Germans and Allied nationals. Among the Americans was waist gunner Joe Musial who was being repatriated because of his severed foot.

At Kreuzlingen, the actual exchange was under the control of the Swiss government, the "Protecting Power" for both the United States and Germany. With great relief, Daniels knew that he was no longer a German prisoner and had gained his freedom. From there, they boarded a train on January 18 and traveled through the Alps and crossed into France. Along the way, they stopped where a U.S. army unit was located and had their first real American meal since many months ago.

Their final destination on January 19 was the French seaport of Marseille on the Mediterranean Sea where they went through a series of administrative procedures and got "cleaned up." They then boarded the U.S. Army hospital ship *Ernest Hands* where they received full medical treatment, were debriefed, and given full details about the war in both Europe and the Pacific.

On January 21, Repatriations Order #1 listing 2nd Lt. Richard Daniels as a Class III Patient and Order #3 listing T/Sgt Joseph Musial as a Class II Patient officially removed them from their overseas station and attached them to Halloran General Hospital on Staten Island, New York, for further hospitalization and disposition.

Daniels wrote to his wife Ginny, "The barbed wire and prison life are far behind me now. The Swiss people have been very kind and the Y.M.C.A. and the Red Cross are super. Again I'll say the Red Cross has been an ace in the hole. I'm now on a hospital ship taking it easy, seeing some movies and shows and getting civilized. Medical treatment and food are really great." Folks back home may or may not have known the extent of the boys' injuries which made the men worry and wonder "how Mom was going to take it." They didn't want sympathy and pampering when they got home but simply to get back to a normal life again.

Daniels and the others boarded the *SS Gripsholm*, a Swedish cruise ship operated by the Red Cross, on January 23 and remained on it for several days while repatriated prisoners from other camps arrived. Life on board the ship was luxurious. There were comfortable cabins, a large movie theater, a swimming pool, barber shop, game and reading lounges, massage and exercise rooms, bars, a dining room with waiters, and lots of good food. After 17 days of waiting on board, their ocean voyage across the Atlantic finally departed Marseille, France, on February 8, 1945. The *SS Gripsholm* arrived in New York Harbor on February 21. It was a very emotional moment for the men to view the New York skyline and the Statue of Liberty.

SS Gripsholm

After arriving in the States, Joe Musial was taken to the Haddon Hall wing at Thomas M. England General Hospital in Atlantic City, New Jersey, where in the later part of May four more inches of his leg were amputated. It was there that he met his future wife, Eleanore Curran from New York City, who was a volunteer. They were married on July 12. Musial had flown a total of 78 missions during the war and called his flight into matrimony his 79th although he said he didn't think this one would be as rugged as the others."

Eleanore and Joe Musial on wedding day
with Joe's older sister, Sophie Vachitis

By early 1945, the war was going badly for the Germans. The vaunted Wehrmacht was falling back on all fronts with Allied forces poised to overrun Hitler's homeland. In the west, Allied ground troops stretched along the Rhine River and surrounded the great industrial valley of the Ruhr. Meanwhile, Soviet armies in the east were streaming across Poland toward Berlin seeking vengeance for the atrocities the Germans had committed on them earlier in the war. Across eastern Germany the Nazis began death marches, herding thousands of suffering political prisoners and Allied captives west toward approaching American forces from whom the Germans expected better treatment than from the dreaded Red Army.

The "Black March"

With the Russian offensive fast approaching, the Germans decided to abandon Stalag IV at Gross Tychow, and on February 6, POW #2154 Roy Holbert was among more than 6,000 prisoners who were ordered to leave the camp on foot with only a few hours notice. Some 1500 POWs who were not physically able to walk were evacuated by train. By this time, Joe Musial had left the camp for repatriation back to the U.S. It was a march of great hardship and became known as the infamous "Black March" during which the prisoners were forced to march 500 miles across Pomerania in the snow and rain for 86 days.

January and February 1945 were among the coldest winter months of the 20th century in Europe, with temperatures as low as –13 °F. Even until the middle of March, temperatures were well below freezing. The POWs were ill-prepared for the evacuation having suffered months of poor rations and wearing clothing ill-suited for the appalling winter conditions.

From Grosstychow, they headed west back to Schwenemunde and were ferried across the Oder River at Stettin, marching across Pomerania to Anklam, Germany, down to Zehdenick and then northwest almost as far as Hamburg before turning south. The men lived in filth and slept in barns or fields. A huge problem was lice, a carrier of typhus. They lived on 770 calories a day when the normal amount for an American soldier was 3,500 calories.

Fortunately, the Red Cross parcels added another 600 calories or many would have starved to death. Holbert said, "We slept in barns and fields at night and were fed whatever the Germans could get their hands on. A lot of the food was potatoes cooked in vats for the hogs." On several occasions, Allied planes attacked the Germans, and the strafing would kill a horse or a nearby cow which was a blessing to the prisoners who were then able to eat some meat courtesy of the "Flying Quartermaster Corps."

Blisters became infected and developed into ugly abscesses that had to be opened. Mud and cold brought on frostbite, in turn bringing on gangrene and amputations. Men collapsed from hunger, weakness, fear, and pain. During the march, they would pass other prison camps where they were usually able to leave the most serious medical cases. Medics made up a slogan, "Keep on marching and your blisters will turn into calluses and your aches into muscles."

Sanitation approached medieval standards and as a result there was disease, suffering, and death. Hundreds of men suffered from malnutrition, exposure, trench foot, exhaustion, tuberculosis and other diseases, but the worst was dysentery which just overwhelmed them. The roads became lined with the sad spectacle of prisoners relieving themselves. Approximately 1,300 perished from disease, starvation, or at the hands of German Guards.

Near the end of March, they arrived at Stalag 357 (Stalag XI-B) near Fallingbostel, Germany, but only stayed there for about a week. Then on March 29th, Holbert and other POWs were put on trains, with seventy-eighty men to a box car, at Uelzen and transported to Altengrabow. There for 10 days, 8,000 men of many different nationalities (Sikhs, Hindus, Gurkhas, French, Scots, Poles, G.I.s and others) were crowded into tents, five to six hundred to a tent. It looked like and smelled like a circus. Once again, food and sanitation (only three pit toilets) were a major problem, as well as nationality differences.

Every day there, they watched the British Royal Air Force's (RAF's) bombs light up the sky at night and the Americans' bombs fall during the day on Magdeberg, a medieval city on the Elbe River, and on Berlin, the capital of Germany. The bombs shook the ground as air raid sirens sounded every hour of the day. Finally on April 26, 1945, their misery ended when the Germans marched them to the American lines of the 104th Infantry Division to surrender at Bitterfeld, Germany, on the Elbe River. On May 23, 1945, Holbert returned home after 444 days, 22 of them in solitary confinement.

Bodies Discovered ... Identities Sought

Following the liberation of Belgium, authorities began to investigate the disappearance of citizens during the Nazi occupation. Many people had been shot and buried in unmarked graves which had to be located and the bodies exhumed. There was a large community cemetery at an airfield in the village of Gosselies, just north of Charleroi that had been taken over by the U.S. Army Air Forces after the Germans abandoned it, and about 200 people, including American and British airmen, were buried there. In April 1945, Raymond Gervais, the Grave Register of the Belgian Identification Service, began the arduous task of attempting to recover and identify the bodies.

In one of the graves, Gervais found the dog tags of Billy Huish whose corpse had bullet holes in the torso. Opening graves next to that one, Gervais found bodies dressed in U.S. Army Air Force's clothing, some rings, and all having similar gunshot wounds. Based on the state of decomposition, Gervais' estimate of death was April 1944. Assuming the bodies were probably those of the downed airmen, he contacted the U.S. military police and the American Graves Registration Command took over from there.

Through further investigation, the bodies were finally identified as those of George Eike, Robert Benninger, and John Pindroch from the B-17 *Susan Ruth*; Orian Owens, Charles Nichols, John Gemborski from the B-17 *Rationed Passion*; Vincent Reese from the B-17 *Women's Home Companion*; and Billy Huish from the B-17 *Skunkface.* The bodies of the eight airmen, along with those of John Pindroch and Louis Colwart, were then taken and buried at the American Military Cemetery in Margraten, The Netherlands. After the war, the bodies of George Eike, Robert Benninger, and Ross Kahler were brought back to the United States for final burial.

American Military Cemetery at Margraten, The Netherlands

Ross Kahler's parents at his grave, Mount Peace Cemetery, Philadelphia, PA

Warren Cole and Ivan Glaze who had taken off on their own from Camp Rièzes did, in fact, make a harrowing but successful escape through France, into Spain, and on June 26 to Gibraltar. On June 30, 1944, they were back in England.

Retribution

After the war ended and Germany surrendered, many former Rexists were either imprisoned or executed for their role in collaborating with the Nazis. Of the Germans and the Belgian collaborators who had participated in the capture and/or execution of the eight U.S. airmen in the woods of St. Remy, various outcomes took place. At his hearing before the War Crimes Department, Florent Simon provided names of people he thought might have been the betrayers, but sufficient evidence could not be found against them.

Charles Lambinon and Marcel Jaye, commander of the Third Company *Garde Wallonne,* were arrested and sentenced to death but both escaped. Jacques Derby was arrested and detained at the prison in Mons, Belgium. Camille Raccourt was sentenced to ten years in prison. Captain Karl Brenner, chief of the *Feldendarmerie*, was not apprehended. Only Jacques Lefèvre, a non-commissioned officer of the 3rd Company *Garde Wallonne*, was tried by the Belgian government, convicted of crimes against the Belgian people, and hanged.

Execution of Rexists (collaborators) at Liège Prison

Colonel David Marcus, Chief of the U.S. Army War Crimes Branch, said in a letter dated September 18, 1946, to Derwood Eike, George's father, "It may also be stated that the apprehension of the criminals is one of the more difficult problems which is encountered in connection with the prosecution of War Crimes cases." A memorandum dated May 7, 1947, submitted by Colonel C.E. Straight, Deputy Judge advocate for War Crimes, stated, "With no further evidence being available and no reasonable expectation of apprehending other perpetrators herein, this Headquarters is administratively closing this case."

Albert Brouns who was one of the first Belgians at the crash site of the *Susan Ruth* received a visit after the war from two American soldiers who were accompanied by the butcher from village of Chimay. Brouns said,

> *They knew that I had the bracelet (Ross Kahler's) and asked me for it. The next day, they went back to Le Havre before returning to the U.S. Sometime afterwards, I received a letter from the mother of the victim. She thanked me for the identification bracelet and sent me a photo of her son because she wanted to be certain that it was actually him. I could not definitely tell her yes because he was so badly injured.*

Florent and Jeanne Simon stayed on their farm in St. Remy until 1946 and then moved about 10 miles north to Froidchapelle for about three years. While there, they were contacted by a Frenchman, Peter Royer, who had been a political prisoner in Germany with their son Joseph. Peter had seen to it that Joseph received a decent burial and included a few of Joseph's personal effects for identification purposes.

Eventually, the Simons brought Joseph's body back to Belgium where he is buried in the family cemetery plot in Cul-des-Sarts. A picture of Joseph is on the headstone along with an inscription about his tragic death being a result of Nazi barbarism and Belgium citizen betrayal. Jeanne blamed her husband for Joseph's death, saying Florent should never have involved their son in the resistance and underground activities. Her continual harping eventually took its toll. Florent's tremendous guilt and remorse eventually caused him to hang himself after which Jeanne went to live with her daughter Fernande. Jeanne Simon died in 1969.

Simon cemetery plot

A Long Delayed Notification

It wasn't until the fall of 1945, nineteen months after the *Susan Ruth* was shot down, that the families of George Eike, Robert Benninger, and John Pindroch received notification by the War Department that they were "presumed dead." Refusing to accept such a vague explanation, George Eike's father, Derwood, invoked the aid of his Senator from New York, James Mead, who was successful in forcing the War Department to make a full investigation into the matter. When the investigation was finished, Derwood and his wife went to Washington, D.C., and were able to read the completed report (since declassified and containing the testimonies quoted herein) at the Department of War Crimes Department at the Pentagon.

This occurred in early February 1947, three years from when the *Susan Ruth* went down. Derwood Eike wrote to the surviving crew members and the bereaved family members, "Knowing the facts does not help the deep sorrow that has come to all of us, but it does help to know that they did not suffer long and the mental agony that they might have had was of short duration. We pray that they did not die in vain and that generations to come will never forget their great sacrifice."

In remembrance of the tragic events that took place on April 22, 1944, a memorial to the eight airmen and two young Belgian patriots who helped them was dedicated on April 22, 1999. It is located in the Champagne Woods next to the Chapel of the Sacred Heart and nearby the site of the Fontaine's house.

February 22, 1944, Memorial at St. Remy

39
AFTERMATH

More airmen with the Eighth Air Force lost their lives than in the entire Marine Corps. When you consider just the 210,000 men who flew combat missions, the mortality rate soars even higher compared to the number of front line ground troops who were "in combat." There was a higher percentage of being killed, wounded or captured while flying in the 8th AF than if they were in the infantry on the front line.

Hitler ... A Legacy

World War II was the deadliest military conflict in history and changed the world forever. Fighting raged in many places in the world with more than 50 nations taking part. Hitler inflicted more pain on the human race than any other person in history. It was not enough to dominate them; he was intent on killing them. He was completely pitiless and detached from human empathy. Human life counted for nothing, even German life as he first began killing his own citizens: the old, disabled, incurably sick, the insane, gypsies, homosexuals, and political opposition. Hitler was determined to destroy everything in the world that did not serve his purpose.

He wanted to reduce Moscow to rubble and then cover it with a lake so that it completely vanished. He wanted to level Leningrad and London and render them uninhabitable. He ordered merciless savagery against the Poles and Russians. Hitler was constantly ordering and urging his armies and police to be utterly merciless since he believed mankind was valueless. By the time the war ended, nearly everyone in the world had been affected by the terror he brought.

Many high ranking German Army officers of the Wehrmacht were not only unsympathetic to National Socialism (Nazism) but opposed to it. They regarded warfare as an honorable occupation and were horrified by the atrocities of the SS and the dishonor they were bringing upon the fatherland. Even so, none of them dared to openly protest. Hitler in turn disliked the military and their foolish idea of honor. He was aware that they sometimes sabotaged his plans to exterminate entire populations. To overcome this, he eventually assumed supreme military command of the armed forces himself, but his contempt for and ridicule of his generals continued. Generals were relieved of duty, reduced in rank, and treated like servants and schoolboys.

His orders were inflexible, and he surrounded himself with yes men who agreed with everything he said. Hitler continually abandoned his armies to their fate, refusing to allow them to retreat or withdraw under any circumstances. As a result, hundreds of thousands of German soldiers needlessly perished. He blamed defeats on mediocre field generals and viewed them as potential traitors. It became a vicious circle; as defeats mounted and he needed his generals the most, the more he hated them and the more bad decisions and blunders he made.

Officers of the Wehrmacht made several attempts to kill Hitler with the closest occurring on July 20, 1944, inside his field headquarters, the Wolf's Lair, near Rastenburg, East Prussia. The purpose of the assassination attempt was to seize political control of Germany and its armed forces from the Nazi Party and obtain a peace settlement with the Allies. The failure of both the assassination and the military *coup d'état*, called operation Valkyrie, led to the arrest of 7,000 people by the *Gestapo* with 5,000 being executed. In 2008, the movie *Valkyrie* was released starring Tom Cruise as Colonel Claus von Stauffenburg, one of the key plotters in the assassination attempt.

The estimated death toll of the war ranges from 60 to 80 million people. Civilians killed totaled from 38 to 55 million, including 13 to

20 million from war-related disease and famine. Total military dead range from 22 to 25 million, including deaths in captivity of about 5 million prisoners of war. Of the major nations, the Soviet Union suffered the highest losses estimated at 20 to 25 million, followed by China 10 to 20 million, Germany 7 to 9 million, Japan 2.5 to 3 million, France more than 550,000, United Kingdom 450,000, Italy 450,000, and United States more than 400,000.

A total of 350,000 men served with the Eighth Air Force in England, and of this number 26,000 were killed and 18,000 were wounded. In addition, 28,000 crewmen ended up in POW camps and 4,000 evaded capture. More airmen with the Eighth Air Force lost their lives than in the entire Marine Corps. When you consider just the 210,000 men who flew combat missions, the mortality rate soars even higher compared to the number of front line ground troops who were "in combat." There was a higher percentage of being killed, wounded or captured while flying in the 8th AF than if they were in the infantry on the front line.

In just over 1,000 days of combat, the Eighth Air Force burned one billion gallons of gasoline, fired 99 million rounds of machine gun ammunition, dropped 732,000 tons of bombs and destroyed 18,810 enemy aircraft. The B-17 and B-24 bombers themselves had a short period of survival with the average bomber listed in service for only 147 days. Approximately 6,000 bombers were lost with another 2,000 written off as a result of extreme damage. Additionally, more than 3,000 fighters were destroyed.

The 306th Bomb Group itself flew 9,600 sorties and dropped 22,500 tons of bombs, and lost 177 B-17 bombers. Thirty-Eight men were killed in flying accidents, 738 men killed in action (KIA), 305 missing in action (MIA), 145 wounded in action (WIA), 885 men became prisoners of war, and 44 evaded capture.

However, the damage the Eighth Air Force inflicted on Germany was tremendous. The significance of its full domination of the air, both over Germany's armed forces and over its economy, cannot be overstated. Even a first class military power, as rugged and resilient as Germany was, could not live long under the relentless, full-scale attacks over the heart of its territory. By the beginning of 1945, even before the invasion of its homeland, Germany was reaching a state of helplessness. Its armies were still in the field, but with the impending collapse of the supporting economy, indications were that they would have had to cease any effective fighting within a few months. Germany was mortally wounded.

After the British Royal Air Force (RAF) abandoned their initial policy of only bombing buildings of direct military importance and changed to "area bombing" (the bombing of housing and civilian centers), it proceeded to destroy one major urban center after another. Except in the extreme eastern part of the *Reich*, there was no major city that did not bear the mark of the attacks. While the death of civilians was never explicitly recognized as its aim, the results of area bombing were inevitable. About 800,000 German civilians were killed by Allied bombings with the most devastated cities being Berlin, Hamburg, and Dresden.

The German capital of Berlin endured the longest prolonged period of bombing. Between 1940 and 1945, Berlin was the target of 363 air raids by the British, Americans and Soviets. Between 20,000 and 50,000 Berliners lost their lives in the sustained bombing during World War II, and many times more people were left homeless.

Berlin

During the last week of July 1943, referred to as "Blitz Week," RAF bombing mission called "Operation Gomorrah" obliterated Germany's second largest city of Hamburg. The severity of the bomb blasts, which continued for eight days and seven nights, created a deadly "*feuersturm*" that reduced more than eight square miles of the city to ashes. Some 3,000 aircraft took part in the raids, which left 42,600 dead and 37,000 wounded. It is estimated that another 1,000,000 civilians fled the city. In total, 9,000 tons of bombs were dropped in an operation of such scale and force that mainland Europe had never seen the likes of it before or since. No subsequent city raid shook Germany as did the one on Hamburg.

Hamburg

From February 13 to 15, 1945, 1,300 bombers from a combined RAF and USAAF dropped more than 3,900 tons of high explosives and firebombs upon Dresden. The British wanted to demonstrate the wanton destruction Hitler had brought down upon the German people and break their spirit. Fifteen square miles of the city center were utterly destroyed by the devastating firestorm that swept through the streets—the hot winds driving people back into the deathtraps that were their houses—killing 25,000. Dresden temperatures reached 3,000 degrees Fahrenheit, enough to melt a stone wall.

Dresden

The city area raids not only left their mark on German cities, but on the German people as well. Prior to the actual occupation of Germany itself, these attacks gave them a horrid lesson of the devastation and disadvantages of war. The morale of the German people deteriorated under the constant Allied aerial attacks, with the night raids feared far more than daylight raids. The people lost faith in the prospect of victory, in their leaders and in the promises and propaganda to which they were subjected. Most of all, they wanted the war to end.

If they had been at liberty to vote themselves out of the war, they would have done so, well before the final surrender. In the Nazi police state, however, there was a big difference between dissatisfaction and expressing opposition. The German people lacked either the will or the means to make their dissatisfaction evident. However, they had themselves to blame by allowing themselves to be seduced by Hitler and become intoxicated with the dreams he painted. They became willing victims and suffered mightily for it.

Even though under ruthless Nazi control, the German people showed surprising resistance to the terror and hardships of repeated air attack, to the destruction of their homes and belongings, and to the conditions under which they were reduced to live. Their morale, their belief in ultimate victory or satisfactory compromise, and their confidence in their leaders declined, but they continued to work hard until the end.

World War II resulted in the downfall of Europe, especially England, as a center of world power and led to the rise of the U.S. and Russia as super powers which brought about the Cold War and the nuclear age.

our party the night before. Danny, Benny, Eike & I had been on a little spree at the Falcon with some of the boys & were feeling surprisingly well for the condition we were in a few hours before. There is nothing like oxygen to clear up a fellows blood.

We flew at 24,000 going in. We flew a good 10 m.p.h. to fast & consequently were putting excessive power. The day was lovely way up there,

with an almost solid layer of billowing milky white clouds beneath us. The sky about was a bright almost pastel blue

We had a new ship which was performing beautifully & as we were in the lead squadron it was easy to fly good formation.

There were several abortions in the lead group; one fell out with an inboard engine on fire & as I lost sight of him below he was under control & the fire seemed to be less.

Excerpts from Howard Snyder's diary

40

RETURN, REUNION & REMEMBRANCE

What impressed him the most, he said, was the stark contrast in the attitude of the G.I.s to that of the strict German Nazis. "The calm and relaxed demeanor of the Americans told me everything would be all right now," Dr. Delahaye said. "We knew we made it through."

Dr. Paul Delahaye and the Belgian American Foundation

Howard kept in touch with his Belgian helpers, especially Ginette Gadenne, Nelly Tilquin, and Raymond Durvin, writing letters several times a year. He said, "They were wonderful people, brave people, who risked their lives to keep me from being captured. They treated me like royalty—giving me their bed and sleeping on the floor; giving me food while they went hungry. They couldn't do enough for me."

In 1983, Ruth and Howard made a trip to Belgium for the first time since the war to see some of his helpers: Ginette Gadenne, Nelly Tilquin, Maurice and Ghisliane Bailleux, Raymond Durvin, and Gabrielle and Emile Albert. Ruth wore a cross pendant that the Tilquins had made from the Plexiglas nose of the crashed B-17 *Susan Ruth* and had sent to Ruth in 1944. When Howard and Ruth went to visit Ginette Gadenne, she happened to be attending an anniversary party and was wearing a silk blouse that her mother had made out of Howard's parachute.

Howard Snyder with Ginette Gadenne and husband André in 1983

Howard with Ghislaine and Maurice Bailleux in 1983

Howard Snyder and Nelly Tilquin in 1983

Mary and Raymond Durvin in 1988

In 1988, Howard received a letter from Dr. Paul Delahaye living in Momignies, Belgium, who had obtained Howard's contact information from Nelly Tilquin. Dr. Delahaye informed Howard that he had formed the Fondation Belgo-Américaine (Belgian American Foundation) to honor and remember American troops who liberated his country from Nazi rule. He invited invited Howard and Ruth to come to Belgium and be his guests at the Foundation's Annual Liberation Celebrations and to the dedication of a monument to the first U.S. troops killed on Belgian soil. Surprised by Dr. Delahaye's letter, Howard and Ruth debated about whether to go or not, but after receiving a program of events and seeing Howard's name listed as a speaker, they decided they had to go.

Dr. Paul Delahaye, founder of Belgian American Foundation

Paul Delahaye was born October 2, 1931, in the little village of Beauwelz near Chimay where the southern region of Belgium meets France. By the end of the decade, war and Nazi occupation had come to the area, and seeking refuge, Paul's family along with the rest of the villagers piled their wagon full of their belongings and started out for northern France.

Unfortunately, the Delahayes were soon forced to turn back due to fighting near their intended destination of Dunkirk, France. Along the return route through the forest of Nouvion, France, nine-year-old Paul witnessed the bloated bodies of dead horses and decaying bodies of human corpses scattered along the road. German aircraft had sprayed the route with machine gun fire killing townspeople who had fled from their homes just 12 hours after the Delahayes.

In late May 1940, Adolf Hitler decided to set up his headquarters in Brûly-de-Pesche, near Couvin, Belgium, in the Ardennes forest which was known as Wolfsschlucht (wolf's den) where he stayed for 22 days. During this time, people in more than twenty-nine nearby villages were forcibly evacuated from their homes. The German *Gestapo* rounded up intellectuals, including Paul's father who was a school teacher and principal, and held them hostage to ensure Hitler's security.

In August 1940, Dr. Delahaye said a Nazi unit took over the Beauwelz entertainment center across from his home. "Every evening, a 'belt party' would occur," he said, in which 20, 50 or 100 lashes of a belt were doled out as discipline to soldiers, depending on how disrespectful they had been to Hitler. "I had a firsthand account of fierce German discipline. During some particularly harsh punishment, I would hear screams at first and then nothing." It was at that point he feared for his life, for as he said, "If the Nazis treated their own that way, surely it would be worse for an outsider."

Paul's father was arrested at machine gun point by the *Gestapo* while Paul, his pregnant mother, and his sister stood terrified in the hallway of their house. His father would return home the next day, but many others were less fortunate. They were beaten and tortured with some driven to commit suicide. "There was starvation and deprivation all around," Dr. Delahaye recalled. "Prisoners would return home from the *Gestapo* interrogation facility just to die. We were in a constant state of fear and anxiety."

He was 13-years-old in 1944 at the time the Germans were finally forced out of his town, and the first time he met any Americans. He remembers it was precisely 2:45 p.m. on liberation day when an eccentric local priest rode his bike through the town proclaiming the arrival of U.S. troops. "He was hollering, 'The Americans are coming! The Americans are coming!'" Delahaye exclaimed. "He was spreading the good word as a priest should."

What impressed him the most, he said, was the stark contrast in the attitude of the G.I.s to that of the strict German Nazis. "The calm and relaxed demeanor of the Americans told me everything would be all right now," Dr. Delahaye said. "We knew we made it through." That feeling made a lasting impression on him, he said, and became the driving force behind the creation of his foundation in 1984 and the memorials and monuments he would eventually build.

"After going through hell for four years, I cannot describe the overwhelming joy everyone felt," Dr. Delahaye explained. "I thought to myself, this must be what heaven is like. I set up the memorials because I wanted concrete reminders to make U.S. soldiers' stories come alive. To me, it's a duty to honor these men for what they gave us. When living through those hard times, and then good times, there's no way to forget. If not for these troops, we would be speaking German today."

In 1986, Dr. Delahaye refurbished a dilapidated shed into a museum dedicated to the U.S. effort to liberate his country and filled it with hundreds of pieces of memorabilia, including many from the *Susan Ruth* and its crew. It was inside this cramped little brick farming shed in southern Belgium where U.S. Army 2nd Lt. Claude B. Cook from Randolph County, Alabama, had cooked an impromptu egg breakfast with his weary troops on September 2, 1944. Hearing a firefight nearby, he peeked his head above the windowsill and was hit by a wayward .50 caliber bullet. Lt. Cook was killed instantly and became the first U.S. soldier killed during the liberation of Belgium.

Thereafter, the tiny brick building, called Musée 40-44, came to symbolize the sacrifices of all U.S. servicemen on the Belgian front in the eyes of the local residents.

Paul said he collected World War II stories and memorabilia, ranging from German communication equipment to parts of Lt. Cook's mess kit, while making house calls as a Doctor of Veterinary Medicine over the years. "If I noticed a man of a certain age and felt he might have some useful information, I would ease into a conversation to learn more," he said. "We can never forget. We have a duty to honor these soldiers. They died for the liberation of a country not their own, and for people they didn't know. We must continue to thank them."

Musée 40-44

The little museum was one step on Paul's lifelong journey to honor Allied troops for their sacrifices in his homeland. He was instrumental in the creation of various other monuments throughout his hometown province of Hainaut. Belgium's liberation began when American troops entered at the border hamlet of Cendron, near the village of Forge-Philippe, and the memorial there depicts an angelic figure of liberty made of white stone unchaining a prisoner, while simultaneously stomping down on a German soldier. A plaque in Beauwelz pays tribute to the 39th Infantry Regiment, credited with liberating the village. Paul also created a memorial to Canadian troops in his hometown of Momignies, recognizing their contribution to the Belgium's freedom.

The first fighting for the liberation of Belgium took place on the ridge of Monceau Imbrechies and the memorial there has 12 grave markers to honor the 12 G.I.s who were the first to die. Only five names of the 12 men are known and the others are "Known but to God." The markers are flanked on the left by an M-47 "Patton" tank and on the right by an anti-aircraft gun. Behind the markers are seven flags of the Allied countries—Belgium, France, Canada, U.K, Luxemburg, Netherlands and the U.S. In front of the monument is a large star standing upright on a stone in the shape of Belgium. It was for the dedication of this memorial in 1988 that Howard and Ruth along with waist gunner Joe Musial were honored guests.

Howard Snyder's dress uniform jacket hanging in Musée 40-44

The following year, a monument in Macquenoise was constructed to honor the B-17 *Susan Ruth* and its crew. Their plane crashed there in 1944, and the monument features the aircraft's propeller. In 1989, when the *Susan Ruth* monument was dedicated on August 28, all four remaining crew members attended with their wives: Howard and

Ruth Snyder, Joe and Eleanore Musial, Roy and Levonia Holbert, and William and Jeanne Slenker.

They relived the life changing experiences of so many years ago, visiting many of the locations where their memories took place, and reuniting with the Belgian patriots who helped them survive. The celebrations took place over several days and included many activities: visiting the museum, speeches, parades featuring World War II vehicles, and tent parties with bands, food, and lots of Chimay beer. As usual, the celebrations were attended by many local Belgium citizens as well as the U.S. Army Garrison representatives from the Benelux Installation Management Command Europe, headquartered at Chievres, Belgium.

B-17 *Susan Ruth* Memorial at Macquenoise, Belgium

Snyders, Musials, Holberts, and Slenkers at dedication of *Susan Ruth* Memorial in 1989

Joe Musial, William Slenker, Roy Holbert and Howard Snyder accepting Principality of Momignies commemorative pewter plates in 1989

Howard and Ruth visited Belgium one last time in 1994, accompanied by their daughter, Nancy, and son, Steve and his wife, Glenda, for the 50th Anniversary Celebration. This was their final time seeing Nelly Tilquin.

Howard Snyder and Dr. Paul Delahaye in 1994

All the crew members are now gone with Roy Holbert being the last to die in January 2010. Of the five crew members who fell in Belgium, the families of George W. Eike, Robert J. Benninger, and Ross L. Kahler brought their fallen loved ones back to the United States. George is buried next to his brother, Dick, at Arlington National Cemetery. Louis J. Colwart Jr. is buried at Ardennes American Cemetery and Memorial, Neuville-en-Condroz, Belgium, and John Pindroch is buried at the Netherlands American Cemetery and Memorial, Margraten, Netherlands, as are John Gemborski, Vincent Reese and Billy Huish. At the time of this writing, William Slenker's wife, Jeanne, and George Eike's wife, Helen who remarried, are the only spouses still living. Former *Luftwaffe* pilot, Hans Berger, is still working at 90 years of age, as a translator in Munich, Germany.

Dr. Paul Delahaye died on July 6, 2013, at age 82. The Belgian American Foundation's name has since been changed to L'Association du Devoir de Mémoire de Momignies. Paul's two daughters, Christel and Severine, carry on his legacy and The Duty to Remember.

ACKNOWLEDGEMENTS

First, I must thank my wonderful wife, Glenda, for her encouragement and support.

In the back of *Shot Down*, resource material is acknowledged. Many books and websites were researched to obtain factual and historical information about people, places, and events used in the book. An important source of information was the 306th Bomb Group Association website's Archives, Photo Album, and over 35 years of articles contained in the Association's publication, *Echoes*.

A substantial amount of quoted material was taken from a variety of sources. They include: personal letters written by crew members, their relatives, and Belgian helpers; crew member written accounts; crew member recorded oral accounts; translations from Belgian newspapers, and U.S. War Department, War Crimes Office, Judge Advocate General's Office, File No. 6-150.

I am grateful to all the people who provided me valuable information in one form or another via email about the crew of the *Susan Ruth*, Belgian helpers and/or historical events: Jeanne Slenker, wife of William Slenker; Romona Reed, niece of Louis Colwart; Bob Norman, cousin of George Eike; Donna Bersaglieri, daughter of Richard Daniels; Joe Des Rosier and Robert Des Rosier, grandsons of Joe Musial; Robert Kahler, brother of Ross Kahler; George Pindroch, nephew of John Pindroch; Bill Slenker, son of William Slenker; Kyle Holbert, son of Roy Holbert; Chris Holbert, grandson of Roy Holbert; Anne-Sophie Gaudry, great grandaughter of Eva and Jack Martin; Philip Mundel, 306th Bomb Group ball turett gunner and togglier: William Houlihan, 306th Bomb Group medic; historian Edouard Renière; historian-author Eric Mombeek and Christel Delahaye.

In particular, much appreciation goes to Hans Berger, a former *Luftwaffe* pilot, who provided wonderful insight from the perspective of a German pilot who fought against the U.S. Air Force during World War II. Remarkably, Hans was one of the Focke-Wulf fighter pilots who shot down my father's B-17 bomber on February 8, 1944.

Special acknowledgement needs to go to three other people: First, my thanks go to Dan Frey for his publication *Chimay—Life, Death and Murder in World War II*. Next, my sincerest appreciation goes to Jacques Lalot for allowing me the privilege of using the material in his unpublished manuscript *Champagne Woods—April 22, 1944*. The depth of Jacques research into the events that surrounded that infamous day is simply astonishing. I cannot thank Jacques enough for the amazingly, detailed documentation and numerous pictures he gave to me to put in my book. Jacques wrote to me:

> *Be sure that I'm not disappointed of the situation* (that his work will never be printed nor published). *With your book, the people who are highly interested in this sad story (I mean the relatives of the crew) will be provided with all the details that will help them realise what really happened on the 22d of April 1944.*
>
> *It was unexpected by me but in the long run, thanks to you, all these nice people will be able to read a comprehensive account of the odyssey their dear ones had to undergo during that dark period of the war.*
>
> *Through your book, I reached my goal. I have the opportunity to inform the relatives of the crew what happened here in 1944. You tell all of them that the Belgian citizen, Jacques Lalot, has been very pleased to inform them about their dear ones.*

Finally, I am really unable to express the deep debt I owe and the amount of gratitude I have for the late Dr. Paul Delahaye. Without his efforts to honor and keep alive the memory of the young Allied soldiers who liberated his country, little would be known about the people and events that took place in southern Belgium 70 years ago. It was through his formation of the Belgian American Foundation and his tireless work to research and record history that the story of the *Susan Ruth* crew is able to be told. My book includes many interviews and testimonies he documented. Without Paul, there would be no book, *Shot Down*.

All of the above enabled me to write my manuscript. Turning it into a professionally published book required the assistance of a group of highly qualified professionals. Knowing absolutely nothing about book publishing, I wasn't sure what to do after I finished writing. Fortunately, through what must have been divine guidance, I found Judith Briles, The Book Shepherd. As my book consultant, Judith guided me step-by-step through the entire process from start to finish. From her vast experience and expertise, she enabled me to produce and publish a book of which I am extremely proud.

Chief Editor was John Maling of Mile High Press who did a marvelous job of editing my work. John's ability to relate to the war years and his personal interest in the story created a common bond between us. The greatly talented Nick Zelinger of NZ Graphics did all the graphics and layout which was no easy task considering the number of pictures that were included in the book. Nick was extremely easy to work with and the visual appearance of the finished product could not have been any better.

ABOUT THE AUTHOR

Steve Snyder is a native Southern Californian with a degree in Economics from UCLA. After graduating, he soon began a career-long association with California Vision Service in 1973 which became Vision Service Pan (VSP) a few years later. He retired from VSP as Eastern Division Vice President in 2009 after 36 years in national sales and sales management. Steve traveled extensively throughout the U.S. during his career, becoming a million mile flyer on several airlines in the process.

Soon after retirement, he began a quest to learn about the World War II experiences of his father, pilot Howard Snyder, and his crew of the B-17, *Susan Ruth*, named after his older sister. It became his passion and has resulted after several years of dedicated research in his book, *Shot Down*. One result of his "new career" as a World War II historian is that he is a member of numerous World War II associations and is on the Board of Directors of the 306th Bomb Group Association.

He and his wife Glenda split their time between Calfornia, taking long walks along the coastline, and hiking in Arizona near their second home when not traveling. An avid gardener, his garden is a Southern California botanical paradise featuring nearly 100 palm trees!

Steve is available for speaking engagements and may be contacted by email at *Steve@SteveSnyderAuthor.com* or through his book website at *SteveSnyderAuthor.com*.

CONNECT WITH THE AUTHOR

WEBSITE: SteveSnyderAuthor.com

EMAIL: Steve@SteveSnyderAuthor.com

FACEBOOK: http://bit.ly/SteveSnyderAuthor

LINKEDIN: http://bit.ly/ShotDownAuthor

TWITTER: https://twitter.com/uclasny

GOOGLE+: https://plus.google.com/109638180386464562111

PINTEREST: www.pinterest.com/uclasny

AMAZON: http://bit.ly/ShotDownBook

SOURCES

Books

Alling, Charles, *A Mighty Fortress: Lead Bomber Over Europe* (Casemate, Havertown, Pennsylvania, 2002)

Air Forces Escape & Evasion Society, *Air Forces Escape and Evasion Society*, (Turner Publishing Company, Paducah, Kentucky, 1992)

Ambrose, Stephen E., *D-Day: The Climatic Battle of World War II* (Touchstone/Simon & Schuster, New York, New York, 1995)

Ambrose, Stephen E., *The Wild Blue: the Men and Boys Who Flew The B-24s Over Germany* (Simon & Schuster, New York, New York, 2001)

Anderson, James, *The World War II Yanks In England, As Remembered by the Brits* (398th Bomb Group Memorial Association Flak News Volume 11, Number 2, April 1996)

Astor, Gerald, *The Mighty Eighth: The Air War In Europe Told By The Men Who Fought It* (Penguin Group, New York, New York, 1997)

Bendiner, Elmer, *The Fall of Fortresses: A Personal Account of the Most Daring-and Deadly-American Air Battles of World War II* (G. P. Putnum's Sons, New York, New York, 1980)

Bove, Arthur P., *First Over Germany, A Story of the 306th Bombardment Group* (Battery Press, Nashville, Tennessee, 1982)

Bowman, Martin W., *US Eighth Air Force in Europe: Eager Eagles: 1941-Summer 1943* (Pen & Sword Aviation, South Yorkshire, U.K., 2012)

Brinkley, David, *The World War II Memorial: A Grateful Nation Remembers* (Smithsonian Books, Washington, D.C., 2004)

Cravens, W.F., *The Army Air Forces in World War II* (7 Volume set) (Office of Air Force History, Washington, D.C., 1983)

Delahaye, Paul, *2 Septembre 1944 Cendron Liberté* (Imprimerie Provinciale du Hainaut, Jumet, Charleroi, Belgium, 2009)

Dowden, Leland, A., *One and One Half Missions: Maine to New York the Long Way* (Western Book/Journal Press, San Mateo, California, 1989)

Freeman, Roger A., *B-17 Fortress At War* (Charles Scribner's & Sons, New York, New York, 1977)

Freeman, Roger A., *The Mighty Eighth War Manual* (Cassell & Co., London, U.K., 1984)

Hastings, Max, *Victory in Europe: D-Day to VE Day* (Little Brown and Company, Boston, Massachusetts, 1985)

Hatton, Greg, *Stories My Father Never Told Me: the Journal of the San Antone Rose* (unknown binding, 1993)

Hirshson, Stanley P., *General Patton: A Soldier's Life* (Harper Collins, New York, New York, 2002)

Hoppes, Jonna Doolittle, *Calculated Risk: The Extraordinary Life of Jimmy Doolittle – Aviation Pioneer and World War II Hero* (Santa Monica Press LLC, Santa Monica, California, 2005)

Hubbard, Jack C., *Patriots Will: Surviving the Great Depression and World War II Combat* (1st Books Library, Bloomington, Indiana, 2003)

Kaplan, Philip & Smith, Rex Alan, *One Last Look: A Sentimental Journey to the Eighth Air Force Heavy Bomber Bases of World War II in England* (Abbeville Publishers, New York, New York, 1983)

Leckie, Robert, *Delivered From Evil: the Sage of World War II* (Harper & Row, New York, New York, 1987)

McCullough, David, *Truman* (Simon & Schuster, New York, New York, 1992)

McLachlan, Ian & Zorn, Russell, J., *Eight Air Force Bomber Stories: Eye-Witness Accounts from American Airmen and British Civilians of the Perils of War* (Patrick Stephens Limited, Somerset, U.K., 1991)

Miller, Donald L, *Eighth Air Force: The American Bomber Crews in Britain* (Aurum Press, London, U.K. 2013)

Miller, Donald L., *Masters of the Air: America's Bomber Boys Who Fought the Air War Against Nazi Germany* (Simon & Shuster, New York, New York, 2006)

Mombeek, Eric, *Defenders of the Reich Jagdgeschwader 1 Volume Three 1944-1945* (Classic Publications, Surrey, U.K., 2003)

Payne, Robert, *The Life and Death of Adolf Hitler* (Praeger Publishers, New York, New York, 1973)

Shirer, William L., *The Rise and Fall of the Third Reich: A History of Nazi Germany* (Simon & Schuster, New York, New York, 1990)

Straubel, James H., *Air Force Diary: 111 Stories from The Official Service Journal of the USAAF* (Simon & Shuster, New York, New York, 1947)

Strong, Russell A., *First Over Germany, A History of the 306th Bombardment Group* (Hunter Publishing Company, Winston-Salem, North Carolina, 1982)

Unpublished

Caplan, Captain Leslie, *Flight Surgeon, Death-March Medic* (Air Force Association, Washington, D.C., nd)

Carroll, Major James J., *Physiological Problems of Bomber Crews in the Eighth Air Force During WWII* (Air Command and Staff College Research Report, 1997)

Frey, Dan, Chimay: *Life, Death and Murder in World War II* (unpublished, 1999)

Lalot, Jacques, *Le Bois De la Champagne: Le 22 Avril 1944* (unpublished)

McHale, Tom, *The POW Story* (Air Force Association, Washington, D.C., nd)

Westgate III, Major USAF Charles J., *The Reich Wreckers: An Analysis of the 306th Bomb Group during World War II* (Air Command and Staff College Research Report, Maxwell Air Force Base, Alabama, 1998)

Websites

Air Field Information Exchange—
http://www.airfieldinformationexchange.org/

Air Force Historical Research Agency—
http://www.afhra.af.mil/

Air Forces Escape & Evasion Society—
http://www.airforceescape.com/index.html

Allied Flight Gear in WW II—
http://www.alliedflightgear.com/

Ancestry.com—*http://home.ancestry.com/*

ArchiveGrid—*http://beta.worldcat.org/archivegrid/*

Army Air Forces in WW II—
http://www.ibiblio.org/hyperwar/AAF/VI/AAF-VI-17.html

Army Air Forces Collection—*http://www.aafcollection.info/*

Army Air Forces Online Forum—
http://www.airfieldinformationexchange.org/community/forum.php

Aviation Archeological Investigation & Research—
http://www.aviationarchaeology.com/default.htm

Axis History—*http://www.axishistory.com/*

1st Bombardment Wing

91st Bomb Group—*http://www.91stbombgroup.com/*

381st Bomb Group—*http://www.381st.org/*

398th Bomb Group—*http://www.398th.org/*

482nd Bomb Group—*http://www.482nd.org/*

40th Bombardment Wing

92nd Bomb Group—*http://92ndma.org/*

305th Bomb Group—*http://www.305thbombgroup.com/*

306th Bomb Group—*www.306bg.org/*

41st Bombardment Wing

303rd Bomb Group—*http://www.303rdbg.com/*

379th Bomb Group—*http://www.379thbga.org/*

384th Bomb Group—*http://384thBombGroup.com/*

94th Bombardment Wing

351st Bomb Group—*http://www.351st.org/*

401st Bomb Group—*http://www.401bg.com/*

457th Bomb Group—*http://www.457thbombgroup.org*

B-17 G Diagram—*http://i-ota.net/B-17Nine-O-Nine/*

B-17 Flying Fortress Queen of the Skies—
http://www.b17queenofthesky.com/index2.htm

B-17 Flying Fortress Queen of the Skies (German version)—
http://www.b17flyingfortress.de/eng/index.php

B-17 Pilot Training Manual—
http://www.stelzriede.com/ms/html/mshwpmn1.htm

B-24 – 392nd Bomb Group—*http://www.b24.net/index.html*

BBC History World War Two—
http://www.bbc.co.uk/history/worldwars/wwtwo/

Belgian Escape Line Research and Remembrance—
http://home.clara.net/clinchy/

Belgian Resistance Historic Overview—
http://www.pbs.org/lastbesthope/programfeature.html

Belgian Underground in WW2—
http://www.belgium.under.ground.freeservers.com/index.html

Brief History of Bedford—
http://www.colindaylinks.com/dayspast/bedfordoverview.html

Carentan Liberty Group—
http://carentanlibertygroup.forumgratuit.org/

Pictures of WW II Royalty Free—
http://historylink101.com/ww2_color/index.html

Commemorative Air Force—*http://www.azcaf.org/*

Control Towers—*http://www.controltowers.co.uk/*

Eighth Air Force Historical Society—*http://www.8thafhs.org/*

Eighth Air Force Operations History—
http://www.8thafhs.com/index.php

European Theater of Operations—
http://www.ibiblio.org/hyperwar/ETO/index.html

Fields of Honor Database—
http://www.adoptiegraven-database.nl/index.php/home

Find A Grave—*http://www.findagrave.com/*

Fold3—*http://www.fold3.com/*

Forgotten Camps—
http://www.jewishgen.org/ForgottenCamps/index.html

German Pilot Perspective—
http://freepages.military.rootsweb.ancestry.com/~josephkennedy/German_Pilot_Perspective.htm

Historic Bombers of the U.S. Air Force—
http://webspace.webring.com/people/qb/b31640/bombers.html

History WW II—*http://www.history.com/topics/world-war-ii*

Life as Prisoners of War—
http://www.angel45-2b.com/lifeasaprisonerofwar.html

Little Friends—*http://www.littlefriends.co.uk/*

Lone Sentry—*http://www.lonesentry.com/*

The Luftwaffe Archives & Records Reference Group—
http://www.lwag.org/index.php

Mighty 8th Cross Reference—*http://mighty8thaf.preller.us/*

National Archives—*http://www.archives.gov/*

National WWII Museum—
http://www.nationalww2museum.org/index.html

100th Bomb Group—*http://www.100thbg.com/*

PBS Detective Techniques Military History—
http://www.pbs.org/opb/historydetectives/technique/military-history-wwii/

Remember History—*http://www.remember-history.com/*

September 2, 1944 Le Passage de la Muese—
http://www.patrimoinemosan.net/Blaimont.html

Stalag Luft VI and IV—*http://www.stalagluft4.org/*

Strategic Bombing Statistics—World War II—
http://hewittmbm.com/strategic/index.php

U.S. Air Force Academy—*http://www.usafa.af.mil/*

U.S. Department of Veteran Affairs—*http://www.va.gov/*

War History Online—*http://www.warhistoryonline.com/*

Wartime Memories Project—*http://www.wartimememories.co.uk/*

World War Photos—*http://www.worldwarphotos.info/*

World War II Archives—
http://www.wwiiarchives.net/servlet/action/index

World War II Database—*http://ww2db.com/*

World War II Today—*http://ww2today.com/*

WW2 History Club—*http://www.ww2hc.org/*

World War 2 POW Archive—*http://www.ww2pow.info/*

World War Two & Aviation History—*http://acepilots.com/#*

WW II Escape and Evasion Information Exchange—
http://www.conscript-heroes.com/escapelines/index.htm

WW II Netherlands Escape Line—
http://wwii-netherlands-escape-lines.com/

INDEX

C

D

E

L

M

T

U

V

W

Y

our party the night before. Danny, Benny, Eike & I had been on a little spree at the Falcon with some of the boys & were feeling surprisingly well for the condition we were in a few hours before. There is nothing like oxygen to clear up a fellows blood.

We flew at 24,000 going in. We flew a good [illegible]

with an almost solid layer of billowing milky white clouds beneath her. The sky about was a bright almost pastel blue

We had a new ship which was performing beautifully & as we were the lead squadron [illegible]

had the same trouble on a previous raid, so I gave the ship to Eike & proceeded to pull the emergency release when I saw the bombs drop from the lead ship.

They released without any trouble & we made a sharp turn to the right & got the hell out of there. Flak continued to break all around us as we left the target area.

Flak doesn't scare me any more but I still feel my heart speed up as if it were thrown into high

No enemy fighters or flax were met on the way in. The usual intensive flax was met over the target. It was barrage flax & fairly accurate. One burst pitted the windshield in front of me & I [illegible] bullet proof

connection with his work hidden & one more or less would make little difference. Of course persons, dates & places shall remain anonymous & I shall attempt to write in a somewhat vague manner in hopes of further safety.

It is impossible to know whether I shall be able to finish my adventu[re]

This story is being attempted primarily to occupy my time which hangs heavily over my head & secondly it may prove of greater interest than a verbal account later.

I have refrained from writting this account before for fear that it might fall into improper hands & cause serious results to those who have so kindly befriended me. However M. has assured me that he has a great many secret papers in

Printed in the USA
CPSIA information can be obtained
at www.ICGtesting.com
LVHW021217061223
765524LV00092B/3072

9 780986 076015